ZEN EFFECTS
THE LIFE OF ALAN WATTS

From the 1950s until the early 1970s when he died, Alan Watts influenced the spiritual search of a whole generation—with Zen, Taoism, mystical Christianity, and the use of psychedelics. Today, a quarter-century after his death, his teaching remains as fresh as ever.

ALAN WATTS ON:

SAFETY: "What we have to discover is that there is no safety, that seeking it is painful, and that when we imagine that we have found it, we don't like it."

KNOWLEDGE: "All knowledge of self is knowledge of other, and all knowledge of other is knowledge of self."

SANITY: "No one is more dangerously insane than one who is sane all the time: he is like a steel bridge without flexibility, and the order of his life is rigid and brittle."

GOD: "God likes to play hide-and-seek, but because there is nothing outside God, he has no one but himself to play with. But he gets over this difficulty by pretending that he is you and I and all the people in the world, all the animals, all the plants, all the rocks, and all the stars. In this way he has strange and wonderful adventures, some of which are terrible and frightening."

LIVING: "The point of music is discovered in every moment of playing and listening to it. It is the same, I feel, with the greater part of our lives, and if we are unduly absorbed in improving them we may forget altogether to live them."

Monica Furlong (1930–2003) was a British author and journalist known especially for her biographies of spiritual figures. Her numerous books include *Merton: A Biography; Visions and Longings: Medieval Women Mystics;* and *Women Pray: Voices through the Ages, from Many Faiths, Cultures, and Traditions* (SkyLight Paths).

Also Available in the *SkyLight Lives* Series

By Robert Coles
with a new foreword by the author

A brilliant portrait of this strange and controversial figure and her mystical experiences.

6 x 9, 208 pp, Quality Paperback

978-1-893361-34-8

By Margaret Cropper
with a new foreword by Dana Greene

One of Underhill's closest friends captures the spirit, journey and wisdom of the influential spiritual thinker.

6 x 9, 288 pp, b/w photos
Quality Paperback

978-1-893361-70-6

By Charles F. Andrews
with a new foreword by Dr. Arun Gandhi, Gandhi's grandson & cofounder of the M. K. Gandhi Institute for Nonviolence

Provides fascinating insight into the spiritual, political and historical environment that affected Gandhi, playing key roles in the development of his thought and action.

6 x 9, 336 pp, b/w photos, Quality Paperback

978-1-893361-89-8

Walking Together, Finding the Way®

SKYLIGHT PATHS®
PUBLISHING

Sunset Farm Offices, Route 4, P.O. Box 237
Woodstock, VT 05091
Tel: (802) 457-4000 Fax: (802) 457-4004

www.skylightpaths.com

ZEN EFFECTS

THE LIFE OF ALAN WATTS

Monica Furlong

With a new foreword by the author

Walking Together, Finding the Way®

SKYLIGHT PATHS®
PUBLISHING
Woodstock, Vermont

Zen Effects:
The Life of Alan Watts

2012 Quality Paperback Edition, Third Printing

Library of Congress Cataloging-in-Publication Data
Furlong, Monica.
Zen effects : the life of Alan Watts / Monica Furlong.
p. cm. — (SkyLight lives)
Originally published: Boston : Houghton Mifflin Co., 1986.
Includes bibliographical references and index.
ISBN-13: 978-1-893361-32-4 (quality pbk.)
ISBN-10: 1-893361-32-2 (quality pbk.)
1. Watts, Alan, 1915–1973. 2. Philosophers—United States—Biography. 3. Philosophers—England—Biography. I. Title. II. Series.
B945.W324 F87 2001
191—dc21
[B]

00-054915

10 9 8 7 6 5 4 3

Manufactured in the United States
Cover Design: Drena Fagen
Cover Art: Elizabeth Cornaro

Walking Together, Finding the Way®
Published by SkyLight Paths Publishing
A Division of LongHill Partners, Inc.
Sunset Farm Offices, Route 4, P.O. Box 237
Woodstock, VT 05091
Tel: (802) 457-4000 Fax: (802) 457-4004
www. skylightpaths.com

In advanced particle physics some remarkable phenomena occur when two particles bearing opposite charges are forced to collide. Some of these events can be explained by standard theory, but others — zen effects — cannot be explained in terms of any known processes.

Contents

Foreword to the SkyLight Lives Edition

Alan Watts rose to prominence in the 1960s and early seventies as one of the key figures in that cultural wave that included the hippie movement, "flower power," psychedelics, rock music, and a general throwing off of the shackles of convention—all elements of a phenomenon that came to be known as the "counterculture." Though many aspects of this movement may now seem quaintly naive to us, there was a vision to it—one of a life simpler and more humanly attractive than one characterized by consumer greed. Along with it there came a new respect for the religious traditions of Asia, and these Eastern philosophies began to make inroads into the Judeo-Christian certainties of the West. The new ways of thinking also contributed to the civil rights and anti-war movements. The traditionally Protestant societies of America and England were taken over by a brief bohemianism, which brought a sense of joy and fun, of play, that never entirely went away again. The movement also laid the foundations for ecological concern, something which, forty years later, has fostered a worldwide dialogue on the subject.

The enduring influence of the counterculture is nowhere more evident today than in the "normalization" of Eastern religion: the seeds planted by Watts and others in the 1960s have grown to the point where today Eastern religions are considered mainstream—in the past decade the practice of Buddhism alone among Westerners has more than doubled by most estimations—and their continuing presence in our culture has altered the way we think about the religious traditions of the West.

In the fifteen years since this book's original publication, the legacy of the counterculture has increased rather than diminished. Thus, this new edition of *Zen Effects* comes at a time when it is more important than ever to examine the lives of the people who, like Alan Watts, are counted as the movement's movers and shakers. These leaders were a mixed bag of academics and singers; poets and painters; Buddhist, Hindu, and Christian teachers; adepts of Zen. Watts, arguably the most influential among them, was an Englishman who had literally "gone West," eventually finding his home in California, after sojourns in New York and Chicago. Classically educated at a British private school, a follower of

Buddhism in his teens, for a time an Episcopalian clergyman, he gradually abandoned the more conventional aspects of Western life along with Western dress, which he regarded as constricting. In 1951 Watts moved to San Francisco, where he helped set up the American Academy of Asian Studies to meet the growing interest in all things Asian. The school quickly acquired some remarkable pupils, including the poet Gary Snyder, a whole group of important artists, and the people who later went on to found the Esalen Institute, the center and retreat dedicated to the exploration of human potential. Watts's intention was less an academic one than it was a wish to bring about a transformation of consciousness in his pupils. He certainly succeeded in bringing some extraordinary people together, many of whom became friends for life.

Like almost everyone caught up in the vision of transformation, Watts experimented with psychedelics. Unimpressed at first, he became fascinated at the timeless vision of the world they showed him. In the early days, Watts, like others, did not guess how destructive drugs could become. Watts, however, always saw them as a temporary aid to consciousness, a cleansing of perception which, like psychotherapy, you gave up when they had taught you what they could: "When you've got the message, hang up the phone," he would say.

By 1969 Watts had become an icon of the movement to the extent that his celebrity made life sometimes difficult. One woman described to me how, at this period, dining with Watts in a restaurant in San Francisco, she was embarrassed by a disciple who came in and knelt before him, disregarding a roomful of onlookers. Perhaps we understand more nowadays about that sort of fame—the sort where people have an awed need to touch, or at least to stare.

Watts's philosophy, carefully developed over the years with study, had a freshness and honesty about it. He had read deeply in Christian theology and felt that many of its symbols had lost their power as a result of being taken too literally, and needed to be rediscovered. He worked at meditation, read Jungian psychology, studied Oriental religious ideas of all kinds, visited Japan. Out of much thinking, reading, and talking, he developed a language that spoke to Westerners who wanted a religion, or at any rate a way of life, that was not totally trapped in rationality. He felt that religion tended to suffer from mystification and the use of a mandarin language that excluded most people, except as timid followers of leaders who then abused their power. His own teaching moved between ways of talking about huge imponderables—suffering, death—to the everyday—the kind of food, clothes, relationships, ways of living that might be appropriate for human beings.

Few, if any, human beings can cope well with becoming a guru or icon. Alan Watts handled it better than some, mainly because he had good friends, and he had a sense of humor that put his fame into perspective, but he was stressed by the exposure and at times his head was turned by it. Watts is not a man on whom it is possible to deliver an easy verdict—he escapes labels. He had an extraordinary wisdom, a lot of knowledge, and a rare ability to put both into language that ordinary people can understand. He still has much to teach anyone searching to find belief—his short and deceptively simple little books are remarkable guides. He was sometimes vain, a know-it-all who could be thoughtless of others, but he was invariably kind in what he said about other people. "He was fond of lifting the elbow," Dom Aelred Graham wrote to me, "but I never heard him say a harsh word about anybody." There are not many of us of whom the Recording Angel will be able to say as much, and it was perhaps Watts's capacity to live out the life he wanted, with all its ups and downs, its failures and successes, that left him so attractively free of envy. His children, I noticed when I interviewed them, were both clear-sighted and truthful about him, but also had loving memories, as had his friends.

He was both an inspired leader and, like all of us, flawed—in Gary Snyder's words, "he sowed problems wherever he went." Watts knew himself quite well, and used to describe himself as a "genuine fake," an expression that catches not only his ambiguities, but also the ambiguities of the human condition, not least when we are trying to be religious. This book tries to explore both the genuineness and the fakery.

Monica Furlong
London
January 2001

Acknowledgments

My principle thanks go to Joan Watts Tabernik of Bolinas, California, Alan Watts's daughter and executor, who encouraged me to write the book and was full of useful information. I was also most grateful to Ann Andrews who talked with me at great length about her father and the family history, and showed me much personal kindness. Mrs. Mary Jane Watts was very generous with her time.

Other members of the Watts family who helped with time, memories, photographs, tapes, and diaries were Mark Watts, Joy Buchan, Leslie and Peggy Watts, Sybil Jordeson, and Jean McDermid. Mrs. Dorothy Watts wrote to me at length about Alan Watts.

Watts had many close and loving friends; those I talked with about him were Elsa Gidlow, Roger Somers, Gary Snyder, Gordon Onslow-Ford, Toni Lilly, June Singer, Robert Shapiro, Ruth Costello, Sandy Jacobs, Virginia Denison, and Watts's niece by marriage, Kathleen.

Others who gave information were Bishop John Robinson,

Theodore Roszak, R. D. Laing, members of the San Francisco Zen Center, Episcopal clergy who remembered Watts from his Christian days, and Joanne Kyger. Dom Aelred Graham corresponded with me about the trip he and Watts made to Japan, Felix Greene about broadcasting with Watts, and Patrick Leigh Fermor about being at King's School, Canterbury.

King's School, Canterbury, provided archive material, suggested contacts, and described to me what the school must have been like in Watts's day.

John Snelling of the Buddhist Society of Great Britain gave me good advice, and the Society produced some interesting photographs.

For much of the research on the book I was away from home, and on my various visits to the West Coast of the United States I much appreciated the hospitality of Ann Andrews, Andrew Weaver, Daniel McLoughlin, and Ruth Costello. Frank and Mary Lee McClain of Winnetka, Illinois, gave me a temporary home while I researched Watts's years in Evanston and suggested a number of local sources of help. As on so many visits to the United States, the principal sources of help, encouragement, and hospitality were Fred and Susan Shriver of Chelsea Square, New York.

Introduction

When I began to write about Alan Watts I paid visits to the *Vallejo*, to Druid Heights, and to the lonely stupa on the hillside behind Green Gulch Farm. In that last place, wanting to pay tribute to a fellow Englishman so far from home, I picked a few of the California poppies that grew in the grass and laid them in front of the little grave.

Watts puzzled me, then and later. The combination of spiritual insight and naughtiness, of wisdom and childishness, of joyous high spirits and loneliness, seemed incongruous. Wasn't "knowledge" in the Buddhist sense of overcoming *avidya*, or ignorance, supposed gradually to lead you into some sort of release from craving, and yet there was Watts drinking and fornicating all over California? On the other hand Jesus had said that those who lived in "the Way" would have life and have it more abundantly than others, and everything I knew about Watts gave me to think that he had abundant life of a kind that made most of the good people seem moribund. He brought others to it, as well. Many more puzzled or troubled than he were introduced by Watts to a new way of seeing themselves and the world, and sometimes to a much more rigorous regime of spiritual exercises than he would have dreamed of undertaking himself, by way of *zazen* (Zen meditation) and Buddhism in its various manifestations.

Another thing that puzzled me about Watts was that he seemed terribly familiar to me. Among clergy in the Christian churches and gurus I had met in other forms of religion, some of them, often less remarkable than Watts, had almost all his characteristics. Though so splendidly and individually himself, Watts was at the same time a type, a type that nobody talked about much in the churches or in other religious communities because representatives of the type were something of an embarrassment, they were very often the subject of scandal. Certain sorts of disgrace tended to follow them, yet of the ones I had known well, there often seemed to be a special sort of *grace* as well, as if they were people who helped to break up rigid social patterns, forcing us to ask questions about them. We seemed to need them.

I had read of shamans who performed a function of this kind, but it was not until I met Gary Snyder and he told me about Coyote, the "trickster" hero of the Shoshone and the Californian Indians, that I could take the idea a bit further. Coyote, a favorite hero in Shoshone stories, was a bit of a rogue, but he knew something important, something other people needed. He was the one who brought fire to the earth by stealing it — it was owned and treasured by a group of flies. In the process of bringing it to his tribe he caught his tail alight and nearly burned himself to death; this was one of a long list of catastrophes that made up his life. He was also the one who brought death to mankind, accidentally. In the process he inadvertently made life worth living, but when his own child died and he really began to understand what death meant, he tried to reverse the process. Too late.

Coyote is a great folk hero, but is contradictory in nature, because his approach to issues of good and evil is an ambiguous one. When he performed "good" actions, they had a way of turning out wrong. When he was "bad," and he was often bad, goodness seemed in some mysterious way to emerge. He resisted the categories beloved of moral majorities; what had appeared comfortingly simple until he came along was thrown into comical confusion. "I think the most interesting psychological thing about the trickster," says Snyder, "was that there wasn't a clear dualism of good and evil established there, that he clearly manifested benevolence, compassion, help to human beings, sometimes, and had a certain dignity; and on other occasions he was the silliest utmost fool."

Maybe it is in this contradictory way that Watts is best seen.

In a poem called "Through the Smoke Hole," Snyder tells the Indian story of "the world above this one." This world is a wigwam with a hole in the roof through which the smoke of the fire goes. There is a ladder that goes out through the roof, and through this hole the great heroes climb on their shining way to the world above. It is our good fortune, however, that a few make the journey in reverse, tumbling, backside first, through the hole, to rejoin us in this world and give us hints of what they know. Such a one was Coyote. And so, possibly, was Alan Watts.

One

The Paradise Garden

1915-1920

ALAN WATTS was born at twenty minutes past six in the morning on January 6, 1915, at Chislehurst in Kent, England, the child of Emily Mary (née Buchan) and Laurence Wilson Watts. Emily was thirty-nine years old and had begun to despair that she would have a child.

Emily came from a big family of five boys and two girls. She was the fifth child, followed by her favorite brother William (Willy) and another girl, Gertrude. Her father, William, was a patriarchal figure who ran a haberdashery and umbrella business in London. Sternly Evangelical, he prayed with his staff each morning before the shop opened, and was so unwilling to dismiss employees when times were bad that his business itself finally foundered. Alan, who could not remember him, pictured him as a sort of wrathful Jehovah who filled his mother with guilt and Protestant inhibition without giving her any real feeling for the spirit of religion.

An equally important figure to the Buchan children was their father's sister, Eleanor, an elegant, wealthy lady who lived at

Bakewell in Derbyshire and who worked in subtle ways to undermine William's austere regime. "I *hope* Eleanor is saved," her brother used to observe doubtfully. Eleanor took a particular interest in the girls, having them to stay and generally encouraging them. As a result of her enthusiasm and her financial help, both Emily and her sister Gertrude were able to carve out careers for themselves. While Gertrude trained as a nurse at the London Hospital, Emily trained as a teacher. She taught physical education and domestic economy at a school for missionaries' daughters, Walthamstow Hall, at Sevenoaks in Kent, but her real talent was for needlework. She was remarkably gifted at embroidery—there are examples of her work still to be found with a fine sense of color and design—and she became a teacher and designer for the Royal School of Needlework, where some of her designs are still used.

Emily was not a pretty girl, she had a brusque way of telling people exactly what she was thinking—a relative remembers that if she didn't like your hat she would tell you so straightaway—and she had a keen intelligence that she never bothered to hide. None of this made her particularly marriageable by the standards of the period, but in 1911 she met Alan's father, Laurence Wilson Watts, and they fell in love.

Laurence was four years younger than Emily. He was the second of five boys and was educated at the Stationers' School (a school originally for poor boys, financed by the Stationers' Guild. In Laurence's day quite well-to-do families sent their sons there). Since his father had a good job with a big silversmithing firm, Laurence grew up in comfortable circumstances at Stroud Green in North London. Perhaps a less dominant personality than Emily, he was a gentle, tolerant, humorous man, well liked by those who knew him. He is remembered in the Watts and

Buchan families as "a ladies' man like all the Watts men." At the time he met Emily, he was working for the Michelin Tyre Company at a job that took him on regular trips to Europe.

Perhaps Laurence liked taking care of Emily, or perhaps she brought to the relationship some sort of forcefulness that he lacked. Whatever the cause, they remained a most loving and devoted couple for the rest of their lives. Their marriage in September 1912 started off on a good note when they found a very pretty cottage in which to set up house at Chislehurst in Kent. Still a rather attractive suburb of London, Chislehurst had acres of unspoiled commonland, a village of old world shops, a fine old church (Saint Nicholas's), and a village pond. Three Holbrook Cottages, as their house was then called, was tiny, with the charming air of a doll's house, and it was surrounded by a large and beautiful garden. Emily and Laurence could not have been more pleased with it. They planted a mountain ash or rowan tree in the front garden and called their new home Rowan Cottage.

From the time of their wedding they seemed to be happy, as Emily's letters to her brother Willy in the United States make clear. "Laurie is so good to me. He always comes down and lights the fire for me in the morning, then brings up a tray with tea and we have it in bed. It is nice and warm by the time I go down to make porridge. He thoroughly enjoys our real Scotch brand of porridge. Laurie is quite a Buchanish man and does all sorts of things to help me."[1]

Their financial prospects seemed quite rosy to them as well. Laurie was earning £250 a year, plus some money his firm kept back to invest for him. In another two years he would get £300 a year, with an eventual prospect of £400 or £500.

Despite the happiness the new marriage brought, child-bearing did not come easily for Emily. She had conceived immediately after marriage and on June 19, 1913, Emily gave birth to a baby boy, Brian, who lived for only two weeks. She herself was very ill and took a long time to recover; she worried desperately about Laurie and about who would care for him during her stay in the hospital. This tragic sequence, though common enough in those days, must have made Emily wonder whether she would be able to bear a child, since she was now nearly thirty-eight. By Christmas she was thinking of consulting a specialist, presumably about her gynecological difficulties.

In 1914 Emily had a miscarriage, but finally in January 1915 Alan was born. Emily's sister Gertrude was present to assist at the birth and to look after Emily. (Gertrude was to be an important member of the family for much of Alan's childhood—"a pretty, vivacious tomboy,"[2] as he remembered her.) Though delighted to have a baby at last, Emily did not find motherhood easy. A relative of Emily's remembers seeing her once with a neighbor's baby and noticed that she seemed to have no idea of how to hold it or what to do with it. She found it charming, but seemed to have no natural feeling for babies, and its mother was glad to take it back.

Natural mother or not, Emily longed for a daughter, and in 1919 she gave birth to another child, a boy, who lived only a few days. The Buchan women tended, tragically, to lose their babies after birth; not until the next generation was this known to be due to the rhesus (Rh) factor. Many of the Buchan women had Rh negative blood, which meant that a baby born to them with Rh positive blood was endangered and needed an immediate blood transfusion. Alan's blood group may have been Rh negative, which would have enabled him to survive.

Emily was not, in any case, burdened with the physical care

of Alan, for she hired a trained child nurse to look after him. One of Alan's Watts cousins, Leslie, once shared his nursery for a few days, and Leslie's mother told him later how shocked she was when she realized the nannie's severity, particularly with Alan: "Wouldn't let a child have a biscuit, or a cuddly toy in bed. Wouldn't let Alan have his toys much at all."

Emily herself was a loving woman, but she had an austere puritanical streak and believed in "firmness"; Alan was not to be indulged.

Nonetheless, Alan had some good memories of his early childhood, especially of the cottage and surrounding garden where he was free to play. He remembered the hedge of sweetbriar in the front garden and "an arbor of jasmine and a magnificent tree of green cooking-apples upon which we used to hang coconuts, sliced open for the delectation of wrens and blue tits." He loved the hours spent in the garden, getting lost in a forest of tomatoes, raspberries, and beans on sticks stretching far above his head, seeing himself surrounded by "glowing, luscious jewels, embodiments of emerald or amber or carnelian light, usually best eaten raw and straight off the plant when you are alone." There was a blissful time when part of the garden was allowed to go fallow "with grasses, sorrel and flowering weeds so well above my head that I could get lost in this sunny herbaceous forest with butterflies floating above."[3] For the rest of his life Alan remembered the taste of the peas, potatoes, scarlet runner beans and pippin apples that came out of that garden.

Beside the garden was a piece of land that the Wattses owned and behind that the playing fields of a girls' school, Farrington's. Beyond that was an immense estate of fields and forests. On the boundary between the school and the Wattses' land was an enormous sycamore tree, ninety feet high, which was important to

Alan in later memory, as he describes. There "the sun rose, and . . . in the late afternoon my mother and I watched glistening pigeons against black storm clouds. That was the axle-tree of the world, Yggdrasil, blessing and sheltering the successive orchards, vegetable gardens and (once) a rabbit farm which my father cultivated in times of economic distress."[4]

From all accounts, Alan was a precocious little boy. When he was three Emily described him in a letter to her brother Willy and his wife as "a gay little chap and an adorer of trains. Never still and always talking. He has a splendid imagination and is not short of words — and makes up a good many for himself — very expressive they are too. He can say the whole of the Lord's Prayer by himself. You would both be rather pleased with the bairn."[5]

Alan was aware from an early age of the love his parents had for each other — he remembered their holding hands under the dining room table — and of the total acceptance and love he received from his father. He had an early memory of playing with a piece of dry excrement as he lay in his crib. "What have you got there?" his father asked him, with the perfect courtesy of a Victorian gentleman. Alan handed it to him, he examined it carefully, and politely handed it back.

Laurence, in fact, never seemed to get over a kind of reverent wonder at this tiny child in their midst, and his proud astonishment at his son's achievements must have done wonders for Alan's self-confidence. Writing, in old age, a preface for his son's autobiography, Laurence tried to say a bit about what his experience as a father had been:

> What may appear to be . . . odd . . . is that a person of Alan's breadth of outlook and depth of thought should have sprung from the parentage of a father who inherited much of the Victorian outlook and tradition and a mother whose family were Fundamentalists

> to whom the Bible was the Truth, the whole Truth, and nothing but the Truth. . . . As a child a gift of narrative showed in him before he could read or write, and an early need was to keep him supplied with material for illustrating the tales he invented. . . . Plenty of white kitchen paper, pencils, and coloured chalks had always to be on hand.[6]

Alan's drawings, writings, and sayings were cherished to a degree unusual in a period less interested in "expression" in children than our own. As soon as he could talk he composed an interminable serial (complete with illustrations) that he dictated to Gertrude about an imaginary country called Bath Bian Street.

The Wattses were extraordinarily lucky in that the First World War seemed to affect them very little. Laurence was saved from conscription by a carbuncle on his neck, though he used to drill with a Territorial unit on Chislehurst Common. (The unit marched to the sound of drums and bugles produced by a group that Alan called "Daddy's band.") Night air raids usually resulted in the unexpected pleasure of cocoa in the dining room for Alan. And once when a bomb did fall in the middle of the village green no one was hurt.

Even without the intermittent excitement of the war, the social and domestic life of Chislehurst was interesting to a little boy. The milkman arrived amid clanging cans with his horse and cart. Next door lived Miss Augusta Pearce, "Miss Gussy," Alan called her. On Sundays church bells rang across the Common, and Alan would go to Christchurch with his mother, or, if Emily was ill, to the Anglo-Catholic delights of Saint Nicholas's with Miss Gussy. On Sundays, too, uncles and cousins sometimes came to visit — to be born into the Watts/Buchan families was to be part of an immense, devoted clan that frequently met and consumed enormous meals together.

Shopping expeditions to the village brought their own joy with visits to the sweet shop run by a Miss Rabbit, the bakery run by Miss Battle, the stationery shop and the grocer's smelling of "fresh coffee, smoked meats and Stilton cheese." There was a chemist's shop called Prebble and Bone, which displayed enormous glass jars of colored water in the window, and a dress and drapery shop run by the Misses Scriven, which gave Alan terrible nightmares. The sisters "displayed their dresses upon 'dummies,' headless, armless and legless mock-ups of female torsos, having lathe-turned erections of dark wood in place of heads. . . . In the midst of an otherwise interesting dream there would suddenly appear a calico-covered dummy, formidably breasted (without cleft) and sinisterly headless. This thing would mutter at me and suggest ineffable terrors. . . ."[7]

As with any small child, however, the life that mattered most was at home, with father and mother, and with the routines of everyday life. Looking back on his childhood from his fifties, Alan divided the house in two: upstairs and downstairs. Upstairs seemed filled with nameless longings, fears, desires, dreams, and nightmares, as well as with boredom, pain, shame, and humiliation. Downstairs was interesting, fun, sociable, the heart of culinary and aesthetic joy. Upstairs was his bedroom, which, as a small child, he shared with his nannie, and which looked across vegetable smallholdings and trees to the spire of Saint Nicholas's Church. He was sent there continually, it seemed to him, for interminable siestas, for bedtimes while the sky was still light, and for punishment. He disliked the bedroom so much that for the rest of his life he never slept in a bedroom if he could help it, preferring some kind of bed that unfolded or unrolled in the sitting room.

Worse than the bedroom was the unheated bathroom, which he associated with all the humiliations of constipation. Emily and her nannie attended to Alan's bowels with Protestant thoroughness.

"They seemed to want, above all things, to know 'Have you *been?*' They invaded the bathroom with an almost religious enthusiasm to discover whether you had made it. They insisted that you 'go' every morning immediately after breakfast, whether or not you felt so inclined."[8] Failure to "go" resulted in a dose of Californian Syrup of Figs, followed by senna pods, cascara sagrada, and in the last resort, castor oil.

Apart from the miseries of constipation, the bathroom was the place where Alan got spanked by his mother "seated on the crapulatory throne," was told Bible stories by his nannie, and was taught prayers by his mother. The first prayer he was taught was "Gentle Jesus, Shepherd, Hear Me":

Gentle Jesus, Shepherd, hear me:
Bless thy little lamb tonight.
Through the darkness be thou near me;
Keep me safe till morning light.

Let my sins be all forgiven;
Bless the friends I love so well.
Take me when I die, to heaven,
Happy there with thee to dwell.

Doubtless intended to comfort little children at nighttime, this prayer had the effect on Alan of making him feel frightened of the darkness and worried that death was an imminent possibility. He had heard of people "who died in their sleep," and thought that this misfortune might happen to him. (Revealingly he mispronounced the fifth line as "Let my sins be awful given.") Later for Watts the Christian religion would seem to be as bleak as this bathroom, a desert without beauty, where an impossible cleanliness seemed to be the sine qua non of godliness, where it was always Judgment Day, and where there seemed no appropriate attitude but that of shame.

Fortunately there was also the "downstairs" life of the Watts household, a life as rich and interesting as the upstairs life was drab and depressing. Emily taught the little boy to feed the birds and to imitate birdcalls (years later in California he was to teach mockingbirds to sing like nightingales), and as soon as he was old enough, his father took him on bug- and moth-hunting expeditions. They would catch the moths by putting a treacly preparation on the trunks of trees. It is typical of Alan that, forty years later, he remembered exactly what the chemical mixture was that attracted the moths. All his life he was fascinated by technical information.

The beautiful garden was the center of his childish world, but one other place had an importance for him that he was too young to understand. In the dining room there was a huge monstrosity called "the Housetop," a combined chest of drawers, roll-top desk, and hanging cupboard. In the cupboard Emily kept plum puddings wrapped in cheesecloth, fruitcake, brandy, preserved fruits, and the family silver and glass. In the desk were small pigeonholes and drawers filled with delightful things: checkbooks whose ink gave off a wonderful smell, pens, pencils, rulers, ivory gadgets, and playing cards.

> In the center of this bank of drawers and pigeonholes was a small cupboard flanked by Corinthian columns with gilded capitals. It contained mostly photographs, postcards and old letters, but there was a secret way of pulling out the whole unit to get access to two hidden compartments behind the columns. . . . From as far back as I can remember I always had the fantasy that, somewhere, the Housetop contained some mystery, some hidden treasure, some magical entity, that would be a key to the secret of life.[9]

While the Housetop was mysterious for the young boy, his mother's drawing room was positively magical. The drawing room, used only on special occasions, contained Emily's collection of

Oriental treasures. There was a round brass coffee table from India, a Korean celadon vase, two Chinese vases, and some Japanese embroidered cushions. It was not so very unusual for houses to contain a little chinoiserie or japonerie, the odd vase or hanging, or the Indian curios brought back from the far reaches of the British Empire, but Emily's deep feeling for Oriental art, her taste, her profound sense of color, and her knowledge of embroidery transformed what might have been just a room full of knickknacks into a place of wonder and beauty. Alan knew that these ornaments were his mother's choice. He recognized, later, that through her he was heir to a kingdom that might not otherwise have been his. "She turned me on, bless her, to color, to flowers, to intricate and fascinating designs, to the works of Oriental art."[10]

Yet despite all this he sensed that something was wrong in his feelings for his mother as far back as he could remember. He valued her skills, her care of him, her conviction that God was planning great things for him when he became a man. He knew her for a good woman, honest, truthful, generous, and he knew his own childish dependence on her. Yet he had a worrying sense of disappointment in her. She did not seem to him as pretty as other women, perhaps because she was older than the run of mothers, and he couldn't stand the way she looked when she woke up in the morning.

Sometimes it seemed to him that his lack of positive feeling for his mother came from the sense that she disliked her own body, and he wondered if that was because she was so frequently sick after her marriage. "When she spoke of people being very *ill* she would swallow the word as if it were a nasty lump of fat, and take on a most serious frown."[11] In fact, for the rest of Alan's childhood, and indeed the rest of her life, Emily's health was frail. She suffered recurrent hemorrhages from her lungs as a result of an attack of pleurisy from which she never seemed to make a complete recovery. Alan's cousins remember that the family often went home early from family gatherings because "Emily doesn't feel well."

Somehow underlying Emily's lack of prettiness, her illnesses, and her dislike of her own body, Alan could sense the influence of the fiercely fundamentalist Protestantism her father had passed on to her. It was not so much that Emily herself had taken on rigid beliefs — she might have been much more cheerful about it if she had — as that she had been force-fed with them and had lived with an uneasy and half-digested religion ever since. Intellectually she was a tolerant and widely read woman; she and Laurence enjoyed exploring all sorts of religious ideas. It was the unexamined and partly unconscious aspects of fundamentalism — in particular in connection with the body — that Alan felt he detected in her.

Watts was reserved about his feelings for his mother when he came to write his autobiography, perhaps mainly out of consideration for his father who was still alive and who took a keen interest in the book. But to friends in private Watts spoke of the difficulty he had in loving her. This puzzled many of Watts's family and friends who found her gentle, lovable, and caring. Although Watts would not have disputed her having those qualities, he felt he lacked from his mother cuddling and sensual appreciation. What he got instead was a dour religion that she didn't fully believe in herself, which got mixed up with condemnation of his nascent sexuality and with the rigor of Californian Syrup of Figs. Any infant in a Christian fundamentalist world was necessarily unsatisfactory, unacceptable, guilty, and ashamed, an example of the fallen and unredeemed human state. For Watts sexuality became something surreptitious, associated with beating or other sadomasochistic fantasies, or with dirty jokes. It seems significant that after writing about his mother and her religion in his autobiography Watts at once moved on to a limerick mocking the Trinity, and the Holy Ghost in particular.[12] For most of his life Watts was to enjoy a reputation for his impressive repertoire of funny and risqué limericks, often connected with religion.

Watts's relationship with his father was less intense, but warm and happy, giving him a level of self-confidence that Emily could never give. Laurence always seemed to have time to spend with his little boy. He read aloud to him, Kipling being a favorite, sang hymns and Edwardian ballads to him, and taught him to shoot with a rifle and a bow. In many ways Alan's childhood was amazingly secure, with the middle-aged couple pouring love and attention on one little boy.

Two

The Education of a Brahmin

1920-1932

ALAN'S PRECOCITY AND CLEVERNESS made him an object of attention and amusement in the limited circle of grown-ups he knew. He was, as people used to say then, "a proper caution." Once when he was ill in bed the doctor came and proposed to give him an injection.

"Only," said the dignified small child, "if you will give me two shillings first." He got his fee.

In photographs he looks a rather owlish little boy, bespectacled, scrubbed, combed, and very neatly and smartly dressed. He knew he was something extraordinary — Emily had made that very clear to him, as well as to all her relatives. Leslie Watts, Alan's cousin, remembers how it was simply taken for granted by everybody that Alan was "very clever."

Despite this early promise, Watts found school to be a letdown. He went, enthusiastically enough, to the Saint Nicholas kindergarten, just across the green from Rowan Cottage, a school for children up to the age of about eight. As an only child, he was interested in the other children, but for the most part, he was bored in the school. Emily had already taught him to read, he found multiplication tables uninteresting, and he didn't like the sort of "prissy paintings" they did, being used to bolder artistic sorties at home. So he spent a lot of time just gazing out of the window at the village green.

On one particularly awful day his teacher, Miss Nicholas, chose him as the blind man in blindman's buff. He was fond of Miss Nicholas, mainly because she was so pretty, but groping round the room, unable to see, chasing giggling knots of boys and girls, made him feel as if he had been singled out for humiliation. Furious at this indignity he went home and drew a picture of Buckingham Palace, which he took back to school next morning. King George V was lying dead with an arrow in his heart, and knights in armor with flaming eyes were saying, "How dared you do that to Alan?"

Miss Nicholas cannot often have been taken to task so severely by the children she taught, and she did not take kindly to it now. Showing the offending picture to the whole school, she gave Alan a lecture on his failings. School, he decided, was a waste of time.

Outside of school he spent much of his time in the "Paradise Garden" of Rowan Cottage, and there conducted elaborate funeral ceremonies for dead birds, bats, and rabbits. He still believed in fairies and magic. On the whole he preferred the company of girls, and in his autobiography he describes how, with "two adorably feminine tomboys," Margaret and Christine, he explored a local stream from end to end. He found them rather intimidating.

While Watts was carrying out his funeral ceremonies, Emily was beginning to make plans for him. In the England of those days, if you hoped to end in a distinguished profession, you needed to have a strictly prescribed, and very expensive, education — the education of a Brahmin, as Watts later called it. You abandoned the company of your little friends at the local kindergarten, junior, and secondary school, and you underwent the rigors of the private preparatory school, usually at age eight, followed by the public school at age eleven. Both were usually boarding schools, both gave you a good grounding in Greek and Latin, both were usually noted for their spartan standards.

Emily and Laurence did not have much money, but they lived very modestly and were prepared to save every penny they had to give Alan a Brahmin's education. Alan was clever; Emily believed this as an article of faith, even though his performance at kindergarten had revealed little sign of it. Still, she knew that the way to shine in the world was to pass through the series of ordeals and initiations provided by private education.

So, Emily enrolled Alan, aged seven and a half, at Saint Hugh's, in Bickley, a nearby town. It was rather early to go to a prep school, but Emily felt that Alan's "real education" could not begin soon enough, and although the school was close enough for him to attend as a day boy, Emily, no doubt suppressing some of her own longings for her child's company, decided that Alan would go as a weekly boarder. She felt strongly that an only child should not be "indulged."

The boys had to wear a uniform to which Alan took an instant dislike, finding it uncomfortable and rigid: "Tight, dark grey pants, a black waistcoat or vest with lapels and cloth-covered buttons, and a black monkey-jacket known as a bumfreezer, obviously designed for the purpose of making the bottoms of small boys more readily presentable for flogging."[1] There was also a large, white starched collar worn outside the jacket, and a straw boater, beribboned with school colors, in this case salmon pink with a white fleur-de-lis at the front.

Emily and Alan traveled on the bus to Saint Hugh's, Bickley.

Though proud of the importance of going to a new school, Alan nevertheless broke down in panic.

"Please, please, let me stay at home," he begged, adding pathetically that he was "too young" to go away. Emily was adamant. She said it would be good for him to have to hold his own in the hurly-burly of boarding school.

Alan found himself placed in a six-bed dormitory. After he had said goodbye to his mother, he went down to supper and found the food so unpalatable that he ate nothing except white bread. Going hungry to his dormitory he had a harsh introduction to Saint Hugh's. There was bullying of new boys — beating and other initiation rites. There was a new vocabulary of lavatory and sexual words. The puritan world of Rowan Cottage, in which he was the center of his parents' existence, and where every precocious word he uttered was received with admiration, was a poor preparation for this sudden descent into hell. Fear, loneliness, homesickness swallowed him up. How shocked Emily would have been if she could have read his summing up, written in middle age. "My first lesson [at Saint Hugh's] given at night in a . . . dormitory by the other occupants, was in the vocabulary of scatology and sexual anatomy, with a brief introduction to buttock fetishism."[2]

The next morning the seven-year-olds assembled in the classroom of Miss Elsie Good, "a precise and serious lady with a sharply pointed nose, who instructed us in English, French, Latin, Arithmetic, History, Geography and Holy Scripture. I suppose all this was, as my mother called it, 'good grounding,' but the whole process was carried out under such duress that only exceptionally gifted Englishmen survived it and retained any lifelong fascination with arts and letters."[3]

History was taught with a notable slant towards the splendors of the British Empire, and French by a system so idiosyncratic that

Alan would find himself translating: "Do you have some pretty jewels? No, but I have given some water to the owls."[4] Algebra remained an ominous mystery to him, and his attempts to question its dark edicts resulted in his being struck with the blackboard pointer. Music was the most depressing lesson of all. He was a naturally musical child with, at least later in life, a fine singing voice, but the severity of the teacher and the boredom of the Czerny studies and "children's pieces" he was obliged to play on the piano set up a mental block that lasted for years.

Life in the classroom was lived under a peculiar form of tension. In order to avoid being ritually whipped on a Saturday morning, the boys had to get fourteen "good" marks during the week, marks arbitrarily given by any teacher who happened to be pleased with a boy. This nerve-racking system did not serve Alan well, and he was beaten a lot. To go home briefly to Rowan Cottage after these dreadful weeks to parents who, though loving, would not really have understood his suffering even if he had known how to tell them about it, convinced as they were that it was "good for him," in fact only heightened the contrast between home and school. Sunday was passed in a gloom of apprehension about the coming week. Yet he felt he was expected to be grateful for his interminable ordeal. "My parents knocked themselves out financially to send me to this amazing institution."[5]

At least home gave him the opportunity to eat a decent meal. Though there were a few things at Saint Hugh's he could eat and enjoy — the fried sausages, and suet pudding with Lyle's Golden Syrup on top of it — Alan found most of the food disgusting. A worried school informed his parents at one point that he was eating nothing but bread.

School shattered, or at least badly damaged, the strong sense of self-esteem he had shown at Saint Nicholas's. The feeling that he was a prince among his peers vanished. "I have been told, in later years, that I look like a mixture of King George VI and Rex Harrison, but *then* the boys told me I was a cross-eyed and buck-toothed weakling."[6]

Apart from all the other hardships of school he missed the company of girls, hitherto his closest friends. No longer could he dream of marrying a schoolmate. Such love as existed at Saint Hugh's was between older and younger boys, pretty younger boys seeking the protection of strong older boys as part of the daily battle for survival. Alan was not regarded as "pretty."

Inevitably he learned in time, however, how to make the kind of compromises necessary to survival in such a place. He learned to swim and eventually got into the school rugger team, though he could never reconcile himself to cricket, having an ocular defect that prevented him from seeing the ball quickly. He enjoyed milk chocolate bars, smutty schoolboy jokes, and the quirks of the more eccentric teachers. Like all preparatory and public schools of the period, Saint Hugh's put most of its energy into teaching boys the classics.

As the years passed, the terrors of school grew somewhat less, though Alan never quite recovered from his initial shock. This plunge into a world of sadism and sexual innuendo left the puritan child in him with the lingering impression of shameful excitement and prurient curiosity. Whenever he writes of this grim rite of passage, it is with a dryness that seems understandably defensive. The brutality of upper-class British schools, he says, is already so notorious and has been so extensively described that he sees little point in going into details. "I was sent off to boarding school for instruction in laughing and grief, in militarism and regimented music, in bibliolatry and bad ritual, in cricket, soccer and rugby, in preliminary accounting, banking and surveying (known as arithmetic, algebra and geometry) and in subtle, but not really overt, homosexuality."[7]

Saint Hugh's was, like all such schools, devoutly Anglican, and while Alan was at the school, Emily did some of her exquisite needlework on the altar cloths. This brought Alan into contact with Charles Johnson, a brother of the headmaster and a gifted architect and designer, who carved the new reredos and generally supervised the work. Johnson, who was known to the boys, was regarded by them as wildly eccentric; some said he was mad, others that he was under the influence of drugs. One of the stories was that he needed a male nurse constantly in attendance, disguised as a butler-cum-chauffeur. Alan was surprised to find that he liked him very much. Johnson, who had lived for years in Mexico, built himself a Spanish-Mexican house in the grounds in splendid contrast to the school's drab architecture, and this became one of Alan's refuges from school. Johnson himself became the first of a long line of older mentors, male and female, who instructed Alan in the arts of living. Like all such people, he struck Alan as "urbane" and "utterly removed from the crickety-militaristic atmosphere of his brothers' school."[8] (The school had two headmasters, the Rev. Frederick Johnson and Alfred Johnson.) Watching him at work designing or carving, Alan thought that Charles Johnson gave him more education in five minutes than his brothers would give him in five years, mainly through his pleasure and meticulous care in his craft.

Despite his resentment of school, Alan also admired Alfred Johnson. Alfred had a real feeling for literature and even more feeling for music. He had a passion for Wagner, and taught the boys to sing parts of *Die Meistersinger*, one of Schubert's masses, and Brahms's *Requiem*. Unfortunately, Alfred's enormous pleasure in music did little to redeem the harm that the Saint Hugh's music lessons had done.

But more important than either Charles or Alfred to Alan's development was their sister Elvira and her husband, Francis Croshaw (also widely believed around the school to be a lunatic). Alan had found a friend at school, Ivan Croshaw, and Ivan took him home to a household which for some years was to be a delight to him and a powerful influence on his interests and taste. Elvira was, in Alan's view, "handsome, witty, and sophisticated," in contrast to his own mother, and she "spoke exquisite French," was "Continental and Parisian" in style, and was also very funny. Her son always referred to her as POM (short for Poor Old Mother), and in Watts's words, "she controlled us simply by casting an influence. I never saw her punish her son, nor lose her temper. . . . I cannot remember any adult with whom I felt so completely at ease, and she, if anyone, is responsible for my adoption of what is sometimes called an un-English style of life. For me she became the archetypal representative of relaxed, urbane society, seasoned with wit and fantasy."[9]

Francis Croshaw, who was too wealthy to work, was also a glamorous figure. He smoked black Burmese cigars, "the kind that are open at both ends, nubbly in texture, and burn with a blue flame and hiss," and he shared these with the eleven-year-old boys. Croshaw was given to taking off in his car for a day and not reappearing for a week, having suddenly taken it into his head to have a look at Wales; he walked about in a Moorish dressing gown carrying a dog whip (though he had no dog), and he read French paperbacks by the score. Alan was slowly finding the sort of friends he would relish for the rest of his life.

He particularly enjoyed their cosmopolitan qualities, their lack of insular "Britishness." Even his reading at this age revealed his dislike of narrow, jingoistic attitudes and "clean-limbed" heroes. At the age of eleven his passion, instead, was Dr. Fu Manchu. He fancied himself as "a Chinese villain, keeping servants with knives hidden in their sleeves, who appeared and disappeared without a sound."[10] He wanted a house with secret passages, with screens, with lacquer bottles of exotic poisons, with porcelain and jade and incense and sonorous gongs. He began filling his bedroom at home with cheap Chinese and Japanese ornaments, until Emily, who had already given him a copy of the New Testament in Chinese, took the hint and decorated his room with some fine Oriental hangings, including a Japanese *kakemono* of two herons watching a flight of tumbling sparrows. The beauty, the simplicity, but above all, the "alienness" of Oriental culture appealed to a child already feeling alien within the culture in which he was brought up. An affinity for all things Japanese was already growing in him; it was a secret link between him and his mother, a doorway to the sensuality he felt she had mislaid.

He missed the presence of girls in the male world of school, but consoled himself as best he could with his female cousins. His favorite was Joy, the daughter of his mother's brother Harry, about his own age, and "ruddy and joyous." Joy was shy in adult company, while Alan was talkative and mischievous, but Alan would talk to her and tease her until she came out of her shell, doing drawings to make her laugh. He corresponded regularly with her, as he did with other girl cousins, very often decorating his letters with rabbits (modeled rather obviously on Peter Rabbit). Even as a child, he had a "way with women."

In the Watts/Buchan clan, family was of immense importance, and there are many photographs of the various relatives gathered in the garden of Rowan Cottage, or out in the countryside on weekend or holiday walks. On Sunday nights the family often gathered at Uncle Harry and Aunt Et's house in Bromley (a local town) for a tremendous high tea, which Alan, in his less sophisticated moods, thoroughly enjoyed. The evening ended less enjoyably for Alan with hymns round the piano. He was later to feel that he had been fed relentlessly with hymns for the whole of his childhood and youth, and moralistic and maudlin as many of them seemed, they somehow never ceased to haunt him with their dignity and beauty. But the Sunday evenings were as much a statement of family solidarity as religious feeling, and gradually Alan could feel himself pulling away from the dowdy, if worthy, Protestant milieu, turning towards a world more glamorous and more cosmopolitan.

He was beginning to travel a little outside the environs of Chislehurst, and in later years the sight of Chislehurst station still recalled the thrill of going away, alone or on family expeditions. "Much as I loved my home, that station — with the knock-knock sound of tickets being issued, the tring of the bell announcing an approaching train, and the murmuring rails as a train came in from the distance — was a center of liberation."[11]

Meanwhile at home, Alan and his friend Ronnie Macfarlane roamed the countryside around Chislehurst on bicycles, carrying an air rifle. Ronnie and he despised, on the one hand, contemporaries who played cricket and talked in the affected accents of the upper classes. On the other hand they did not want to be identified with lower-class boys who dropped their aitches, talked in a "common" accent, and revealed signs of poverty and meager education. So they set themselves up as a pair of independent adventurers — the Japanese word *ronin* summed it up — needing nobody, but alive to the excitements and wonder of the world around them.

But times were growing hard for Emily and Laurence. Laurence, like so many in the Great Depression, had lost his job. The Wattses had lived simply, apart from the cost of Alan's education, pleased with all that they had, thrifty and saving. They had a little money saved, which they tried to eke out with Emily's embroidery and a rabbit farm that Laurence set up beside the house, but there was much family discussion about how they could be helped. Should they emigrate to America and join Emily's brother Willy? They wrote to ask Willy's advice. How could they keep Alan at boarding school? Saint Hugh's, pleased perhaps to help a boy of considerable intellectual ability, agreed to reduce the fees.

One burden was taken from their shoulders when, in 1928, Watts won a scholarship to King's School, Canterbury. King's School is probably the oldest school in England, with a long list of famous former pupils, including the poet Marlowe. Standing beside Canterbury Cathedral, the school is integrated into the life of the cathedral, and therefore into one of the most ancient sites of Christianity in England, the place where Saint Augustine of Canterbury initiated the conversion of a whole people, the seat of Edward the Confessor, the heart of Anglicanism.

It was a setting to which no boy with any feeling for history or visual beauty could remain indifferent. The poet and writer Patrick Leigh Fermor, a friend and contemporary of Watts's at the school, remembered the deep awe he felt at his surroundings when he first went to King's.

> I couldn't get over the fact that the school had been founded at the very beginning of Anglo-Saxon Christianity, before the sixth century was out, that is: fragments of Thor and Woden had hardly stopped smouldering in the Kentish woods: the oldest parts of the buildings were modern by these standards, dating only from a few decades after the Normans landed. There was a wonderfully cobwebbed feeling about this dizzy and intoxicating antiquity—an ambience both haughty and obscure which turned famous seats of learning, founded eight hundred or a thousand years later, into gaudy mushrooms and seemed to invest these hoarier precincts, together with the wide green expanses beyond them, the huge elms, the Dark Entry, and the ruined arches and cloisters—and while I

> was about it, the booming and jackdaw-crowded pinnacles of the great Angevin cathedral itself, and the ghost of St. Thomas à Becket and the Black Prince's bones — with an aura of nearly prehistoric myth.[12]

Watts too was affected by these ancient surroundings. He described the Canterbury of his boyhood as

> a garden enclosed — walled and gated on all sides. . . . Almost every building was of pale grey stone, and the architecture Romanesque and every variety of Gothic. The whole atmosphere was strangely light and airy, full of the sound of bells and the cries of jackdaws floating around the great Bell Harry Tower of the Cathedral, and when March came in like a lion the air swept through the buildings, slamming doors and rattling shutters, and seeming to cleanse the place of human meanness.[13]

The great cathedral seemed to him romantic and heraldic, reminiscent of the tales of King Arthur and the Holy Grail. He was moved by this central shrine of English religion, the "corona" of Canterbury.

> All around this corona are tall narrow windows of stained glass, predominantly blue — as good as anything at Chartres — which, with their colours reflecting on the pale grey stone, give the whole place a sense of light and lofty airiness, jewelled transparency and peace.[14]

The school was, in many ways, in a good phase. It had an original and enlightened headmaster in the person of Norman Birley, and it attracted a number of lively and able teachers as staff. It gave, as most public schools did, an excellent education in the classics. However, it also showed an interest in the arts and gave boys active encouragement to pursue them, which was an unusual practice for public schools at the time.

Sports, to Watts's dismay, inevitably figured largely in the curriculum as well, but even there those who were bored could escape: "In summer, having chosen rowing instead of cricket, [I] lay peacefully beside the Stour, well upstream of the ryhthmic creaking and exhortation, reading Gibbon and gossiping with kindred lotus-eaters under the willow-branches."[15] In many ways it was a very civilized and cultured way of life.

Watts was in Grange House, with a housemaster, Alec Macdonald, whom he liked and admired. Macdonald had been a pilot in the Air Force in the First World War, but, perhaps because of this, he was "a man of peace" as well as a man of culture. He was a good linguist, with a deep knowledge of European classics, and a music lover who played classical records to the boys. He had also invented a new method of musical notation — just the sort of thing to fascinate Watts — and in general was much the sort of person Watts hoped to become.

There were difficulties and tensions at King's School for Watts, though perhaps fewer than at Saint Hugh's. Many years later Watts was to tell his second wife Dorothy that he had minded being "a scholarship boy," that this had given him feelings of inferiority. Since his father was by now unemployed, and since even when he had been employed he had worked in "trade" instead of being a "gentleman," it is possible that Watts was mocked or despised for these reasons. "Trade," in that prewar England, was still "not quite nice." Watts suffered, however, from a sort of unwilling snobbery on his own part, a fascination with the ease and style that went with wealth, and it must have been painful to return to a home where every penny was counted, where his admired father was out of work, and where his mother did what she could to make money by embroidery.

He had learned a lot at Saint Hugh's about survival, and he

reflected that, whereas he had been frequently beaten there, at King's he managed "by sheer guile and skulduggery to avoid it altogether — only to learn the curious fact that the man who uses brains against brawn is, by the brawny, considered a sneak, a cheater, and a coward — almost a criminal."[16]

At one point early on he attempted to run away from King's School. He had written a Latin exercise in Gothic script with a decorated initial capital, and his teacher decided that this attempt to "be different" was a wicked prank. His running away, though, was half-hearted, mainly because he could not see an alternative to the school. Clever non-Brahmins went to the local "county school" where, public school boys believed, everyone said "ain't" instead of "isn't," and he could not contemplate such a fate. But if he dreaded the county school, he felt that he did not really "fit in" at King's School. Instead, he acquired an armor of bravado, superiority, and clever criticism that he was rarely to shed during the rest of his life.

During Watts's first year at Canterbury, Archbishop Cosmo Gordon Lang was enthroned at Canterbury. The magnificent cathedral was packed to the doors with robed bishops and clergy, with government ministers, with royalty — the whole panoply of church and state. The archbishop's procession wound through the nave and up the long flight of steps to the high altar with Watts, wearing knee breeches, silk stockings, and buckled shoes, carrying the long red train. Already a performer and a lover of ritual, he thoroughly enjoyed it, and Emily and Laurence were overwhelmed with pride.

At thirteen he was more at home in the elegant clothes of ritual than in the drabber garments required for everyday life. The uniform for boys below the rank of sixth form was, as Watts says, designed for "dowdy dandies," an affair of a speckled straw boater, with a blue and white ribbon, a starched wing collar with a black tie, and a black jacket with Oxford gray trousers.

The food, as at Saint Hugh's, outraged Watts's growing interest in gastronomy: "a diet of boiled beef, boiled cabbage, boiled onions, boiled carrots, boiled potatoes, and slabs of near-stale bread."[17] The serious eating in such an establishment was all extracurricular. One of the pleasures of life was to nip down to the Tuck shop run by a Mrs. Benn beneath the arches of the medieval hall and to feast on barley sugar, butterscotch, toffee, marshmallow, a chocolate bar, or an ice cream soda. Before being long at the school boys acquired their own Primus (methylated spirit) stoves, and learned to cook sausages, eggs, and bacon for themselves. Sometimes Watts brewed a sort of curry made from two onions, six frankfurters, a handful of raisins, salt and pepper, curry powder, and cooking oil. As in all such schools there was a tea shop within bounds where coffee and scones and cake were on hand, and as soon as boys began to look even remotely grown-up they would cycle out into the country to drink the excellent Kentish ale at local pubs.

In his second year at King's, Watts was prepared for confirmation — it was the routine initiation into Christian practice for boys of his background, one of the common rites of puberty. The teaching that accompanied the rite included dark warnings against masturbation, homosexuality and playing around with girls. Among the dangers they were given to understand attended masturbation was syphilis. Alan dimly wondered, as no doubt they all did, just what they were supposed to do with their nascent sexual feelings. The answer seemed to be: "When aroused, go and dangle your balls in cold water" — of which there was plenty.

Like another schoolboy at an English public school during the same period — Thomas Merton — Watts was depressed by the absence of girls in school life, and by the homosexual preoccupation that this lacuna seemed to impose. Officially dedicated to discouraging homosexuality, the school tried to control it by forbidding friendships with younger boys.

Patrick Leigh Fermor, more daring than most, remembers kissing a very nice fair girl, a maid at the school called Betty. He approached her first in the corridor. "She looked very surprised, then went into fits of laughter and dashed off. It happened two or three times — 'Now don't be a Silly Billy' and 'You'll get me shot!' she would say."[18] There would have been a frightful row if they had been caught by the authorities.

Later in his school career, Leigh Fermor had a more serious heterosexual encounter. He was "very smitten," as he puts it, with Nelly, a knockout beauty who was the daughter of the local greengrocer. The two of them used to sit and hold hands in the back of her father's shop. Eventually the affair was discovered and Leigh Fermor was expelled from the school. He had liked the place but had had a stormy career there largely because of an enthusiasm, adventurousness, and wild originality that the school regarded as outrageous. "Frequent and severe beatings" made not the slightest difference to his conduct, as he continued to live out his own courageous brand of romanticism. Watts, in later life, described his own response to the unbalanced life of school.

> I would not go so far as to say, with Kenneth Rexroth, that English public schools are positively seminaries for sodomy, buggery, pederasty, and sadomasochism. But monastically separated from girls as we were, a good deal of this kind of thing went on, and my first serious love affair was with a younger boy. We did nothing about it physically except hold hands, and as soon as I could escape from school I sought the company of girls, but found it strangely difficult to consummate any relationship until the age of twenty-two. . . . I was afraid of rejection.[19]

Confirmation, when it came, was supposed to be one of the high spots of school life. At least half expecting to be filled with the Holy Spirit, Watts renewed his baptism promises and then went forward to kneel before the bishop. With the bishop's hands on his head, he listened to the confirmation prayer: "Defend, O Lord, this thy child with thy heavenly grace, that he may continue thine for ever; and daily increase in thy Holy Spirit, more and more, until he come unto thy everlasting kingdom." When the service was over and he left the cathedral, he could detect no difference inside him, no white-hot religious fervor or tendency to speak with tongues. Of course, the laying on of hands did mean that he could now receive the wine and the bread at Holy Communion. This too turned out to be a disappointment, lacking in any of the feeling of conviviality and joy that he instinctively felt ought to accompany it. "No sense of being turned-on, but only an intense and solitary seriousness. Everyone in his own private box with God, apologising for having masturbated, fornicated or adulterated."[20] He felt that there must be some other way of approaching the deep mysteries of existence, but no other way, at least at Canterbury, seemed to be on offer.

Religion apart, life at school was getting quite interesting. He was making very rapid progress through the academic curriculum. He was very gifted at Greek and Latin verse, and in history his teacher had already marked him down as a candidate for an Oxford scholarship. He had a passionate pleasure in learning that surprised his more philistine schoolmates — he was continually looking things up in encyclopedias and checking on the origin of words in dictionaries, an astonishing enthusiasm in a world that cared more for sport than for learning.

With Leigh Fermor he led a rich imaginative life, discussing all kinds of ideas and interests on long bicycle rides. Leigh Fermor remembered how much he loved to laugh and what a strange effect the very slight cast in Watts's eye gave — "an amusing obliquity to his glance — and you sometimes didn't know which eye was looking at you."[21]

Watts was also beginning to discover the joys of public speaking, partly under the rather questionable influence of a Welsh teacher, Mr. William Moses Williams. Mr. Williams would arrive late at the school debating society, knowing nothing of the subject for the evening, nor on which side he was down to speak. Immediately he would pitch in to the side that took his fancy, speaking with irresistible eloquence, without notes or even very much knowledge. Watts said that he learned from Williams "that you can pitch a good argument for any cause whatsoever." In later life Watts himself was a master of effortless eloquence.

At the age of fourteen, casting round in his mind for a subject for the junior debating society more original than the usual ones about war, coeducation, and corporal punishment, he remembered his own deep pleasure in Japan. He took as his title "The Romance of Japanese Culture." Mugging up his material for the occasion, he spoke of Zen Buddhism and Shintoism, of the martial arts, of calligraphy, and of painting. Japan was not a subject that British schoolboys knew much about at the period — the Japanese would probably have come, like most foreigners, under the general condemnation of being "wogs" — but Watts talked so well that their curiosity was aroused and they asked many questions. It was perhaps the first time that he had thought seriously about Zen Buddhism and its rituals.

Much of his life at the time was taken up with another set of rituals — those of High Anglicanism. The Dean of Canterbury, the famous "Red" Dean, Dr. Hewlett Johnson, had a passionate enthusiasm for Anglo-Catholic practices, a meticulous sense of the way elaborate ceremonies should be carried out and processions conducted. Watts, with his natural gifts as a performer, was a favorite server and a keen apprentice at the altar. "I have even," he reminisced, "served as master of ceremonies at a pontifical Solemn High Mass, celebrated from the throne. . . . [Hewlett Johnson] reformed the style of services in the Cathedral and, among other things, taught us how to process in the right way — not marching and swaying in close order, but gently strolling, about two yards from each other."[22] It was a much more congenial form of Christianity than Uncle Harry's hymn singing and his mother's uncompromising Protestantism. Anglo-Catholics, he found out (with the possible exception of the Red Dean who slept on a camp bed in the open air and ate a strange diet), tended to like the good things in life. One such local high churchman, Canon Trelawney Ashton-Gwatkin, was the rector of Bishopsbourne, a country parish. Watts would bicycle out there on a Sunday, enjoy a delicious meal, followed by a Balkan Sobranie cigarette, and would admire the fine collection of books belonging to the wealthy canon and his wife. It was a world away from the boiled cabbage of school.

Francis Croshaw and the witty Elvira (POM) remained Watts's favorite grown-ups, and these two broadened his horizons immeasurably by taking him abroad to Saint-Malo in 1928. At fourteen he was enchanted by the delicious, unfamiliar food and wine, much of it eaten out of doors. Forty years later he still remembered the taste of the pâté de foie gras, the œufs en gêlée with truffles, and the intoxicating local cider. He was taken to Mont-Saint-Michel, to the races, to a bullfight down in the Basque country, and to a casino at Biarritz. The pleasure of all these sophisticated adventures, and the excellent food consumed so assiduously along the way, were like a revelation, a revelation that made what he called the "boiled beef" culture of England seem particularly crass. Not surprisingly, "from then on, the curriculum, the sports, and the ideals of King's School, Canterbury seemed, with some few exceptions, to be futile, infantile and irrelevant."[23] Feeling himself now to be a man of the world, Watts became rather more self-consciously arrogant, endlessly "one up" on his hapless fellows with their passion for cricket and football, a self-styled "European" in the heart of British culture.

The Croshaws' style, and Watts's growing interest in becoming a man of the world, contrasted rather poignantly with life at home, where Laurence's unemployment had brought matters to a crisis. In 1928 Emily had started an embroidery business in Widmore Road, Bromley. Her brother Harry owned two houses there, which he used for furthering foreign missions, and he allowed her to have a workroom in one of them. She took embroidery commissions, gave lessons in embroidery, and made small items such as tea and egg cozies, which were displayed for sale in a showcase outside the house. The embroidery business grew, and Laurence helped with the commercial and accounting side of it, but they still could not make ends meet. Laurence even wrote to ask Willy in Minneapolis about the prospects of work there, but more seriously considered borrowing money to buy one of the houses from Harry, letting rooms in it to pay for the mortgage and other expenses, and letting Rowan Cottage. In the end Harry rented the property in Bromley to them, and they let their beloved Rowan Cottage and its cherished garden on a seven-year lease. It was a painful move, one to which Watts does not refer in his autobiography. It meant that they saw more of the Bromley relatives. Uncle Harry held a religious occasion every Sunday afternoon known as PSA, a Pleasant Sunday Afternoon, designed to offer a little uplift in place of more worldly occupations. He persuaded Watts to conduct one of these, which he did with enthusiasm, getting Joy to illustrate some of his points on the piano. It was perhaps the first religious occasion he ever conducted. Ultimately Uncle Harry would be poles apart from Watts in matters of religion, but he nevertheless managed to convert Watts to a lifelong passion for one thing: tobacco. Cigars, pipes, cigarettes often smoked through an elegant holder — Watts was rarely without one or another for the rest of his life.

As painful as the financial bite of the Depression was Emily's failing health. While trying to start a business, she was contending with repeated hemorrhages from the lung. "The doctor assures us that there is nothing in the way of disease there and that all that was needed to effect a cure was rest so that she has spent the best part of the last fortnight in bed," Laurence wrote. "Alan is very well and happy at his school in Canterbury. I went down to see him on Friday last. While waiting for him I spent a very pleasant hour wandering round the precincts of the Cathedral, in which the School is situated. Afterwards we had a good walk together. He is growing up very fast and is a very companionable sort of boy. Both the Headmaster and his Housemaster think well of him."[24]

Watts's talent for Latin and Greek and his intense enjoyment of academic work took him into the sixth form, the top class of the school, at the age of fifteen. Now he wore a dark blue band round his boater and carried a silver-topped walking cane. He became a prefect and a monitor.

His passion for Chinese and Japanese art, always encouraged by his mother's taste, was leading him deeper into questioning his own Christian inheritance. Canon Ashton-Gwatkin's son Frank, who had worked at the British Embassy in Japan, gave Watts some hanging scrolls and a Japanese dictionary. Francis Croshaw, who had Buddhist inclinations himself, lent him books from his library, including one by a writer unknown to him, Christmas Humphreys.

One day, wandering in Camden Town during the holidays, Watts bought a fine brass Buddha and a book by Lafcadio Hearn entitled *Glimpses of Unfamiliar Japan.* He bought the book because he was under the impression that it had a lot about ghosts in it, but what ultimately delighted him was the author's description of his own house and garden at Matsue, so much so that many years later Watts went there on a pilgrimage. The poetic discourse on frogs, insects, and plants fired the boy. He felt "a certain clarity, transparency, and spaciousness in Chinese and Japanese art. It seemed to float."[25]

By reading another book by Lafcadio Hearn, *Gleanings in Buddha-Fields,* he learned about the concept of nirvana. For some time he had felt a profound distaste for public school religion and even for the adventurous liturgical life of Canterbury Cathedral; above all, perhaps, he longed to reject the repressive fundamentalism of his mother's family. Christianity, he considered, was all about accusation — God the Father was, in effect, always "telling you off" for your wickedness. The essay on nirvana gave him a "convincingly different view of the universe" — it seemed to see ultimate reality quite differently. "The ground of it all was, instead, something variously known as the Universal Mind, the Tao, the Brahman, Sinnyo, alaya-vijnane, or Buddha-nature, wherewith one's own self and being is ultimately identical for always and always."[26]

Having seen this, Watts acted. Not without a certain pleasure at the one-upmanship involved, he made it publicly known both at school and to his astonished relatives that he had become a Buddhist. There were not many Buddhists in the Britain of the 1930s, least of all among public schoolboys. (Patrick Leigh

Fermor responded to Watts's startling declaration with gratifying awe: "Do you really mean that you have renounced belief in the Father, Son and Holy Ghost?") Watts wrote off confidently to the Buddhist Lodge in London, addressing his requests for information to Christmas Humphreys, the judge, who was the best-known English Buddhist of his generation. Noting both the address and the intelligence of his correspondent, Humphreys believed for some time that he was writing to a master at the school.

Watts's Buddhist conversion was less admired by the Watts and Buchan families, and bent on persuading them all, Watts wrote a small pamphlet that he circulated to them and to his school friends. Laurence, then and later, was driven to defend his son by saying that God was a mountain to whom many different people looked up from many different angles, and Alan was entitled to his angle. Aunt Gertrude, on the other hand, wrote back suggesting that Buddhism was a selfish belief, and that its attitude to suffering would not help those who suffered as much as a belief in a loving Jesus Christ. She also suggested that Buddhism ignored women.

In a correspondence with Gertrude that allowed him to expand upon the beliefs he had set out in the pamphlet, Watts took up the cudgels, first defending Zen intellectually: "Now I have just set forward a nice little theory which is intended to be understood by the *intellectual* faculty. The Zen master aims at giving you a much wider vision of the same Truth through the *intuitional* faculty, so that you have it not as a *conclusion*, but as a *conviction*." Against a charge Gertrude had made about meditation, Watts replied, "Of course constant meditation — the constant adoption of an impersonal attitude to Life — is a remarkably difficult thing to keep up — I do not pretend to be able to do it for more than five minutes at a time."[27]

Watts refuted Gertrude's claim that suffering is a "test." "I find it impossible to believe in a personal, loving God when the world is so full of suffering and ignorance. If you say that suffering is a test for us, I must ask, why have a test?" Man, says Watts, has made God in his own image:

> I'm afraid it is hard to put faith in a man-made God. Then put faith in what? In the immaculate Law of which all things are transient manifestations. How is this done? By looking at life from a universal instead of a personal standpoint; by seeing all things as the functioning of Reality; by annihilating the distinction between "I" and "not I," between "self" and "not self," between subject and object, and by seeing all things in terms of Reality — as being just so.[28]

None of this is likely to have appealed very much to a Christian of Aunt Gertrude's Evangelical stamp. The personal relationship with Jesus, the awareness of personal sinfulness redeemed by the suffering of the Savior, the need for effort at overcoming personal failings, the acceptance of suffering as God's will, the belief in a transcendent God owing nothing to anthropomorphic projections, were all very different from Watts's puzzling talk of "I" and "not I." And besides, Buddhism felt strange and uncongenial — the sort of thing foreigners would like, as did Alan in his state of adolescent rebellion, but scarcely the sort of thing that would do in Chislehurst.

At school, a less pained and a more intellectual approach was brought to Watts's new beliefs. Watts had a new housemaster, R. S. Stanier, whom he admired so much that he copied his handwriting for a while — a useful ploy in forging permissions for boys to stay in Canterbury out of school hours. Stanier took a strongly Calvinist line against Watts, but knew his own theology so thoroughly and argued so well that they both enjoyed their verbal battles. Watts claimed that "inadvertently" Stanier taught him "all the fallacies of Western logic."

Norman Birley, a liberal and intelligent headmaster, well-accustomed to the ephemeral phenomenon of adolescent fervor, seemed not at all put out by the boy's change of faith, to Watts's secret annoyance. In the spirit of one who believed in encouraging all things educational, he sent Watts off to represent the school at a weekend conference on religion. William Temple, then archbishop of York, presided, and in spite of his own contempt for Christianity, Watts was won over by the archbishop's good mind, his humor, and his geniality. Temple had presence, a quality helped by his enormous belly and a laugh so loud that it made the room shake. Smoking a pipe with the boys late at night he told them two stories that a Zen master might have told. One had to do with the musician Walford Davies. Teaching a hymn to a choir, Davies was heard to say that they must on no account *try* to sing it, but should simply think of the tune and let it sing itself. (Both Watts and Christmas Humphreys later used this story in books to illustrate the Zen approach.) The other story was about Temple's own difficulties in composing Latin poetry as a boy: "I was working by candlelight and whenever I got stuck and couldn't find the right phrase, I would pull off a stick of wax from the side of the candle and push it back, gently, into the flame. And then the phrase would simply come to me."[29]

Back at school Watts continued to develop his religious and other interests with passionate enthusiasm. He was studying Vivekananda's *Raja Yoga*, a book that recommended abstaining from meat, alcohol, and sex, and suggested yogic exercises; despite ridicule he managed to perform yoga at night in his dormitory cubicle. Later, to his pleasure, he got the flu and was transferred to the school sanatorium. Alone in his bedroom he was free to practice all the spiritual exercises he pleased; it also gave him more freedom to read — his appetite for books just then was voracious. He enjoyed a mixed diet of religion, politics, and psychology in such authors as D. T. Suzuki, Keyserling, Nietzsche, Lao-tzu,

Feuchtwanger, Bergson, Madame Blavatsky, Anatole France, Havelock Ellis, Bernard Shaw, Robert Graves, and Carl Jung; and in such works as the Upanishads, the Bhagavad-Gita, and the Diamond Sutra.

His change of religion had not noticeably diminished his arrogance. He challenged the headmaster to abolish flogging on the grounds of "its sexual complications." Norman Birley seems to have received the admonition with his usual good-natured interest in Watts's precocity, without feeling a compelling need to act on his advice. Another of Watts's targets was the Officers' Training Corps, common in those days in most public schools. While most students accepted such a militaristic body unquestioningly, Watts expressed open contempt for the violence it represented.

To become opinionated, even eccentrically so, was not frowned upon for boys in the senior part of the school. In fact, such schools encouraged that kind of confidence, self-assurance, and independence of mind. So there was some grudging admiration for Watts's determined support of unpopular causes and unusual beliefs. No doubt he delighted to shock — as much as his contemporaries were delighted to *be* shocked — when he defended conscientious objection or attacked capital punishment. At school debating societies he talked about Chinese and Japanese art — material entirely new to the British school curriculum — and gave lectures on Omar Khayyám and the Japanese poet Basho.

Teachers do not always appreciate the sort of outstanding intelligence that goes its own way, a way often quite different from that of the examination syllabus. Watts's teachers hoped that he would win a history scholarship at Trinity College, Oxford. His chances of doing so were, one might think, excellent, and without such a scholarship there was no chance of the Wattses' being able to afford to send their son to a university.

But Watts did an odd thing. Instead of simply sitting the examinations like anyone else and doing the best he could with them, he took it into his head to answer the questions in the manner of Nietzsche, a whim so quixotic that it lost him his scholarship. Various explanations come to mind. Was it pure arrogance, a feeling that he should be allowed to do anything and get away with it? Was it a kind of contempt for Oxford and its examinations? Was it a fear of failing so great that he felt a need to provide himself with a perfect excuse? To have tried openly and honestly and then failed might have felt like an intolerable humiliation. Or was it that he needed to escape from the pressure of his parents' high expectations? His own, later explanation of his action and failure was that he was bored by school and by the idea of Oxford, and was much more interested in his own program of reading, thinking, and experience than anything the university was likely to provide.

It is easy to accept his suggestion that nothing was lost by his missing Oxford, that on the contrary he gained by getting a more unusual education. Certainly his mind was naturally scholarly, and he combined this quality with an originality of thought shown by few academics. Yet it is difficult also not to suspect a hurdle he was afraid to jump, dreading competition from others possibly more clever than himself, a possible blow to his self-esteem. The gesture of failing the scholarship, apart from being a bitter disappointment to Laurence and Emily, started him off on a career as an outsider, one he was often later to regret. He had stepped off the path prescribed for Englishmen entering the professions — prep school, public school, university — and was never able to find it again. It could have been a courageous act, or an act of protest against the elitism of the Brahmins, but it looked a lot more like pique or loss of nerve.

By the time he sat the scholarship examination, of course, he was thoroughly impatient with the whole system — the Anglicanism, the "boiled beef" culture, and in particular the absence of girls. He longed to get to know girls, but was shy about it when opportunity offered.

By the autumn of 1932 he had become head boy of his house, the Grange, and no longer had to live in a cubicle in a dormitory. His own room was Elizabethan, with fine windows and ceiling moldings, which lent dignity and prestige to its temporary owner. More important, it also gave him privacy. In the winter he could light a fire in the grate and sit up late studying, and here he began to learn about meditation. At first he sat and puzzled about what it was that the Oriental masters of meditation described, his mind picturing all the theories he had read about snapping round his heels like little dogs. He writes of his first successful attempt at meditation, "Suddenly I shouted at all of them to go away. I annihilated and bawled out every theory and concept of what should be my properly spiritual state of mind, or of what should be meant by ME. And instantly my weight vanished. I owned nothing. All hang-ups disappeared. I walked on air."[80]

Three

Christmas Zen

1932-1938

CHRISTMAS HUMPHREYS was a man with the kind of panache that had already appealed to Alan Watts in other models. Initially he enjoyed the security and confidence of a wealthy patrician background, but this confidence was badly shaken when his brother was killed during the First World War. It was then that he began to seek something that offered him more than the conventional and unquestioned Anglicanism of his class. This search gradually led him to Buddhism. As an undergraduate at Cambridge he had read Helena Petrovna Blavatsky's works, and in company with Henry Dicks, later a distinguished psychiatrist, he had taken up Theosophy. He was called to the bar and eventually became a well-known judge. In the twenties he became seriously interested in Buddhism, and he started what was known as the Buddhist Lodge in London.

At a time when many Britons showed a kind of imperialist contempt for religions other than Christianity, it was unusual for a man of Humphreys's social and professional distinction to show a deep and abiding interest in Eastern religion — this interest revealed his originality, his openmindedness, his almost unshakable self-confidence, and, maybe, his wish to be singular. As the Buddhist Lodge began to grow, his fellow British Buddhists recognized that he was larger than life, a born performer with just a touch of ham, a kindly and generous man who did much to further the knowledge of Buddhism in England. "One cannot fairly characterize Mr. Humphreys as a great spiritual original," a fellow Buddhist wrote after his death in 1983, "one who attained deep insight or realization, nor as a guru or spiritual teacher in the strictest sense. Rather he was a great proselytizer, popularizer and energizer — a great catalyst, in fact. He got ideas — Buddhist ideas — circulating; he got groups going; he got things happening. And he was able to do this because he was endowed with a unique combination of talents and advantages — most of them of an unusually high order."[1]

Having corresponded with Toby, as Christmas was known to his friends, while at school, Alan Watts started attending Buddhist Lodge meetings during the holidays, which took place in the flat of Toby and his wife Aileen (she was known as Puck) in Pimlico. Emily and Laurence, with their habitual loyalty to Alan and his enthusiasms, accompanied him on his voyage outside the Christian faith, Emily as an occasional visitor, Laurence eventually as a practicing Buddhist who later became treasurer of the Lodge. Humphreys introduced a very English, and curiously Protestant, note into the proceedings — Emily, who had reason to know, complained that he ran the Lodge like an old-fashioned Sunday School.

The young Watts, however, found in the silence, the conversation, the ideas, the obvious admiration for him of Toby and Puck, who had no children of their own, exactly the spiritual home he was looking for. For his part, Humphreys felt some special quality in Watts.

"The boy didn't just talk *about* Zen," Humphreys used to say later, to fellow Buddhists, "he *talked* Zen."

Watts began to go more and more to the Humphreyses' flat—it was

> a hideaway with a bright fire, Persian rugs, incense, golden Buddhas, and a library of magical books which promised me the most arcane secrets of the universe. . . . Toby and Puck gave me an education which no money could possibly buy, and the depth of my gratitude to them is immeasurable. Even though I now [that is, in 1973] remonstrate against some of Toby's interpretations of Buddhism, I shall love him always as the man who really set my imagination going and put me on my whole way of life.[2]

To begin with, Watts was probably as fascinated by Theosophy as by Buddhism. He was avid for "arcane secrets." All his life he was someone who loved to "know," either the kind of secrets that gave him technical mastery, or the deeper kinds of knowledge that offered intellectual grasp or control—there always seemed something boyish about this, as of the little boy convinced that the adults were conniving at keeping some essential secret from him.

One of the appeals of Buddhism for Watts was that it seemed to offer some release from the guilts of Christianity with its deep-dyed sense of sin, and from the lonely responsibilities of Protestantism. The Buddhist belief in karma, which suggested neither praise nor blame, merely a recognition of the energy bubbling through the universe, was much more congenial. Buddhist *bodhi*, or wisdom, seemed to Watts more loving in practice than Christian *agape*, or love.

Humphreys resisted Watts's attempts to turn him into a guru, but for some years Watts's life centered on the flat in Pimlico, and many of his friends, ideas, and aspirations were filtered to him through it. In some ways Humphreys was a natural successor as a role model to Francis Croshaw — the easy wealth, the aesthetic taste, the unconventionality, the interest in the exotic were all there. His arrival in Watts's life at this time was fortunate; Croshaw had just suffered a tragic death by falling from an upstairs window in his home in circumstances that might have indicated suicide.

Like Croshaw, Humphreys loved travel and the arts. The Diaghilev ballet was in London, and Toby and Puck introduced Watts to the sweeping staircases, velvet curtains, and glittering chandeliers of Covent Garden. Toby dressed splendidly for the occasion in a cape and top hat; he carried white gloves and an ivory-handled cane. Watts, used to his parents' more sober tastes at home and the austerity of school life, was captivated by it all.

Through the Humphreys and the ballet Watts got to know many Russian émigrés and acquired a love of Russian music. He was also introduced by Humphreys to a *budokwai*, a school of judo and *kendo* (fencing), as well as a Japanese form of exercise, *ju-no-kata*, rather like what many people know now in its Chinese form as tai chi. He never became a great exponent of any of these arts, but said that they taught him "how to use my feet, how to dance, how to generate energy by following the line of least resistance."[8]

Humphreys's glowing admiration for the boy who talked Zen was in strong contrast to the feelings of many of Watts's own relatives, who could only see him as a boy who had thrown away on a whim his chance of attending a university. The Great Depression was not a promising time to emerge into the adult world without either the degrees of the professional man or the skills of the workman, and family councils were held about "what to do with Alan." Laurence, with the help of Uncle Harry, had recently got himself a job as a fundraiser in an organization called the

Metropolitan Hospital–Sunday Fund. By pulling strings he managed to get the seventeen-year-old Watts a job there too, and the two of them traveled up each morning from Chislehurst to the Mansion House, the official residence of the lord mayor of London, where the fund had its offices. The job never seemed to engage very much of Watts's attention, but it left him free to pursue his own interests in the evenings and at weekends. In fact, finding himself at last turned loose in London, free of the restrictive world of school, felt glorious to him.

The London of the early 1930s was quite an exciting milieu. The worlds both of the arts and of psychology were hugely enriched by the many distinguished refugees from Hitler's Germany, and politics and religion were widely discussed with enthusiasm. A number of these currents crossed in the Humphreyses' drawing room, and Watts, so alert, so alive, so enthusiastically intelligent about all that life had to offer him, moved enraptured from one enthralling conversation to another. Part of the charm of this new world was that, unlike the world of school, it included women, and Watts was anxious to get to know women. So far he had not overcome a lingering sense of shyness, but he felt he only needed a bit more practice and the help of a willing female accomplice to explore the mysteries of sex with him. Meanwhile he practiced his charm on his cousin Joy, who remembers him affectionately from this period of their lives. To her he seemed a confident, highly articulate youth, one who was kind and thoughtful to his younger and shyer cousin, talking to her at length, doing his best to make her laugh, telling her funny stories, and drawing her pictures.

The main problem facing Watts at this time was that he still lived at home. Like many a young man, he dreamed of a flat of his own where his evenings and any potential romances would not be cut short by his need to catch the late train home. Not surprisingly, he also longed to get away from Emily. His relationship with her had come to be one of courteous emotional distance, as it would be for the rest of their lives. His friendship with his father, on the other hand, bloomed and flourished:

> He went for long walks with me on weekends through the hills of Kent, during which we discussed all the basic problems of life, admired haystacks, views of the Weald, and ancient churches and mansions. We drank beer and ate excellent bread and cheese — the tart and solid Cheddar, and sometimes the blue Cheshire — at village pubs. Almost invariably he accompanied me to sessions at the Buddhist Lodge. . . . He is a quiet, serene man who never says anything unless it is really worth saying, and I cannot imagine a more companionable father.[4]

Laurence Watts might, one supposes, have expressed his disappointment that Alan had not lived up to his parents' hopes of a university scholarship, but Watts says he fell readily in with his son's plan to design his own "higher education." Maybe Alan had convinced his father that "no literate, inquisitive, and imaginative person needs to go to college unless in need of a union card, or degree, as a certified lawyer, or teacher, or unless he requires access to certain heavy and expensive equipment for scientific research which he himself cannot afford."[5] Laurence had a way of thinking almost everything about Alan perfect, at least until a later phase of his life when he profoundly violated his father's moral code. Still, on the long tramps through the Weald and over the lunches of beer and bread and cheese, Watts's father was an important source of companionship and support.

Quite quickly after leaving school Watts was able to get to know, mainly through Humphreys's introductions, a circle of friends that would have shocked his Evangelical relatives if they had known. One of these was a young man, Nigel Watkins, who ran an esoteric bookshop in Cecil Court in Charing Cross Road. The shop carried books on a most extraordinary range of subjects: "Oriental philosophy, magic, astrology, Masonry, meditation, Christian mysticism, alchemy, herbal medicine and every occult and far-out subject under the sun."[6] The shop was also a Mecca for an extraordinary range of customers: serious seekers of knowledge who could not satisfy their curiosity elsewhere in sober England, visiting Asians, people like Watts who wanted to learn "arcane secrets," and quite a few who were frankly curious about much that seemed to be left out of a conventional education. It thus became the haunt of a wonderful blend of gurus, priests, witches, psychotherapists, lamas, and mahatmas, and ordinary office workers who happened to have wandered in during the lunch hour.

Watts quickly became friends with Watkins, and especially appreciated the fact that Watkins was frank about which material in his shop he regarded as genuine and which as rubbish. He was well informed and equally frank about what various gurus in London had to offer. One day he introduced Watts to another customer also called Alan Watts, who, for a brief period, was an important influence on his young namesake. The elder Watts was living with a woman young Watts regarded as stunningly beautiful, and, emboldened by this fact perhaps, Watts asked all the questions about sex that he had never felt prepared to ask anyone at home or at school. The older Watts not only answered those questions sensitively and helpfully, but he also introduced him to the works of Freud and Adler and to the theory of psychoanalysis. Finally, he began to speak of a very special guru he consulted himself, Dmitrije Mitrinovic, from Yugoslavia, who, he told the young Watts, was probably "a high initiate into the mysteries of the universe."

Watts needed no more. This was just the kind of person he was looking for, and he wasted no time in getting to know Mitrinovic, who was exotic enough to live up to Watts's wildest hopes and expectations. Mitrinovic lived in Bloomsbury, on Gower Street, in those days a quiet, early Victorian street in a modest part of London where many writers had lived. Somehow Mitrinovic contrived to make his perfectly ordinary house seem like a secret and exotic Eastern sanctuary, to which it was an extraordinary privilege to be invited. The rooms were dark, heavily scented with incense, decorated with fine Oriental objets d'art and with rare editions of books, often with an Eastern flavor. He lived surrounded by friends who were more like disciples, and by women, all of whom seemed to the admiring Watts to be "adoring" of the masterful Mitrinovic. He often held court late at night — 11:00 P.M. was a favorite time for entertaining — which made it difficult for a young fellow who needed to get back to Mum and Dad in Chislehurst on a train that left before midnight. On one occasion when Watts threw discretion to the winds and stayed on, Mitrinovic sent him home at 3:00 A.M. in a chauffeur-driven limousine. He had what the young Watts most admired — style.

Part of his fascination was his appearance. He had a shaved head, high Slavonic cheekbones, black winglike eyebrows, and eyes that were large and hypnotic. For his rare daytime appearances he was meticulously dressed in a bowler hat, of the kind favored by Winston Churchill, a cutaway black morning coat, and striped trousers. He completed this outfit by carrying a walking stick with an amber handle. He paid all bills in the large, beautiful five-pound notes of the period, white, crisp, and designed to look like legal documents; he drank huge amounts of whiskey, without apparently becoming drunk; and he smoked outsize cigarettes.

Watts realized that he was fascinated by the man, but that he was also quite frightened of him — in Buddhist and Theosophical circles the word was out that he was a black magician. If he was, he never revealed the terrible secrets to Watts.

Mitrinovic obviously liked Watts, took him out with other friends to Hungarian, Russian, and Greek restaurants in Soho and home to long absorbing conversations. At home Mitrinovic put on loose robes and held court sitting on his bed. Watts remembers his discussing the principles of unity and differentiation in the universe — ideas important in Watts's later thinking — and how the two principles went together. In fact he was introducing Watts to what the Japanese call *ji-ji-mu-ge* — an understanding of the mutual interdependence of all things and events.

Although Watts, influenced by Humphreys's Theosophical ideas, went through a period of wondering whether Mitrinovic was one of the secret "Masters" in touch with the ancient knowledge, his relationship with him moved gradually onto a more ordinary level. One of Mitrinovic's ideas was to develop the thought of Alfred Adler on lines that would nowadays perhaps be called co-counseling. Mitrinovic, Watts, the other Alan Watts, a physicist, and a psychoanalyst, embarked upon a "no-holds-barred mutual psychoanalysis." For some months they met on a regular basis for some hours at a time during which period Watts remembered that they "resolutely destroyed and rebuilt each other's personalities."

Mitrinovic was remarkable for his times in that he seemed fully to grasp the kind of threat that Adolf Hitler posed and advocated stern opposition to him by Britain and France. He was a socialist of sorts, who believed in doing away with money and in making workers stockholders in industry. He followed Rudolph Steiner in his concept of the threefold state (with three assemblies, one political, one economic, one cultural) and in a federation of Europe. He invented a movement called the New Britain Movement, which planned to do away with money, and published a magazine outlining his political ideas that Alan tried to sell for him at Piccadilly Circus.

In the years that followed, Watts was to show little interest in politics; rather, his two principal interests would later be psychology and religion, and both of these were foreshadowed by his youthful adventures in London. He became friends with the Jungian analyst Philip Metman and an even closer friend of the psychiatrist Eric Graham Howe. (It was typical of Watts that years later he clearly remembered what Howe had given him for lunch at their first meeting — a fine potato baked in its jacket and smothered with butter.) Perhaps what psychology seemed to offer was yet another form of arcane secrets, knowledge, or power. One day Howe introduced Watts to Frederic Spiegelberg, an Oriental philosopher who was to be important in Watts's life years later in California. Spiegelberg made an indelible impression on Watts: "He wore a hat with an exceedingly wide brim, spoke English with a delicate German accent which always suggests a sense of authority and high culture, and was propagating the theory that the highest form of religion was to transcend religion. He called it the religion of non-religion."[7]

The religion of nonreligion . . . It so happened that about the time he was considering Spiegelberg's ideas, Watts was being introduced by Humphreys to D. T. Suzuki, a tiny Japanese, with pebble glasses and a bow tie, who was to influence Watts and many other Westerners in an extraordinary way. Then in his late sixties, Suzuki had led an interesting and varied life. Born of samurai stock, he had nevertheless grown up in near poverty because of the early death of his father. He had been a clever schoolboy, working hard at other languages including English, and he had been keenly interested in studies in Rinzai Zen. He studied under Kosenroshi and then under Soyen Shaku. Soyen gave the youth the *koan* Mu ("Nothingness" as a subject for meditation) and Rick Fields, the author of *How the Swans Came to the Lake,* movingly quotes his struggles with it:

> I was busy during those four years with various writings . . . but all the time the koan was worrying at the back of my mind. It was, without any doubt, my chief preoccupation and I remember sitting in a field leaning against a stack of rice and thinking that if I could not understand Mu, life had no meaning for me. Nishida Kitaro wrote somewhere in his diary that I often talked about committing suicide at this period, though I have no recollection of doing so myself. After finding out that I had nothing more to say about Mu I stopped going to sanzen with Soyen Shaku, except for the compulsory sanzen during a sesshin. And then all that usually happened was that the Roshi hit me. . . . Ordinarily there are so many choices one can make, or excuses one can make to oneself. To solve a koan one must be standing at an extremity, with no possibility or choice confronting one. There is just one thing which one must do.[8]

In the winter *sesshin* (a marathon of "sitting") Suzuki put all his strength into solving the torturing *koan*, and realization happened. Walking back to his quarters in the moonlight the trees looked transparent, and he knew himself to be transparent too. In 1897, at the age of twenty-seven, Suzuki went to live in the United States, working in Illinois at a publishing house with religious and Oriental interests. He began writing a book in English, *Outlines of Mahayana Buddhism*, a book expressing his passionate belief in the living quality of Buddhism. Later he would return to Japan and marry an American women, Beatrice Lane, in 1911. Together the two of them worked on an English-language journal, *The Eastern Buddhist*, and in 1927 the British publisher Rider combined some of these essays with new ones to bring out Suzuki's *Essays in Zen Buddhism*. It was this remarkable book that more than any other was to attract Westerners to Zen.

It was not an easy book to read. The mixture of learning and playfulness, not to mention the unconventional subject and the ideas surrounding it, left readers interested but baffled. Many people bought it — it soon went into second and third volumes of essays — but few seemed to know quite what to make of it. Japanese scholars at Western universities seemed to resent Suzuki's success and accused him simultaneously of "popularizing" Zen (they meant cheapening it) and of being impenetrably obscure. The American Oriental Society, famed for the austerity of its approach, gave the opinion in its journal that he was a dilettante, and others complained that he was not keen enough on "discipline."

Watts, however, following Christmas Humphreys, felt love, admiration, and reverence for Suzuki. One of the first times Watts ever saw him was during a particularly boring meeting at the Buddhist Lodge. Suzuki was playing with a kitten, and something about the old man's total absorption in the tiny creature gave Watts the feeling that he was "seeing into its Buddha-nature."

Something in Suzuki the man, as well as in his writings, told Watts that he had found the principal teacher for his private university, the master he had been looking for. Suzuki had none of the expensive, ostentatious habits, the easy cosmopolitan airs, or the cultural aims of Watts's other models, but his stillness and his smile touched something lonely and lost in Watts, offered a hint of a way out not merely from acting instead of being oneself, but also from the predicament of being isolated and human, from what Watts often thought of as a "bag of skin." Already interested in Zen, Watts was now fired with a passionate concern to absorb it. Like many writers before him, he found a way to give the utmost concentration to a new enthusiasm — he would write a book about it.

His working days were still devoted to raising money for the London hospitals, but with the self-discipline that was later to mark his use of time, he decided to devote a month to writing *The Spirit of Zen* in his spare time. Instead of spending his evenings eagerly dashing off from the office to fascinating meetings with his new friends, or his weekends haunting the Humphreyses, he went soberly home each night and wrote a thousand words or so, and within a month had fulfilled his aim — a book of around thirty-five thousand words. It is easy to sense the pleasure with which it was written, a particular sort of freshness and enthusiasm that is infinitely touching. He dedicated the book to his master Christmas Humphreys, but wrote a humble and moving preface to Suzuki, saying how much he owes to his writings, and urging the reader to attempt the *Essays*, presumably using *The Spirit of Zen* as a sort of guide.

The book is self-confessedly derivative, but it is an astonishing achievement for a writer of nineteen. Writing a preface to the second edition twenty years later, Watts wished that his knowledge of Chinese had been better when using translated texts, so that he could have been more critical, that he had had a more academic knowledge of Zen, and that, before he began the work, he had seen more clearly the ludicrousness of "explaining Zen." (If the purpose of Zen is to help people "go out of their minds" in order to stumble upon the nonrational truth, then explaining it is not likely to get them very far.)

Whatever failings Watts later perceived in the book, it had, and has, a very special quality, consisting partly of Watts's love for Suzuki and for Zen, and partly of the revelation of a new side of Watts — loving and undefended — which, as he grew older, would appear more rarely in public. There is also intelligence, simplicity, passionate enthusiasm, and the first evidence of a masterly gift for describing religious and philosophical thought lucidly and provocatively. There is nothing youthful in any crude or unskillful sense; it is balanced, thoughtful, and excellently written by a cultured mind.

For the first of many times in his life, Watts describes the isolation of the individual with his or her impossible cravings, and the Zen method of trying to shock or baffle a way out of this "defended castle." Here Watts follows the Buddha's insight into the unity of all living things, and his charge to replace hostility by divine compassion, *karuna.*

Watts sees Zen as a vigorous attempt to come into direct contact with the truth itself without allowing theories and symbols to stand between the knower and the known. The method, he says, is to "baffle, excite, puzzle and exhaust the intellect until it is realized that intellection is only thinking *about.*" Similarly with the emotions, with which the aim is to "provoke, irritate and exhaust" so that it becomes clear that emotion is only "feeling *about.*" All this so that a kind of leap can take place between secondhand conceptual contact and reality itself.

He moves on to look briefly at the history of Buddhism and the aspects of it that interest him most. The Buddha was once asked, "What is the Self?" and he refused for a long time to answer. Eventually he said that "man will find out only when he no longer identifies himself with his person, when he no longer resists the external world from within its fortifications, in fact, when he makes an end of his hostility and his plundering expeditions against life."[9] The alternative to this "philosophy of isolation," as the Buddha called it, was the sense of the unity of living things, and the need to replace hostility with *karuna.*

Watts examines the different views Mahayana and Hinayana Buddhism have on the question of the Self.

> What is found when man no longer resists life from behind the barrier of his person? Because the Buddha denied the existence of any "self-nature" in the person, the Hinayana takes this to mean that there is no Self at all. The Mahayana, on the other hand, considers that a true Self is found when the false one is renounced. When man neither identifies himself with his person nor uses it as a means of resisting life, he finds that the Self is more than his own being; it includes the whole universe. The Hinayana, realizing that no single thing as such is the Self, is content with that realization. . . . But the Mahayana couples this denial with an affirmation; while denying the existence of Self in any particular thing, it finds it in the total interrelatedness of all things. Thus Enlightenment is to deny the self in the castle, to realize that Self is not this person called "I" as distinct from that person called "You," but that it is both "I" and "You" and everything else included.[10]

Watts, in his search for nonseparatedness, was selecting the Mahayana path, and the particular form of Mahayana Buddhism known as Zen. Within that he concluded that "the true Self is not an idea but an experience," the experience which comes to pass when the "mind has voided every metaphysical premise, every idea with which it attempts to grasp the nature of the world." Although in our ignorance, we continually lose sight of this fact, the Self, the experience, is no less than "the Buddha nature." "An ordinary man is in truth a Buddha just as he is"—his difficulty is to be brought to know it.

In *The Spirit of Zen* Watts also recounts many of the famous Zen stories that show pupils, in laughter, pain, anger, grief, suddenly getting the point, achieving enlightenment in a sudden, astounding flash of intuition. By that flash of intuition, *satori*, the willed but painful separateness of egoism is overcome. Even *striving* after Buddhahood implies a fatal distinction between oneself and the Buddha-nature. "While the ego works at its own spiritual betterment it is already separated from the rest of life, isolated from other beings, and this is a lesser form of lunacy, for the lunatic is the most isolated person in the world."[11]

With hindsight we can see Watts preaching to himself the answer to his own painful loneliness and know that, as is the habit of preachers, he was never entirely to benefit from his own wisdom.

Curiously, in the book he treats Zen rather more like a work of art than a living discipline available to Westerners. He describes life in Zen monasteries with a rose-colored attitude that he would later renounce, but he does not seem to expect the reader to wish to try Zen techniques like *zazen*, and he does not trouble to give the outwardly simple details of how this is done. Zen, he says, is "for the few," as elitist a way of life, he implies, as a taste for Chinese and Japanese art is for the handful of people who have developed a "high culture." Later he would change this view, or rather, events would change it for him. But the book remains an important one for those interested in Watts; at the age of nineteen (twenty when the book was published by John Murray in 1935), he had managed to state, in a rudimentary way, most of the ideas that would interest and occupy him for the rest of his life.

He was to see much more of Suzuki. In 1936, "that year of true grace in my life," as Watts called it, the World Congress of Faiths met in London, sponsored by the Himalayan explorer, Sir Francis Younghusband. All kinds of distinguished scholars, philosophers, religious leaders, and writers were there, from many different kinds of backgrounds, but so far as Watts was concerned, Suzuki, with his simplicity, his spontaneity, his humor, stole the show.

> Suzuki's feeling for the basic reality of Zen was . . . elusive, and the moment you thought you had finally grasped his point he would slip from your grasp like wet soap . . . thereby showing that Zen is something like dancing or the movement of a ball on a mountain

stream. But neither is it mere chaos, just as the flow-patterns in flame and water are animated designs of great complexity, which the Chinese call *li*, the markings in jade or the grain in wood.[12]

Suzuki could be very critical of Zen as practiced in Japan, saying that it would be best if all the monasteries could be burned down. He practiced *zazen* only occasionally (it was one of the things his enemies had against him), but was known for being able to slip into *samadhi*, a sort of reverent concentration (or maybe it was sleep, no one quite knew which), at stressful moments. Like Jesus falling asleep during the storm on the sea of Galilee, Suzuki was good at dropping off during turbulent airplane flights, a child at home in the universe, unworried and serene. He seemed to live spontaneously, without calculation, and without rigid conceptual distinctions between himself and others, or between himself and objects or animals. He used the force of gravity, Watts mysteriously claims, "as a sailor uses the wind."

Suzuki gave a paper about Mahayana Buddhism, denying the Western cliché attitude that it was a rejection of life and an escape from it; on the contrary, said Suzuki, it meant total acceptance of all life's vicissitudes, it meant compassion for all sentient beings, and it meant becoming a master of *samsara*—the world of birth and death. Watts introduced the discussion of this notable paper, and thereafter he attended every lecture and seminar that Suzuki gave. The Zen "boom" in which distinguished psychoanalysts and therapists, artists, composers, and writers were to flock to Suzuki, Erich Fromm and Karen Horney among them, did not happen until the 1950s. Suzuki was not the easiest of teachers to follow, because his method was so strange. "Teaching," according to Rick Fields,

> in addition to being a way of earning a living was a way of thinking out loud about whatever books or translations [Suzuki] hap-

> pened to be working on, and it was not uncommon for him to lose students as he crisscrossed the blackboard with a bewildering maze of diagrams and notes in Japanese, Sanskrit, Chinese and Tibetan. Mary Farkas, a student who audited the class occasionally, remembers counting as many as a dozen people sleeping in their chairs one afternoon. Not that it bothered Suzuki. Once, John Cage tells, a low-flying plane drowned out Suzuki's voice in mid-sentence, but Suzuki simply continued speaking, without bothering to raise the level of his voice.[13]

The energy of young Watts was at its height. He was now reading and writing Mandarin Chinese quite well, he was still practicing martial arts at the *budokwai*, he had changed his handwriting to a beautiful italic, and trained himself in a thorough knowledge of graphics, layout, and lettering. He was reading widely not just in Buddhism, but in Vedanta, Taoism, and the Christian mystics; with Eric Graham Howe's advice he was also exploring the writings of Jung.

Would Watts have benefited more intellectually if he had attended a conventional university? Judging by contemporary biographies and autobiographies, relatively few undergraduates of the period read, wrote, or thought as studiously as Watts did. Oriental studies were fairly limited at English universities, and most students would not have had the chance to mingle as freely as Watts did with such an interesting variety of thinkers and talkers. All his life Watts had a knack for finding people who were original without being eccentric and of seeing quickly to the nub of their ideas before making them his own.

If his pursuit of knowledge and of interesting people came easily to him, his pursuit of "girls" did not. Watts had left school with the naive belief that women would be as eager as he was for sexual experiment, and all he needed to do was to find one who attracted him. To his surprise it took him a year or two to find any girls with whom he felt a sense of rapport, and even then, to his disappointment, they seemed unwilling to go beyond the preliminaries. He did not despise the pleasures of what was later to be known as "necking," but when weeks and months took him no further, he became exasperated. It was, as he inimitably put it, "all retch and no vomit." It was gradually borne in on him that girls were conditioned to withhold their sexual favors as a prize that went with marriage (their very real fears of pregnancy seem not to have occurred to him), and this made him feel that he was the victim of an infuriating game. If there could be no sexual freedom without marriage, and if, as he believed to be the case, there was no chance of his affording marriage until he was at least thirty, then the prospects for a lusty young man were deeply depressing.

Part of the torment was that he was not sure whether his failure with girls was due to lack of experience and technique. Infectiously self-confident in most other matters, he felt anxious and unsure about his sexuality. Looking back from the vantage point of nearly forty years later, he puzzled about his failure to consummate a relationship before the age of twenty-two (though this may not have been as uncommon among his contemporaries as he seems to assume). Perhaps in the end it came down to something quite simple: "They were scared, and I was afraid of rejection."[14]

He started his romantic life with a girlfriend named Betty, whose would-be liberated style was somewhat cramped by an overanxious mother. Finally, Betty alienated Watts by joining the Oxford Group, the religious organization later known as Moral Rearmament, which relied heavily on piety, guilt, and group confession. Anything less likely to appeal to the youthful Watts or less promising to the sexual adventurer in him would be hard to imagine. There was another girl called Greta who seemed constantly to promise ecstasies she was never ready to fulfill; in the end Watts got on rather better with her brother, with whom he went on camping expeditions. The most promising liaison was with a Danish au pair girl, Hilda, who would "kiss and hug like a mink," but deeper involvement was always interrupted by Watts's need to go and catch the 11:55 train. Perhaps he was more scared than he later remembered. In any case, the sexual mores of the time were against him. "Nice girls" were not expected to do much more than kiss before marriage, and in addition to warnings of pregnancy, they were told that "men wouldn't respect them" if they gave way to desire. Underlying all of this was a dimly understood belief that Christianity thought fornication was wrong, but also an atttiude toward sexuality that insisted that "ladies" didn't enjoy sex and that there was something beastly in men which regrettably did. It was not a healthy foundation for sexual experience, forcing many into marriage before they were ready for it, as the only "decent" way of satisfying their sexual desires. The young Watts, not surprisingly, was at war with this damaging and unrealistic approach to natural feelings, and there was pain and bewilderment at his initial inability to persuade well-brought-up young women to see the matter as he did. All this changed rather quickly, however, when Eleanor Everett came into his life.

The first time he saw her was at the Buddhist Lodge early in 1937. Her mother, Ruth Fuller Everett, had come to give a talk about her stay at a Zen monastery in Kyoto two years before. Mother and daughter, apparently devoted to one another, had an air of easy American wealth; money and the style that went with it had often fascinated Watts in the past, but this time it came in a new guise.

Ruth Everett, a rather formidable lady, knew more about Zen than Watts. Like many American society ladies she had, some years previously, come under the influence of a man who, like Aleister Crowley or Mitrinovic, could be described as a "rascal-guru," one Pierre Bernard, who owned a sort of ashram in Nyack on the Hudson River and taught tantric and hatha yoga. At Nyack Ruth discovered the existence of Zen Buddhism and, with the sublime self-confidence that marked all her actions, simply took off for Japan with the fifteen-year-old Eleanor and introduced herself to Suzuki, who in turn introduced her to Nanshinken, the famous *roshi* of the picturesque monastery Nanzenji. Ruth insisted on being allowed to sit *zazen* at the monastery, thus making her and Eleanor the first Western women ever to do so, but Nanshinken seemed to prefer Eleanor's company and liked to sit out on his veranda showing her pictures of sumo wrestlers he thought might appeal to her as possible husbands.

Ruth, though she later became a serious student of Zen, was perhaps initially seeking some solace for a wretched marriage. At the age of eighteen she had married Warren Everett, a famous Chicago attorney who represented well-known industrialists. It became clear to her almost at once that Warren was less interested in her as a woman than as a competent housekeeper and a decorative hostess. She had great intelligence and gradually acquired wide aesthetic and religious knowledge as compensation for an empty emotional life, but in the beginning she had been a timid girl with a bullying husband, himself trying to compensate for having been crippled as a child with polio. He was fearfully exacting about how the house was run — Ruth remembered years later how the biscuits served at the table had to have enough fat in them to stain the napkin they stood on — and he took for granted that it was her job to entertain innumerable business acquaintances whose interests were entirely different from her own.

Gradually under these pressures a very powerful woman began to emerge. Eleanor, as the only child of a strong-willed mother and an irascible father, had a hard time simply being her own person. She had money to spend, beautiful clothes to wear, a background of extensive travel to exotic places that took Ruth's fancy, but she did not finish high school, probably because her mother wanted her as a traveling companion. In 1937, however, when Eleanor and her mother came to London, she decided that she wanted to study the piano, and she was working with a teacher named George Woodhouse, a man with a Zenlike approach to piano playing.

It is striking that Watts devoted as much space in his autobiography to Ruth as he did to Eleanor, and it is Ruth who comes across as the stronger and more interesting personality. Perhaps it was Ruth, with her knowledge, her formidable power, and her money who most deeply fascinated and attracted Watts, but the way to be close to Ruth was to be close to Eleanor.

He and Eleanor went to the opera and the ballet and to various piano concerts together, always with the most expensive seats, and she encouraged him to start playing the piano too — he got as far as a Scarlatti sonata. She also persuaded him to dance — a thing most inhibited Englishmen of his generation found almost unimaginable except in the most formal circumstances. Eleanor had picked up the hula on a trip to Hawaii and taught him the swing of the hips that makes true dancing possible.

Eleanor was not precisely pretty, but was a pleasing, slightly plump girl, with a vivacity that made her fun as a companion; she wore lovely clothes that Watts's cousins admired and envied, had money to spend and an air of sophistication. She was talented and appeared supremely self-confident. Always perceptive, Watts probably knew that beneath the culture, the fine clothes, the extreme high spirits, was a girl with little self-esteem who felt intimidated by her mother and unloved by her father. These feelings, however, would have touched on Watts's own weakness — his pleasure in playing a kind of Pygmalion role toward women, to mold them and give them confidence, no doubt in an attempt to relieve fears and neurotic tendencies of his own. Whatever the reasons, a romance had begun, one that caused interested speculation in the Watts/Buchan clan since Watts had committed himself to the point of describing Eleanor to them as "highly satisfactory."

He had other pleasures in 1937, in particular the publication of his new book, *The Legacy of Asia and Western Man.* The *Church Times* described it in a review as a "witty and perverse little book," but Watts himself in later years found it somewhat embarrassing. This may have been because it attempted to cover too much ground, but it is a lucid and interesting book, and it reveals much about the way Watts's mind worked in the period immediately following *The Spirit of Zen.*

In some ways it is a response to the rather shallow arguments against Buddhism that his first book provoked, the sort of criticism of which Watts had been happily and unselfconsciously aware when he began to write. In his second book he felt obliged to tackle questions of whether Buddhism is "impersonal," whether it "devalues" the individual, whether it lacks "love" and social concern.

Watts, however, took on a bigger task than defending Buddhism. He began to see every religion as having special gifts of its own to bring to mankind: Hinduism a very deep understanding of mysticism, Taoism a sense of oneness with the principles of life, Buddhism in all its forms, a developed method of freeing the mind from illusion. Inevitably Christianity, the traditional religion of most people he was writing for, had somehow to be rediscovered for his purposes. He approached it with a certain amount of distaste, still resentful of the guilt and shame that surrounded its moral teachings, still angry about heaven and hell used as carrots and sticks to control the simpleminded, and still dubious of the Christian Church's claim to ultimate truth.

Yet despite distaste for a religion that, it seemed to him, had gone collectively sour, Watts admitted to feeling a kind of pull toward it: "However much we may imagine ourselves to have cut adrift from the Church's symbols, they return to us under many forms in our dreams and phantasies, when the intellect sleeps and the mind has liberty to break from the rational order which it demands."[15]

Because Christianity had lost its life and vigor, Watts felt that modern Western man had lost himself in the "rational," in humanistic, scientific, and technocratic modes that derived from a purely rational attitude to life. "It is precisely to preserve us from a 'rational' civilization that a vital Christianity is necessary."[16] Having thrown Christianity away he began to feel it return like a boomerang.

In *The Legacy*, borrowing from Jung, Watts suggested that Christianity must learn to see itself much more in symbolic and mythical terms than in historical ones, so that, for example, the Passion and Resurrection of Christ become the pain of the individual torn between the contradiction of the opposites, and achievement of their eventual resolution, or the birth of the Divine Child becomes the birth of intuitive love in every person. Watts also believed that assimilating Asian wisdom — in particular the wisdom relating to the relativity of good and evil, and the recognition of the way mankind is torn by duality — gave a chance for escaping the alienation of duality.

The young Watts was applying himself to some of the central questions for Western man, doing his best to grasp the nature of the tragedy. As part of the new understanding he believed that psychotherapy was essential; within the triangle of Eastern religion, Western religion, and psychotherapy, a new beginning for human salvation, a new healing, was to be sought.

In his two books Watts had now outlined his lifelong preoccupations: the synthesis of Eastern and Western thought, in particular the synthesis of Buddhism and Christianity, and the links of both with healing, particularly in the form of psychotherapy. For the rest of his life he would think and struggle, read and argue, teach and discuss, make jokes and tell stories about precisely these questions.

Eleanor shared Watts's Buddhist preoccupations just as Ruth did. Able to sit in the full lotus position, she came with him to Buddhist meetings to sit in *zazen*, and the two of them faithfully practiced meditation together at home. Once when the two of them were walking home together from a meditation session he began to talk about how difficult he found it to concentrate on the present. "Why try to concentrate on it?" Eleanor asked. "What else *is* there to be aware of? Your memories are in the present, just as much as the trees over there. Your thoughts about the future are also in the present, and anyhow I just love to think about the future. The present is just a constant flow . . . and there's no way of getting out of it."[17] Watts found this comment of Eleanor's a minor revelation, one for which he remained grateful to her for the rest of his life. "You could have knocked me down with a feather," he said.

He was just as grateful to Eleanor for her eagerness to embark on sexual adventures. Perhaps it accorded with the more liberal sexual ideas of her new religion, perhaps the sense of wealth made the possible consequences seem less alarming, perhaps she sensed Ruth's rather obvious complicity. Ruth went back to America, leaving Eleanor to Watts's tender mercies, perfectly aware that the two were spending most of their spare time together. They took advantage of the opportunity, two virgins anxious to lose their virginity, two attractive young people who liked each other's company. They very quickly started to believe that they were in love.

Ruth's total cooperation is perhaps a little surprising. Known in Chicago as a social climber, she might have sought and found a better match for her daughter. She might have feared (perhaps with justification) an element of fortune hunting in Watts's courtship of her daughter, not in any crude sense, but in his simple expansive pleasure in the good things of life — good seats at the opera, good restaurants — otherwise not available to him. She probably found him physically attractive, as Eleanor did, and she may have felt that his good manners, his elegant Britishness, his cheery insouciance made up for a good deal he lacked in other ways. Certainly his lack of money, or a career, kept the young people under her control to some extent. It was not that she had any very high opinion of his abilities and potentialities, despite his two published books. When she left England for America her only comment about him to Eleanor was, "He's all right, but he'll never set the Thames on fire."

The two young people continued to try out all the sexual techniques of which Watts had read in books — Eleanor tended to prefer the more conventional methods — and instead of traveling home on the 11:55 train every night Watts often spent the night at Eleanor's apartment, something which cannot have had Emily's approval. "Living together" was still rather frowned on for any but the most bohemian. Perhaps this reason pushed the two of them, young and inexperienced as they were, towards the possibility of marriage.

Watts took Eleanor to tea with Emily and Laurence at Rowan

Cottage — they had by now moved back and had just celebrated their silver wedding anniversary. Eleanor found Rowan Cottage charming and talked, with her easy American manners, about her home in Chicago, her life in London. Emily, a little stiff as always, had put herself out to entertain "Alan's girl," and Laurence was openly delighted with her. It did not surprise him that his son should attract a girl so rich and stylish.

Social expectations swept them along; young people in love were supposed to get married, especially if they could afford to do so. Watts proposed to Eleanor, she accepted, feeling a wonderful sense of release from the tyranny of life with her parents, and the two of them were invited to spend Christmas 1937 with Eleanor's family in Chicago. They sailed for New York on the *Bremen* on December 17, but the day before, an engagement party was held at Rowan Cottage, with all Watts's uncles, aunts, and cousins there to meet the "very sophisticated American fiancée."

The journey to America was a delight to Watts. Although he sensed that the visit to Chicago was set up to be an inspection of him, he had no qualms of his success and dived into the delicious food on the liner with tremendous pleasure. New York was the next excitement — thrilling and beautiful — and then the two of them boarded the *Commodore Vanderbilt* train for the night ride to Chicago. The fields gleamed white with snow under the moon, many of the towns and villages were lit with colored lights for Christmas, and Watts went to sleep to the sound of the old steam whistle as the engine pounded through the night, through towns with magic names like Poughkeepsie, Schenectady, and Ashtabula. In the morning at the La Salle station, they were met by the Everetts' Philippine chauffeur, who tucked them under rugs into a sleek limousine, and Watts was on his way to meet the family for their holiday celebration, given for them on a royal scale.

Warren Everett, who, at the best of times, was a bad-tempered man with a bullying lawyer's manner, was by now an invalid badly afflicted by arteriosclerosis, which did not improve his character. To everyone's surprise, he and Watts took to one another on sight, Watts later thought because they enjoyed some similar vices — smoking cigars, telling ribald stories, and thumbing through girlie magazines. Despite his youth Watts was not frightened of Warren, and he showed a genuine interest in the older man's long and varied career. Although Watts found most of the other Everett relatives he met to be rather boring, he got on quite well with a number of Eleanor's friends. Then it was back to England again on the *Bremen*, to the fun of trying to dance the Viennese waltz on a rolling deck to the music of a Bavarian band.

Before taking him home to visit her parents Eleanor had changed Watts's style of dress, as she was changing so much else in his life. Always biased towards the formal, he had been in the habit of sporting a mustache, a black Homburg hat, a black formal coat with striped trousers, a silver-gray tie, chamois gloves, and a rolled umbrella. Eleanor got him out of this rather pompous and old-fashioned gear and into tweed jackets and colored ties.

Although a date had not yet been set for the wedding — indeed their parents might have discouraged setting one until Watts had a "proper job" — in February 1938 Eleanor became pregnant by Watts, and they immediately decided to get married in April. Eleanor was eighteen, Alan twenty-three. Looking back on it afterwards, Watts "could not understand" how it was that two Buddhists managed to get married in a Church of England ceremony, at Saint Philip's, Earls Court, one at which Eleanor promised to "love, cherish and obey." Perhaps the reason was simply that Ruth could have the big society wedding that she had set her heart on.

The bride, on Watts's insistence, entered the church to the

Meistersinger overture, and the couple left to a theme from the last movement of Beethoven's Ninth Symphony. During the taking of the vows the organist gently played a Tchaikovsky melody, which, years later, when it was turned into a popular song, Watts was amused to notice had the new title "Will This Be Moon Love, Nothing but Moon Love?" These musical details were about the only say the two of them had in the planning of their wedding.

Ruth had taken a maisonette (duplex) for them at Courtfield Gardens in London, a huge Edwardian mansion with vast rooms. Watts does not make it clear whether the house was already furnished, whether Ruth undertook the task for them, or whether he and Eleanor set about spending her very considerable allowance from her parents. But the place was curtained with yellow Chinese damask, carpeted in dark purple, and set about with pieces of Elizabethan and Jacobean furniture. "Almost palatial" was Watts's description of it.

They did not stay long to enjoy the splendor. Even the temporary respite of Munich made it clear for those who chose to see it that war with Germany was bound to come, and that if it did, Watts would be conscripted. He had not the slightest intention of becoming a soldier — the idea appalled him from every point of view — nor did he intend to endure the public obloquy and possible imprisonment inflicted on conscientious objectors. The only alternative was flight, and for the young Wattses flight to the United States was very easy, with moneyed relatives waiting to receive them. Perhaps sooner or later the United States would have lured Watts anyway. Ever since the enchanted journey to Chicago he had been excited by the challenge it offered — perhaps some of the wealth would rub off on him?

So with Eleanor in the last months of pregnancy, they set off for New York. Entering the continent via Montreal Watts was stopped by a U.S. immigration officer who noticed that he carried a stick.

"Whaddya carry a cane for? You sick?"

"Not at all," Watts replied. "It's just for swank."

Once in New York, the young couple was installed by Ruth in an apartment next to hers at the Park Crescent Hotel, at Eighty-seventh and Riverside, and here in November Eleanor gave birth to a daughter, Joan. The future, despite the war, looked personally promising.

Four

The Towers of Manhattan

1938-1941

MANHATTAN SEEMED DANGEROUS, fast, foreign, almost unbearably exciting to the young Alan Watts, entirely different from the familiarity and coziness of 1930s London. He was fascinated by the sight of so many different races of people in the streets and by the enormous streamlined towers beneath which men were as tiny as ants. He loved going to drugstores and inventing amazing sundaes for himself (concoctions that made the later, gourmet Watts squirm at the recollection), such as "vanilla ice cream globbed with butterscotch, ringed with maraschino cherries, topped with whipped cream and chopped nuts."[1] He liked the huge steaks, the food in Jewish delicatessen shops, and the many kinds of exotic cooking. He was amused when he gave his name in stores and they spelled it *Watz*. He thought the New York girls beautiful and beautifully turned out, and never tired of watching the passing show in the streets.

Apart from the joys of exploring New York, it was good to be married, and married to Eleanor. The misery of being without a sexual partner and the humiliation of trying to persuade various unwilling girls to oblige him were things of the past. Marriage to Eleanor had also had the additional bonus of taking him away from the uncomfortable relationship with his mother and the burden of difficult relatives in general. As a young, attractive, moneyed couple, the Wattses found themselves part of an interesting social circle, constantly invited to parties, to weekends in country houses, and to dinner parties with friends. Their friends were musicians, painters, scientists, psychologists (the sort of people Watts was to know and enjoy for the rest of his life), who talked of Buddhism, mysticism, Jungian analysis, and much else. Watts was already a brilliant talker who knew a great deal about these subjects, and he enjoyed an instant popularity. If his rather courtly British manner and "Brahmin" accent seemed slightly affected to his new audience, they nonetheless exerted a perverse attraction of their own.

He was less successful as a father. It was not that he didn't like the baby, more that he was bored by all the daily labor that went with her, which interested him much less than his own ideas and pursuits. In this he was aided by the mores of the time, which did not have high expectations of paternal involvement, especially when, like the Watts couple, the parents could afford "help." Their social life was not seriously disrupted. Little Joan did, however, sleep in their bedroom, and Watts seemed to enjoy what he called her "burbling" and "bubbling" and the way she developed "a lilting language of her own that sounded like a mixture of Hopi, Japanese and Malayan."[2]

Ruth Everett was living next door to them, alone, since Warren Everett was now permanently confined to a nursing home with arteriosclerosis. Pursuing her interest in Zen, she found herself in 1938 a new master, Sokei-an-Sasaki. Funded by a rich Japanese businessman, Mr. Mia, Sokei-an had taken a couple of rooms on

West Seventy-third Street and founded the Buddhist Society of America in May 1931. "I had a house and one chair. And I had an altar and a pebble stone," said Sokei-an. "I just came in here and took off my hat and sat down in the chair and began to speak Buddhism. That is all."[3]

Sokei-an had led an adventurous and interesting life. He had begun by studying art and becoming a painter, carver, and sculptor in Tokyo, with a particular skill in carving dragons, but he had gone on to become a Zen student with the famous master Sokatsu Shaku. With Sokatsu and some of his students he had gone in 1906 to California, where they tried unsuccessfully to farm at Hayward near San Francisco. Sokatsu arranged a marriage for Sokei-an, and he had three children by his wife, Tomoko. Much of his life had been one of conflict, as he was torn between first his Zen studies and his work as an artist, and then between his duty to Tomoko and his children, and his longing to lead a lonely and independent life. Eventually he separated from his wife and returned to Japan where his old teacher was now living; there he gave himself up at last to his Zen studies. At the age of forty-eight he was authorized to teach by Sokatsu and told to return to the United States where his life's work would henceforth be. The first years in New York were painful, as he tried to eke out an existence without money or a permanent place to live. Then Mr. Mia took him up, and slowly he began to acquire students.

By 1938, when Ruth Everett met him, Sokei-an had about thirty students who met for *zazen* for about half an hour. They sat upright on chairs rather than crosslegged on the floor because Sokei-an was convinced that Westerners would not endure the crosslegged posture. His major teaching was not *zazen*—there was no *sesshin* at his *zendo* (room for meditation) either—only *sanzen*, the private interview in which *koans* were assigned and discussed.

Hearing of the remarkable Sokei-an from Ruth Everett, Watts decided to go along and see the master for himself. He found him in "a small temple in a walk-up . . . just one large room with a shrine that could be closed off with folding doors, and a small kitchen. Here Sokei-an lived in extreme simplicity with his Maltese cat, Chaka."[4]

Watts was very taken with both the simplicity and convenience of Sokei-an's way of life and asked the old man if he could become his student, to which Sokei-an agreed. The method of training was that the pupil was given a *koan* that, following the formal method devised by Hakuin, had to be answered in a specific way.

Beginning with enormous enthusiasm, Watts worked extremely hard at his *koans*, only to find that, bored and angry, he reached a point of nearly intolerable frustration and felt as though he were looking for a needle in a haystack. Ironically, in *The Spirit of Zen* he had described this sort of discouragement as an essential stage in the pupil's development, the suffering described as an iron ball in the throat that could neither be swallowed down nor spat out. It was indeed precisely the experience of being driven "out of one's mind" and thus onto another level of awareness altogether that the *koan* so uncomfortably existed to promote.

Perhaps Watts did not have enough trust in Sokei-an to undergo this ordeal at his hands, or perhaps he found the role of apprentice too humiliating to be bearable. Whatever the reason, after some eight or nine months of study Watts lost his temper in *sanzen*, shouting at his teacher that he was right.

"No, you're not right," Sokei-an replied. That was the end of formal Zen study.

Other pupils saw Sokei-an very differently. When he sat in the *roshi* chair to conduct *sanzen*, the small, rather insignificant-looking man inspired awe. He was formidably silent, and the silence created a vacuum in which the pupil was drawn out of his or her habitual self into a new awareness of the One. Ruth Everett, admittedly always deeply fascinated by Sokei-an, felt that, in his teaching guise, he was not so much a man as an "absolute principle."

Sokei-an liked to lecture, which he did hesitantly and with a strong Japanese accent. His astonished audience would see him change before their eyes, becoming the animals or the people or the forces of nature he was describing: a golden mountain or a lonely coyote, a princess or a geisha. According to one of his pupils, in Sokei-an's teaching "there was something of Kabuki, something of Noh's otherworldliness, something of a fairy story for children, something of archaic Japan. Yet all was as universal as the baby's first waah."[5]

Either Watts did not see this or his envy of the rival spellbinder was insupportable. It was not exactly that he had decided that Sokei-an had no more to teach him, rather that he resented the teacher/pupil role. He solved this problem through a kind of surreptitious observation of Sokei-an, a study of how a Zen master lived as he went about his daily life.

There was ample opportunity for him to do this, since Sokei-an was now spending a lot of time at Ruth Everett's apartment, eating with her and going on trips with her, and Watts and Eleanor were frequently invited along. "A photograph of the period shows . . . Alan and Eleanor, Sokei-an and Ruth, out for the evening on the boardwalk at Atlantic City — mother and daughter looking like sisters in their long evening gowns, Watts resembling a young, handsome David Niven in his tuxedo, and Sokei-an, also in evening clothes, but wearing glasses, and a large false nose and moustache, looking very much like a Japanese Groucho Marx."[6]

Watts's observation of Sokei-an at close quarters deepened rather than lessened his admiration. There was something true and somehow inexplicable about his calm, his laugh, his ribald, earthy humor (often rather shocking to American sensibilities; he liked to use farting as an example of a spontaneous Zen moment), his skill as a woodcarver, and his scholarship in the Buddhist classics. Watts noticed that he had none of the nervous embarrassment of other Japanese he had known, but "moved slowly and easily, with relaxed but complete attention to whatever was going on."[7]

Ruth Everett's organizing energy had begun to make a difference to Sokei-an's modest beginnings of a Buddhist society. She had persuaded him that, Western or not, his students must sit crosslegged on the floor, and she took on the editorship of the society's journal, *Cat's Yawn*. She and Sokei-an began working together on a translation of the *Sutra of Perfect Awakening*.

Formidable woman that Ruth was — her granddaughters point out that she was born on Halloween, under the sign of Scorpio, and that her Japanese name meant "dragon's wisdom" — Sokei-an clearly enjoyed her company a great deal.

Warren Everett died in 1940. Even before his death, Watts and Eleanor had noticed, unbelievingly at first, that Ruth and Sokei-an appeared to be falling in love. Watts had wanted to observe the conduct of a Zen master at first hand, but he had scarcely anticipated the experience that now came to him of watching one in "the first bloom of romance." Absolute principle and dragon, this unlikely pair seemed to match one another in power, perhaps both finding love for the first time in their lives, she "drawing out his bottomless knowledge of Buddhism and he breaking down her rigidities with ribald tales that made her blush and giggle."[8]

In November 1941 Ruth set up a sort of house-cum-temple for Sokei-an on East Sixty-fifth Street. Here she took her splendid library and Oriental works of art and set up the First Zen Institute of America. This was intended to be Sokei-an's future home. In

December, however, Japanese forces attacked Pearl Harbor, and almost at once the FBI began rounding up Japanese, American citizens or not. The Buddhist Society was regarded as an object of particular suspicion, and Ruth and Sokei-an were extensively questioned.

In July 1942 Sokei-an was taken to an internment camp in Wyoming. He had just had an operation for hemorrhoids at the time and, according to Watts, was "put in a hut from which he had to walk some fifty muddy yards to the nearest latrine." The major in charge of the camp liked Sokei-an and did his best to ease his living conditions, in return for which Sokei-an carved him a stick with a dragon climbing on it. Ruth hired a famous lawyer to work on his case, and eventually he was allowed to return home, his health seriously undermined. The couple married at last in 1944. In 1945 Sokei-an died, according to Watts with the parting words, "Sokei-an will never die," and to Rick Fields with the saying, "I have always taken Nature's orders, and I take them now."

Meanwhile, the marriage of Alan and Eleanor was running into difficulties. They were very close, too close Watts was later to think, so that the unhappiness of one could pull the other down into deep gloom. This might not have mattered so much but for the fact that Eleanor was becoming seriously depressed. Maybe it was the responsibility of having a child to care for when she was still very young herself, maybe it was, as Watts seemed to believe, the difficulty of living with him instead of a more conventional husband, maybe the sexual disagreements that were later to become central to their marriage were beginning to be apparent. Whatever the underlying reason, Eleanor was deeply sad. She put on a lot of weight, developed eczema and a tendency to put her jaw out, presumably from tension, tended to drink too much, and to worry, quite unnecessarily, over money. No doubt being the rich wife of an unemployed husband posed its own threats to the marriage; at one point, because she wanted to make Watts feel, as he put it, "more of a man," she handed over her considerable holdings in stock to him. They continued to live comfortably off the dividends, supplemented with occasional handouts from Ruth. Eleanor began to have treatment from a psychiatrist friend, Charlie Taylor.

Watts was deeply affected by Eleanor's distress. He entered into her symptoms and the possible cures with the kind of friendly sympathy he always showed to those around him; it was not easy to see what was troubling her. Eleanor "had everything," as people say—money, a nice apartment, an attractive husband who loved her, and a contented baby—yet she was showing signs of severe stress. Watts is oddly silent about the relationship between Eleanor and Ruth at this time.

Eleanor, who had been frightened and controlled by her mother all her life, can scarcely have wished to live next door to her in adult life, nor to have lived off her money, with all the possibilities for power that such an arrangement provides. But getting out of Ruth's pocket would have required Watts to take up a successful career, which he showed no sign of doing. In one sense, Watts was her ally against her mother, an attractive husband who was theoretically on her side. But the trouble was that Watts was deeply fascinated by her mother, perhaps even to a degree in love with her. His previous models in life had been men, rich, clever, eccentric figures, whose knowledge and taste exceeded his own and from whom he could learn. But his mother-in-law was wealthier than Francis Croshaw, cleverer than Christmas Humphreys, better read in the Oriental classics than Watts. Her ideas, her conversation, her library, her style, her taste ("infallible" so far as Oriental objets d'art were concerned) all compelled him in spite of himself. Partly it seemed that wealth had always cast the sort of spell over him that it sometimes does upon the genteelly poor; partly perhaps, in the days of Ruth's unhappy marriage to Warren Everett, Watts sensed a deep sexual frustration that attracted him more than he knew. For all these reasons he could not be free of Ruth, and Eleanor, who despite gifts and talent of her own had never quite emerged from the shadow of her mother, felt more trapped than ever.

Although Watts could not see his way to taking a job, he had none of the characteristics of the layabout or ne'er-do-well. Much as he liked parties and relaxed evenings with friends, he had a natural self-discipline, liked to rise early and use every moment of the day. He spent his time reading seriously and deeply, working at his Zen studies, practicing photography, calligraphy, and painting — he worked in watercolor, ink, and tempera. He also painted icons and sometimes made erotic drawings to please his friends. Ruth suggested that he work for a Ph.D. and take up teaching, but just as he had once felt that he could do better than go to Oxford, now he felt that he could do better for himself than take up the patient molelike digging of the academic life. He was either too proud or too wise, too frightened or too self-confident, too lazy or too easily bored — perhaps a bit of all of these.

In fact, he had begun teaching, though not within the academic system. He lectured at the Jungian Analytical Psychology Club, talking about "acceptance," in the sense of contentment, and he conducted rather successful seminars in Oriental philosophy that were well attended. He turned his Jungian lecture into a book — *The Meaning of Happiness* — which Harper enthusiastically bought. It came out in May 1940 "just as Hitler moved into France and no-one wanted to read about happiness and mysticism," though it was warmly praised by the *New York Times*. As a result of the book's success, Harper began to use Watts as a manuscript reader, and he began to sell the odd article to magazines interested in Asian ideas and religion.

The subject of the book was a simple one. Of what did human happiness consist? The religion and psychology of both West and East maintained that it was about union or harmony between the individual and the principle of life itself—God, the Self, the unconscious, the inner universe. The individual, Watts thought, needed first to become aware of this, and then to recognize that he or she was, as it were, already *there*. Harmony was not, in his view, achieved by tremendous efforts, but by perceiving the real state of affairs:

> At this very moment we have that union and harmony in spite of ourselves; we create spiritual problems simply through not being aware of it, and that lack of understanding causes, and in turn is caused by, the delusion of self-sufficiency. As Christianity would say, the Grace of God is always being freely offered; the problem is to get man to accept it and give up the conceit that he can save himself by the power of his ego, which is like trying to pick himself up by his own belt.[9]

This idea that we are already *there* was to be central to all Watts's thinking thereafter. It had practical consequences for his daily life, in particular that he was unable to follow "systems," as he had been unable to accept the teaching of Sokei-an. Similarly, he was fascinated by depth psychology, but unable to undertake the discipline of psychoanalysis.

The purpose of all disciplines for the mind, it seemed to him, whether religious or psychological, was enlightenment, mystical experience, "transforming consciousness so as to see clearly that the separate and alienated ego is an illusion distracting us from knowing that there is no self other than the eternal ground of being."[10]

What he had against the systems, however, was that they subtly encouraged the disciples to postpone enlightenment to some future in which they were "good enough." A system, it seemed to this supremely confident young man, might be

> an elaborate and subtle ego-trip in which people inflate their egos by trying to destroy them, stressing the superhuman difficulty of the task. It can so easily be mere postponement of realization to the tomorrow which never comes, with the mock humility of, "I'm not ready yet. I don't deserve it." . . . But what if this is just self-punishment and spiritual masochism — lying, as it were, on a bed of nails to assure oneself of "authentic" existence? Mortification of the ego is an attempt to get rid of what doesn't exist, or — which comes to the same thing — of the feeling that it exists. . . . My point was, and has continued to be, that the Big Realization for which all these systems strive is not a future attainment but a present fact, that this now-moment is eternity, and that one must see it now or never.[11]

This idea followed very naturally from the Zen leap, the "direct path up the mountainside," which he had written about in *The Spirit of Zen.* He was older now, however, and his students and contemporaries in the United States were harder on him than the Buddhist Lodge had been on the twenty-year-old boy. At his age, they wondered, what did he know of wisdom, of suffering, of mystical experience? Where was his apprenticeship to a guru, his initiation, his gradual growth into God-consciousness? Wisdom demanded that the disciple work away faithfully until crisis point or breakdown was reached, and in that crisis grasp the truth;

the Buddha himself had followed the pattern. Yet here was young Alan Watts claiming that you could get there without the agony, that you could fly in by airplane, as it were, instead of making the long, painful journey by foot and camel. Who did he think he was?

Close to the question of whether or not discipleship was necessary was another conundrum about religion which Watts set out in an article for the *Columbia Review of Religion.*[12] His thinking about whether one attained mystical experience through a supreme effort of will, or whether the effort was precisely what prevented one from having the experience, reminded him of the ancient Christian dispute between Pelagius and Saint Augustine. Pelagius held that man's salvation must come by his own efforts, and Saint Augustine that it could only come by way of divine gift or "grace." Prompted by Suzuki, Watts had long ago noticed that Mahayana Buddhism struggled with a very similar conflict. There were those, such as the Zen meditators, who pinned their hopes of liberation on *jiriki* (self-power, the effect of one's own dutiful efforts towards enlightenment), and those, like the Jodo Shinshu sect (Pure Land Buddhists), who believed that liberation can only come by *tariki* (other power), the power of Amidha or Amitabha, a transcendental form of the Buddha revered in Southeast Asia. As Watts toiled at these ideas for his *Review* article it began to occur to him that Zen, Jodo Shinshu, and Christianity might all three be approaching the same goal (enlightenment) by different routes. With growing excitement he began to see Christianity as part of the common experience of the human race, instead of a religion he found embarrassingly and uncomfortably unique. If Christians could be persuaded to give up their rigid, defensive stance, their "imperialistic claims to be the one true and perfect revelation," then there might be a chance to rediscover Christianity's mystical depths and, for many Westerners who had never seriously considered it, to discover it for the first time. He also thought that it might be possible for a growing number of people to get into the habit of "passing over" from one religion to another in search of whatever sustenance they needed.

It is impossible to divorce these intellectual struggles of Watts from his emotional conflicts. Throughout his life Watts seemed to need to reconcile his childhood religion with his adopted religion. He had taken in Christianity with his mother's milk, but had digested it uneasily, as Emily had before him. He had longed to find it better than it was, even, perhaps, as he had longed to find Emily tenderer and prettier than she was.

To accept spiritual guidance from a teacher was to put himself back in a state of dependence, and there was in him a mixture of longing and fear, of self-destructive willfulness and calculated self-interest, which made it too difficult to accept help, even from a Sokei-an. He had to be independent and self-sufficient because any kind of dependence brought back the guilt and shame of dependence upon Emily. It seemed to be what mothers, even when disguised as Zen monks, exacted as the price of such nourishment.

It was of course true that many adults made themselves ridiculously dependent upon priests, *roshi*, gurus, and other kinds of teachers, and it was equally true that sometimes in their dependence they believed nonsense that no intelligent person should believe and submitted to all sorts of practices and disciplines that at best were harmless and at worst actually got in the way of real understanding and insight. Often they had little or nothing to do with the inner leap of Zen, or liberation in any of its Western or Eastern forms.

That is not to say, however, that there were no masters from whom Watts could benefit. Indeed, as a young man he clearly longed to find a teacher he could depend upon, and he turned, with varying degrees of success, to Toby Humphreys, Ruth Fuller Sasaki, Sokei-an Sasaki, and possibly D. T. Suzuki, as later in life he would try to trust a psychoanalyst. But in the end his nerve always failed, and he had to detach himself as he had from Sokei-an. To refuse so much wisdom and loving care, however skillfully he rationalized it, reduced him to an isolation, which, for all his marvellous openness, produced a particular kind of rigidity, the rigidity that comes from self-sufficiency, from always "knowing better." It was a lonely path to have chosen.

It was all the lonelier since Eleanor's neurotic problems were growing worse. The jolly girl who had once taught him to dance the hula had turned into a sad woman who felt too miserable to cope with life at all. One day, wandering into Saint Patrick's Cathedral when she felt tired on a shopping expedition, Eleanor had a vision of Christ. It filled her with deep disquiet, and she began a round of visits to priests and others who might tell her what it meant. No one seemed able to do this in a way that she found helpful.

Given the closeness of Watts and Eleanor at that time, it is perhaps not very surprising that Eleanor somehow anticipated his revived interest in Christianity. From the time of his *Review* article onwards, Watts had been taken up with the idea of a work of resuscitation. What had repeatedly shocked him was the sense that few Christians really knew or cared about the "innerness" of their religion. Most knew much about the basic teachings and practices of Christianity, but had no conception of the mystical content that Watts felt gave the religion vitality and meaning. He wanted both to revive the lost mystical tradition of Christianity and to integrate Christianity among the great religions of the world. For Watts it had a place, but not, as Westerners often believed, the sole place.

This was an exciting if ambitious plan for which it is possible to feel some sympathy — an attempt at healing the great divide of East and West, as well as, maybe, the great divide within Alan Watts. It was one of many ways in which he was ahead of his time, anticipating ideas that would not truly come into their own for another twenty years.

This was not enough for him, however. He at once moved on from this position in his thinking to wonder whether, if he was to be listened to in his criticisms of Christianity, he should find a stronger strategic position from which to do it. As he put it, he began to think that the best thing would be to "fit myself into the Western design of life by taking the role of a Christian minister."[13]

However generously Watts's motives are interpreted, it is difficult not to feel a twinge of cynicism about this scheme. A young man who has been a Buddhist for the past ten years of his life suddenly decides to become a Christian priest, not from any sudden conviction that Christianity is the "way of liberation," but because, to put it bluntly, it provides a convenient way of earning a living. Unemployed, tired of living off his wife and his wife's relatives, knowing that he knows a great deal about religion, and that he is a natural speaker, singer, and theologian (much more skillful at all these things than the average parish priest), he adds all of these considerations together and decides that switching religions may be the answer.

Watts did not, in fact, make any pretence of conversion, but such was the enthusiasm of the Christian clergy who encouraged him, or such was the unconscious arrogance in the church that all "right-thinking" people are Christian at heart, that he encountered no difficulties when he proposed to take up paid employment in a religion no longer his own. Such criticism as there was came not from Christians, but from his friends and students.

> Our personal friends . . . were astonished. They knew Eleanor as an earthy girl with a rich belly-laugh, and me as a fathomless source of bawdy limericks with a propensity for outlandish dancing and the kind of chanting which, today, brings calls to the police, the citizens supposing that the Apaches — in full war paint — are in their midst. The . . . possibility of such persons being also a minister and a minister's wife was beyond belief. Were we about to repent our sins and become godly, righteous and sober?[14]

Eugene Exman, the religious editor at Harper, apparently thinking that it was faith rather than a paid job that was the issue, urged him to become a Quaker. Watts's students, not unreasonably, had mixed feelings.

> I had discussed Buddhism as a key to the inner meaning of Christianity in seminars, and many of them, especially those with Jungian inclinations, had no difficulty in seeing Christian symbols as archetypes of the collective unconscious which is common to mankind as a whole. Others felt instinctively uncomfortable with Christianity for, although they could grasp the rationale of my explanations, they could not stand the atmosphere of church and churchy people.[15]

Ruth took the line of "how nice that you dear children have at least found a belief that really means something for you."[16] It was a subtle insult, implying that Buddhism had not really meant very much to Watts, and it is difficult to see how she could regard the change with much admiration.

The most quizzical response came from Robert Hume, Indologist and translator of the Upanishads, who taught at Union Theological Seminary; alone of Watts's friends he questioned the integrity of what was going on. Watts reports his attitude rather scornfully: "How *very* interesting, how really remarkable that I

—Alan Watts—should be contemplating this momentous STEP. He would be fascinated to know in just what ways I had come to feel that Buddhism was insufficient."[17]

Watts's daughter Joan suggests another reason for Alan's "conversion." In 1941 he was in danger of being drafted, and having escaped the war in England he did not propose to have it catch up with him in the United States. As a minister he would be safe from the draft, although it is not a reason he mentions in his autobiography.

With their new plan in mind Watts and Eleanor began shopping around the Episcopal churches in New York. The low churches, which offered simple morning prayer, clearly would not do for such a ritualist as Watts, but on Palm Sunday they discovered Saint Mary the Virgin on West Forty-sixth Street. After attending the blessing of the palms and solemn high mass, all carried out in Gregorian chant, they realized that they had found their new home. They returned for Tenebrae on Maundy Thursday. First there was a prolonged chanting of psalms, interspersed with bits of Palestrina. "One by one they extinguished the candles on a stand before the altar and gradually the church went into darkness. . . . There was undoubtedly magic in that church."[18]

Watts introduced himself to Fr. Grieg Taber, the rector of Saint Mary's, and told him about his wish to become a priest. It is not recorded that Father Taber had any doubts on the subject. Was this because Watts was so plausible, because he really seemed to have the makings of a priest, or because Father Taber was not accustomed to men approaching the idea with quite so much cool calculation as Watts did?

Pages of slightly uneasy explanation and justification are given in the autobiography. Watts had not *abandoned* Buddhism and Taoism, in fact he had always thought the Gospels inferior to the

Tao te Ching. But perhaps it did not matter all that much if he was not very interested in Jesus. What mattered when celebrating mass was conveying the *mystery*, the mystery that all religions celebrated. He could really do a great service to people by suggesting that "Christianity might be understood as a form of that mystical and perennial philosophy which has appeared in almost all times and places."[19] As a priest he would be "sincere but not serious."

The excuses and explanations multiply, but never do they seem to justify such a significant change. What seems to be lacking is any sense of passion, or, as the Christians say, vocation. Becoming a priest for Watts was, in the main, a way of making a career out of religion. An incidental inconvenience was that it also implied some degree of disloyalty to the Buddhist beliefs he had practiced and advocated for years. There is a deep and disturbing sense of his refusal to face the implications of what he did, and underlying that, an unattractive self-seeking. Becoming a priest would solve some urgent problems in his life. His final word on the subject is a chillingly practical comment on his defection from Buddhism and his sudden espousal of a religion he had affected to despise: "It was simply that the Anglican Communion seemed to be the most appropriate context for doing what was in me to do, in Western Society."[20]

Father Taber sent Watts to see Dean Fosbrooke at the General Theological Seminary, and Fosbrooke pointed out his lack of a degree. What a young man like him needed was some academic background, more particularly in history. One way to get into the priesthood without a college degree was to find a bishop who was favorably impressed, and then, with his sponsorship and approval, it was occasionally possible to make a short cut in the academic training. Wallace Conkling, the bishop of Chicago, seemed a likely sponsor, since he was just the sort of Anglo-Catholic Watts aspired to become. And the Everetts, though far from keen churchgoers, were a well-known family in Evanston, with many of the right connections necessary in just this sort of situation.

All went as planned. The bishop took to Watts, and Watts, rather unexpectedly, took to the bishop, deciding he was a *bhakti* mystic (one who achieved enlightenment through devotion) and a man of high culture. Watts was at once sent off to talk to Bishop McElwain, the dean of Seabury-Western Theological Seminary in Evanston, who felt that the degree might possibly be overlooked and that Watts might be enrolled as a special student, if he could show that he had read reasonably widely in religion and history. The reading list that Watts then prepared astounded the old man, accustomed as he was to less scholarly students. The bishop prescribed a two-year course for Watts, with courses in New Testament Greek, the Old Testament, and theology.

The young couple cheerfully packed up their possessions in New York, pausing only for Watts to paint a mural of the tree of life in the white space on the wall left by taking down a Japanese screen. They moved to Clinton Place in Evanston, next door to a flautist in the Chicago Symphony Orchestra, who introduced Watts to the delights of poker, usually played with other members of the orchestra. The new milieu was suburban, and, determined to live like his neighbors, Watts bought insurance, went to football games, and attended church socials and dances, though with a playful spirit that indicated a certain lack of conviction. The chameleon had entered a new phase.

Five

Colored Christian

1941-1947

AFTER THE MYSTERY AND NUMINOUSNESS of Saint Mary the Virgin, the churches of Chicago struck the Wattses as rather arid. The seminary chapel at Seabury-Western did not appeal to Alan Watts much either: "a colorless alley lined with oak choir stalls where the black-gowned seminarists sat in somber rows to chant the psalms of Matins and Evensong."[1]

Nor were his Evanston neighbors all that much to his taste. The main preoccupation of most of them was making money, which Watts thought might be rather fun to do — a clever game, like bridge — only people seemed to have to pretend not to enjoy it.

> It must most definitely be classified as *work*; as that which you *have* to do as a duty to your family and community, and which therefore affords many businessmen the best possible excuse for staying away from home and from their wives. The Nemesis of this attitude is that it flows over into the so-called leisure or non-work areas of life in such a way that playing with children, giving attention to one's wife, exercising on the golf course, and purchasing certain

> luxuries also become duties. Survival itself becomes a duty and even a drag, for the pretense of not enjoying the games gets under the skin and tightens the muscles which repress joyous and sensuous emotion.[2]

Watts clearly was still struggling with his own Protestant roots, using his resentment of them to make observations about the link between work and play.

For him the barrier between work and play did not exist. At Seabury-Western Watts threw himself into reading with a tremendous intellectual appetite. He had been afraid at first that he would have difficulty in keeping up, since unlike most of his fellow students he had not been to college, but his old Brahmin training and his habits of scholarship stood him in good stead. He quickly discovered that his rusty Greek was the best in the class, and that he could manage all the required reading by working one night a week, which left the rest of his study periods free for the reading that interested him. By his second year he was so far ahead that his teachers excused him from classwork and taught him on a tutorial basis. So it came about that for two years Watts gave himself up to serious theological reading, day after day, the study of a man who cared intensely about theological ideas and had a boundless curiosity about what others had made of those ideas. He read Harnack's *History of Dogma*, Clement and Origen, the Gnostics, Athanasius, Irenaeus. There was one period when he threw himself into reading Saint Thomas Aquinas and his modern exponents, Maritain and Gilson. There was a Russian phase when he read Vladimir Soloviev, Berdyaev, the hesychasts. He intensely scrutinized the classics of Christian mysticism — every well-known mystic from Pseudo-Dionysius to Leon Bloy, together with Evelyn Underhill, Friedrich von Hügel, and Dom John Chapman.

Somewhere in all this Watts became fascinated by the "unknowing" tradition of Christian mysticism, as in *The Cloud of Unknowing*: "silence of the mind and being simply at the disposal of God without holding any image or concept of God."[3] It was here, Watts felt, that Christianity and Mahayana Buddhism came close to touching hands.

A chance encounter during this period was with Aldous Huxley. On an Easter visit to Ruth in New York in 1943 Watts was introduced to Huxley, and they both made tentative overtures in what was to be a long, though not close, friendship. Watts found Huxley kind and sensitive, as well as mordantly witty and intellectual. It was a pleasure for Watts to hear again the forgotten cadences of English beautifully phrased and spoken by an English voice. Huxley told him about the group of Englishmen — Gerald Heard, Christopher Isherwood, Felix Greene, and himself, all living on the West Coast — that was studying Vedantist ideas. Heard and Huxley in particular were working towards some sort of synthesis of Christianity and Oriental mysticism, but in Huxley's excellent exposition of it at least, it came across as too "spiritual," too ascetic. Huxley seemed to Watts a Manichaean who hated the body. Watts's own thoughts along these lines were that Christianity's "Word made flesh" must be about a transcendence of the dualism of mind and matter rather than a denial of the flesh, and it seemed to him that this expressed much the same idea as Pure Land Buddhism.

> This very earth is the Pure Land,
> And this very body the Body of Buddha.[4]

At home at Clinton Place Watts and Eleanor had done what they could to make a rented house feel homey. When they arrived it was all painted institutional buff, expensively antiqued on the moldings. They painted it, moldings and all, in pale green. They were living in a style unimaginable for most students and enjoyed the services of a maid.

Eleanor's depression had not notably improved, however. She found it difficult to cope with the demands of a small child, and sometimes turned violently on Joan. She was aware of the popularity her husband found wherever he went, and although she was capable of holding her own socially, she felt left out and envious. All these problems were aggravated by the fact that, soon after they arrived at Evanston, she found herself pregnant once more. She did not want another child yet, but consoled herself with the thought that it might be a son, which she did want. In August 1942, however, she gave birth to a daughter, Ann (often, as a young child, to be called Winkie). Eleanor was disappointed and inclined to blame Watts for her plight. Ann had come into a painful inheritance—a mother who did not want children and who would have preferred a boy, and a father who, both sisters were later to feel, really preferred Joan. From quite early on, unable to cope with all the tensions of her family life, Eleanor was physically cruel to Ann.

Watts's response to Eleanor's growing misery and to the distress of the children was to withdraw still further into his academic work. No doubt he had once thought he could save Eleanor from her various problems, including her mother; now he began to feel her as a drag on his life, and her mother, who had interested him so much, was far away in New York. Eleanor fought with him or had long bouts of crying; she was less and less interested in the sexual side of the marriage. She rebuked Watts continually for not giving enough of his time to the children, and Joan remembers the frequency of rows at Clinton Place.

Watts did not spend much time with his children (either in this marriage or his subsequent one), but this made the time that he did spend with them especially treasured and memorable. On one wonderful weekend, Joan remembers, he set himself to paint the inside of the barn with monsters and demons until he had transformed it into a place of magic. When Watts played with his children he played as if he was a child himself, totally absorbed. He wasn't there a lot, but the time he gave was, says Joan, "quality time."

A few years later Ann found herself sick in the hospital with scarlet fever. Using his position as a minister to get to see her, Watts sat down and produced on the spot a magical chain of cutout paper dolls. He had the sorcerer's gift of producing something out of nothing, a gift that his children loved and remembered. Writing about his children years later Watts had his own sort of guilt about neglecting them, and his own excuse.

> By all the standards of this society I have been a terrible father, with a few disastrous attempts to be a "good" one, for the simple reason that I have no patience with the abstract notion of "the child," which our culture imposes on small people; with the toys and games they are supposed to enjoy, with the books they are supposed to read, with the mannerisms they're supposed to assume, and with the schools in which they become lowest-common-denominator images of each other. I am completely at ease with the infant who still enjoys nonsense and plays spontaneously at unprogrammed games, and then again with the adolescent who is calling the brainwashing into question. But the Disneyland "world of childhood" is an itsy-bitsy, cutie-pied, plastic hoax; a world populated by frustrated brats trying to make out why they are not treated as human beings. . . . If my children have found me distant and aloof, this is the explanation.[5]

Perhaps Watts's children did not so much find him distant and aloof in any emotional sense, as simply *not there*, in the most ordinary physical sense, to which Disney and his artefacts were irrelevant. They needed their father to counter Eleanor's sadness and to control her anger against them, and he was too busy becoming an Episcopalian.

It was not easy for someone who was still basically a Buddhist to pass as a man of Christian conviction. The need for an element of concealment was there, since Watts was exasperated at being constantly in the company of those whose emotions were "colored Christian." He detested the atmosphere of guilt, repentance, and confession, and hated the idea of God as *He*. *She* might have corrected the balance a bit, he felt, but really if he was to speak of God at all (and he found it difficult to take that idea seriously), he would have preferred to use the word *It* or *That*.

His Christian teachers for their part accused Watts of pantheism and wondered if his inability to relate to God as a person might indicate an inability to relate to persons in general. This was a fairly offensive observation, but no doubt they sensed that something was not quite right about Watts's sense of vocation and that he was holding back feelings and thoughts from those who were supposed to be friends and future colleagues.

Watts describes this period of his life in mock-innocent, "Where did I go wrong?" tones: "I chose priesthood because it was the only formal role of Western society into which, at that time, I could even begin to fit. . . . But it was an ill-fitting suit of clothes, not only for a shaman but also for a bohemian — that is, one who loves color and exuberance, keeps irregular hours, would rather be free than rich, dislikes working for a boss, and has his own code of sexual morals."[6] To which the Christians might have replied, if they had understood his rather dubious motives, that no one was compelling him to be a priest.

However, on Ascension Day 1944 Watts was ordained an

Episcopal priest in the Church of the Atonement, Evanston (he managed to get the date wrong in his autobiography); he had put on the ill-fitting suit of clothes and was condemned to wear them for another six years.

He could not imagine himself as a parish priest and hoped that Bishop Conkling might let him be a sort of priest-at-large in Chicago, maybe running a retreat house with a strong emphasis on contemplative prayer. Much later, by the 1960s and 1970s, Christians were to develop a renewed interest in contemplative prayer, but Watts was ahead of this development. The best the church could do for him was to make him chaplain at Northwestern University.

Watts threw himself into the job with a will. It provided a home for his family at Canterbury House on Sheridan Road in Evanston. Canterbury House was designed to be both the chaplain's home and a sort of student center, and it contained within it Saint Thomas's Chapel. Eleanor, who had skill and taste, set to work to give the house a welcoming beauty and style.

Watts meanwhile worked out a program to attract students both to services and to the intensive course of education and discussion in which he wanted to involve them. In one of the pamphlets he had printed for students, he pointed out that at the most, a high school graduate had had 360 hours of religious instruction in school as compared with 1,800 hours of English or mathematics. That meant that a grown-up girl or boy had about reached the third grade where religious teaching was concerned. One of his hopes was to encourage intellectual curiosity about religion.

> The Church is here on campus to provide what college education neglects — a mature understanding of those doctrines and the real answer of Christian philosophy to the central problems of life, in ignorance of which no-one can call himself educated. . . .

> What am I for? What causes me to exist? Is it a mechanical process or a living intelligence? What is God, the ultimate life and reality? Can I have actual knowledge of God, and if so how? These most fascinating of all questions are in the mind of every member of this university, for even the most hard-boiled agnostic has *some* interest in religion.
>
> Through lack of time and resources the religious teaching given in the average Sunday School (or even sermon) is so elementary and superficial as to be actually misleading to a grown mind. Thus the popular impression of Christian doctrine is a wild caricature of the reality. No wonder people don't believe it![7]

The pamphlet that offered this release from religious ignorance advertised a series of lectures at 7:30 on Sunday evenings, many of them given by Watts himself, on such subjects as "Religion and Science," "Christianity and Psychoanalysis," "Popular Religious Art" (with slides for illustration), and "The Painting of Eternity" (also with slides). It also offered individual instruction with the chaplain for any member of the university who cared to ask for it. Individual instruction would cover the following subjects: the aim of religion; the doctrine of God; the doctrine of man; the Incarnation; the Church and sacraments; prayer and the spiritual life; Christian ethics; Christian worship.

In addition to this educational program Watts also offered personal counseling to those who wanted it, and he made it clear that he and Canterbury House were always available:

> Canterbury House is *not* a "social center." It has no "organizations," no "committees," no "programs." It is supported by the Episcopal Diocese of Chicago to serve the spiritual life of Northwestern University, to give proofs of God's existence, his supreme importance and our utter dependence upon him, and of the impossibility of rational life and thought without him; to combat the silly and pernicious views of agnosticism, humanism and pseudo-scientific

materialism so fashionable among modern educators; and to afford you the opportunity to bring your own faith in God and his Church to maturity and conviction.

Although it is not an organized social center, Canterbury House is "Open House," especially on Sunday afternoons from 4 to 6. People are always coming in to talk and pass the time of day; the Chaplain thoroughly enjoys it; you cannot waste his time![8]

This was an enthusiastic and generous approach to a job for which Watts was paid a tiny salary. It was difficult for Eleanor and the children to carry on their family life with such busy coming and going of students, but Eleanor was determined to play the part of "the minister's wife" to the best of her ability. Watts soon became a well-known figure on campus, bicycling from one place to another (bicycling was rare enough at that time to be regarded as eccentric), dressed from head to toe in clerical black. He was bearded too, which was unusual, and it was rumored that he fasted and went in for other ascetic practices.

Fired by the intensive reading of the past few years, Watts had begun a new book entitled *Behold the Spirit: A Study in the Necessity of Mystical Religion*, for which his seminary was to award him a master's degree. In the course of his switch to formal Christianity, which the book represents, he enormously increased his theological knowledge. The intensive course of reading that preceded his ordination introduced him to the Fathers, to the *Summa Theologica*, to the riches of medieval Christianity, and to the Counter Reformation saints, all of which subjects were previously unknown to him. He began to realize that there was more to his native religion than Protestant ethics, guilt, and sentimental devotions to Jesus. Fired by this discovery he recovered the clarity and energy of style evident in his early books about Zen.

Like all Watts's books *Behold the Spirit* asks how liberation, or enlightenment, is to be achieved. The book begins from the assumption that "Church religion is spiritually dead," as evidenced by its organizational busyness, inadequate teaching, excessive moralism, doctrinal obscurantism, lack of conviction, absence of reality, and disunity. What the Church did not succeed in doing was in relating "man to the root and ground of reality and life. . . . At times man *knows* his need of religion; at others he only *feels* it as an unexplained void in the heart."[9]

The problem seemed to be as great among those who went to church and followed Christian spiritual disciplines as among those who had abandoned or never known such practices.

> Christian faith and practice have lost force because the enormous majority of Christians . . . do not know what they mean. Let it be said at once that such knowledge is not a matter of mere learning, of philosophical and theological acumen. Indeed, the theologian has often just as little grasp of the meaning of his religion as anyone else. He knows ideas; he knows the relations between these ideas; he knows the historical events — the story of Christ — upon which these ideas are based. He knows the doctrines of the Trinity, the Incarnation, the Virgin Birth, and the Atonement and can describe them with accuracy. But because he does not know, or even apprehend, what they mean, having no consciousness of union with God, his description of them — while correct as far as it goes — is uninformative and lacking in significance.[10]

The main trouble with church religion, Watts says, is that people are taught to carry out spiritual exercises on a sort of imitative basis. Because the saints said their prayers, received the sacraments, and performed the conventional Christian gestures, others suppose that the way to become saints is to copy them, and if no inner transformation takes place, they are enjoined to practice "holy patience" forever if necessary. But this approach does not take account of the terrible vacuum at the heart of such piety. Imitation does not feed spiritual hunger. "They want God himself, by whatever name he may be called; they want to be filled with his creative life and power; they want some conscious experience of being at one with Reality itself, so that their otherwise meaningless and ephemeral lives may acquire an eternal significance."[11]

Watts suggests that such wistful seekers are ignorant of a vital secret:

> They do not know that the Church has in its possession, under lock and key (or maybe the sheer weight of persons sitting on the lid), the purest gold of mystical religion. Still less do they know that creed and sacrament are only fully intelligible in terms of mystical life. And they do not know these things because the stewards and teachers of the Church do not, for the most part, know them either. For while holding officially that eternal life consists in the knowledge of God—and in nothing else—churches of every kind are concerned with almost everything but the knowledge of God.[12]

For Watts it came down to this:

> Knowledge of God, the realization of one's union with God, in a word, mysticism, is *necessary*. It is not simply the flower of religion; it is the very seed, lying in the flower as its fulfilment and preceding the root as its origin. . . . It is the *sine qua non*—the *must*—the first and great commandment. "Thou shalt love the Lord thy God with all thy heart, and with all thy soul, and with all thy mind." On this hangs all the Law. On this all rules and techniques depend, and apart from it mean nothing.[13]

To suggest that people *must* know God is to say something at once too difficult and too simple to be grasped. Mysticism is not so much a doing as an undoing, a removing of the barriers, a taking down of the defenses, a creating of space, a getting out of the way. Mysticism is "an action in the passive."

The time had come, Watts suggested, to recover the deep mystical sense Christianity had previously known, but with a new emphasis. Medieval Christians had felt at one with God and with religious symbolism in a primitive, childlike way. The Renaissance and the growth of humanism could be seen as a kind of rebellious adolescence, necessary as a movement towards maturity, but not maturity itself. This was followed by a tremendous awareness of human power in action, in science and technology. But this enormous upsurge of energy and action was followed not just by weariness, but by the spiritual maturity of age.

Following Oswald Spengler Watts suggests that Western culture was on the verge of a "Second Religiousness" that in some ways would be quite different. It would be "an interior, spiritual and mystical understanding of the old, traditional body of wisdom. . . . What the child understood as an external, objective, and symbolic fact, the mature mind will see also as an interior, subjective, and mystical truth. What the child received on another's authority, the adult will know as his own inner experience."[14]

Watts goes on to consider what a twentieth-century mysticism could be like. In the past Christian mysticism had had a kind of "unholy alliance" with Manichaeism, denying the fleshliness proclaimed in the Incarnation, "the Word made flesh," by despising the body — supposing it, its senses, and in particular its sexual fulfillment, to be inimical to the life of the spirit. A true understanding of the Incarnation involves a recognition of the redemption of body as well as spirit, that "the eternal life of God is given to man here and now in the flesh of each moment's experience."

Release from our own isolating egoism comes partly from recognizing the hunger for God, partly from a sort of relaxation. Egoism itself is "like trying to swim without relying on the water, endeavoring to keep afloat by tugging at your own legs; your whole body becomes tense, and you sink like a stone. Swimming requires a certain relaxation, a certain giving of yourself to the water, and similarly spiritual life demands a relaxation of the soul to God."[15]

Union is often thought of as a tremendous attainment, needing huge struggles. But there is a whole other method, as in Zen *satori*, which suggests that what knowing God is about is not effort and attainment, but realization: "The soul striving to attain the divine state by its own efforts falls into total despair, and suddenly there dawns upon it with a great illuminative shock the realization that the divine state simply IS, here and now, and does not have to be attained."[16]

Yet there was, Watts suggested, some perverse determination in us that it had to be difficult, some self-regarding romantic picture of our own heroic labors: "We flatter ourselves in premeditating the long, long journey we are going to take in order to find him, the giddy heights of spiritual progress we are going to scale." The tragedy is that we thus miss the obvious:

> God is not niggardly in his self-revelation; he creates us to know him, and short of actual compulsion does everything possible to present himself to our consciousness. In saying that God gives us union with himself here and now, we are saying also that here and now he exposes himself right before our eyes. In this very moment we are looking straight at God, and he is so clear that for us complex human beings he is peculiarly hard to see. To know him we have to simplify ourselves.[17]

Watts makes the very interesting suggestion that the mystical consciousness of God (as opposed to the more direct, beatific vision) may be very like the sort of awareness we have of ourselves:

> For while we cannot perceive our own egos directly, we know that we exist. We do not know what we are, but we know ourselves as existing, and this knowledge is present as an undertone in all other

> knowledge. Similarly, the mystical knowledge of God is a knowledge of God in the act of his presence and union with us, but is not immediate vision and apprehension of the divine essence.[18]

The amazing joy of this sort of apprehension, partial as it is, is that we know ourselves to be part of a "living mystery, which imparts life, power and joy." The price of knowing this mystery is the cutting off of the "possessive will."

Always practical about spirituality, Watts goes on to consider what this view of God means. He is not against formal religion. For some it is a necessary way to discover ultimately that God cannot be possessed. For others it is a precious way of tracing out the symbolic and analogic patterns of God in order to move on to "the Reality beyond symbols." For others again, formal religion has such repugnant associations that it is almost impossible for them to espouse it.

Watts envisages a new flexibility in Christian worship, with a formal liturgy at one end of the scale for those who want it, and wordless contemplation at the other for those who want that. Sermonizing, moralizing (especially where the dubious lever of guilt is employed), and excessive theological speculation, seem to Watts totally fruitless. What the whole religious endeavor is about is in finding God in the most hundrum moments—this, he believes, rather than by "devotions" to Jesus, is the way to discover "the mind of Christ." He would like to see the Church give informal teaching on "digging potatoes, washing dishes and working in an office." There must, he thinks, be a Christian way of washing your hands.

This is an interesting view of Christianity, obviously much influenced by Zen. In his perception of people's hunger for mystical experience Watts anticipated much that was to come within the next thirty years—the search for mystical experience outside the

Church and the renewed interest in contemplative prayer within it. In other ways, too, he was prophetic. He saw that the time was coming when the "male God" would seem incongruous, and that the elevation of the Virgin Mary, though important, did not touch the real need. He saw the need for Christians to undo their Manichaean heritage and finally accept the messy body, able to feel at one with God even when, or especially when, in *flagrante delicto.*

When *Behold the Spirit* came out in 1947 the reviewers were rapturous. An Episcopal reviewer, Canon Iddings Bell, said that the book would "prove to be one of the half dozen most significant books on religion published in the twentieth century," which was high praise indeed. Another Catholic author noted with interest that the book recognized "contributions from Oriental religion which simply are not present in contemporary Western religion. More than this it shows how the traditional Western doctrine of the Incarnation and the Atonement can be reconciled with and combined with the intuitive religion of the Orient, such as that of Zen Buddhism. These are exceedingly important and outstanding achievements."[19]

Meanwhile Watts was setting to work to transform the liturgical experience of students. On Sundays at 11:00 A.M. he conducted a service at the Chapel of Saint John the Divine on Haven Street, which, though it stuck basically to the Book of Common Prayer, managed to achieve colorful and dramatic effects unknown to the Episcopal students before. He introduced incense, the slow, casually formal processions that he had learned about from Hewlett Johnson, short arresting sermons, Gregorian chant and Renaissance polyphony, sung by a specially trained ensemble from the music school. Worshippers came into a church fragrant with smoke, brilliant with vestments and candles, in which the prayers were spoken in Watts's beautiful resonant English and the ritual was performed like the gestures of a play. Something of the mystery that Watts had learned from Friar Taber was there too and something of his own feeling for language and use of intelligence and humor. The students began to flock to Saint John's in large numbers, even though lively liturgy and strong preaching was on offer in the neighborhood of the campus. Watts was one of the latest fashions.

He was also hardworking. In the Anglo-Catholic style he celebrated Mass every morning except Mondays at 7:15 A.M. in Saint Thomas's Chapel, and most of the rest of his waking hours were spent either conducting services, taking seminars, or entertaining students in his own home.

His growing popularity was looked upon a little sourly and suspiciously by colleagues and others. The dean of the seminary wondered aloud what sort of preparation Watts's example would provide for the work his theological students would be taking up in very ordinary parishes where the "bells and smells" of Saint John's would not be appreciated. The mother of one of the seminarians quoted in Watts's biography expressed this point of view more succinctly: "The religion you are giving these people is not the religion of Saint Luke's and Saint Mark's here in town, and from what I can see it isn't the religion of the Episcopal Church anywhere."[20] Perhaps she sensed an element almost of leg-pulling in the sheer elaboration of ceremonies; she had, at least, an inkling that Watts was up to something. He had also managed to upset the scientists on the faculty of Northwestern by attacking their antireligious attitudes.

The students, not surprisingly, took a more adventurous view of his activities. His imaginative liturgies appealed to many of them. They dubbed Richard Adams, a student with whom Alan planned the liturgies, "the Sorcerer's apprentice," a joking recognition of the shaman quality they noted in Watts. They appreciated the individual attention Watts was prepared to give to people in intellectual or emotional difficulties, and they enjoyed the social life of Canterbury House, a mixture of fun and endless discussion, as life with Watts was apt to be. Watts and Eleanor kept open house, and the house, Watts remembered, "was the scene of an almost perpetual bull session, involving students, seminarists and members of the University faculty." On Sunday afternoons there were tea parties, which lingered on into the cocktail hour "and became decidedly merrier than anything ordinarily foreseen in the prospect of tea at the vicarage."[21] On Sunday evenings, when Watts had completed his seminar, people gathered round the piano and sang rather racier material than the hymns at Uncle Harry's. Later there was dancing.

Perhaps because the members of the group at Canterbury House did have such a good time together they appeared as a bit cliquish to those outside, though Watts was welcoming to anyone wishing to join the fun. He was not very interested in being a good colleague to his fellow clergy, or perhaps was simply not very interested in them at all. One former student remembers trying to get him to a surprise birthday party for a curate in another parish and getting a frosty response.

As time went on the parties got wilder, as members of the group around Canterbury House came to trust one another more. Forgetting the proprieties expected of him, or simply sick of them, Watts would play with as much relish as any of his students. Joan remembers him in competitions with students to see who could pee the highest, and making "bombs" with them of matchheads in milk bottles, which they exploded in the back garden. Watts himself remembers one of his students demolishing a streetlight with an air rifle from inside a car, and though he did not actually encourage the student to do it, Watts was driving the car at the time. On another night the same student and he attached a wire and a wad of sanitary napkins soaked in gasoline to a helium balloon, lit it, and let it blow away over Lake Michigan. Chicago's inhabitants, seeing a flame floating in the night sky, excitedly reported sightings of flying saucers to the police.

While Watts had been training to be an Episcopal priest and preparing to write his book about the failures of Christianity, the war in Europe and in the Far East had had little impact on his life. Perhaps the only effect on him was that his parents had been prevented from visiting him in his new country. In 1946 they were able at last to visit Evanston. Apart from the pleasure of seeing their much-loved only child again, they were glad to see Alan apparently so settled with wife and children, making a success in a career that Emily in particular admired. Did they, one wonders, have any inkling when they played with the children, or talked to Eleanor, or saw Alan in the pulpit, that all was not sound? A photograph taken during the visit shows the older couple looking pleased and happy, Watts looking evasive, Eleanor looking unhappy and embarrassed, and Ann looking sad and vulnerable. The older Wattses' visit was much appreciated by the two little girls, who responded to their gentleness and loving interest.

The next year Joy Buchan and Aunt Gertrude set off from England on the exciting trip by boat and train to visit their relatives. Joy went on alone to Evanston from Minneapolis where they had been visiting Uncle Willy. She was met at the Chicago station by Watts, and the only change she discovered in him was his beard. She found the children sweet and attentive and Watts very pleased to see her. He showed her his drawings and paintings, calligraphy and photographs, and gave her a copy of *Behold the Spirit.* The life of a clerical household went on around her: choir practices, in which she took part, discussion groups, people dropping in, visits to the church where Watts preached and celebrated Communion. Like any visitor from Britain in that austere postwar period she was fascinated by the variety of food and wrote at length of delicious meals consumed either in the Watts household or at restaurants. Her companion on some of these jaunts to restaurants was a young mathematics student, Dorothy De Witt ("Doddy"), who was often a babysitter for Joan and Ann. Sometimes too there was a musical evening at Canterbury House, with Eleanor and Ann, Doddy, and a young musician called Carlton Gamer playing for them, or all of them listening to records together.

Joy's diary paints a very favorable picture of the chaplain's household, a portrait of a man faithful in his pious duties, attentive as husband and father, generous and thoughtful as a host, busy and devoted about the occupations of suburban Evanston. Eleanor perhaps emerges as a little distant, performing the duties of a hostess; Joy was, in any case, Alan's cousin, not hers. Emily and Laurence must have loved hearing all the details of the visit when Joy got home again to Bromley. Beneath the conventional happy family facade, however, all was not well.

Six

Correspondence

1947-1950

"MY DEAR BISHOP CONKLING," Eleanor Watts wrote in a cliffhanger of a letter dated June 29, 1950. "I have never taken any steps to acquaint you with this matter as I have hoped it would prove unnecessary for me to uphold my status at the cost of another's reputation whom I cannot bring myself to judge. But Father Taber insists that the time has come when my silence can no longer protect the Church, and that I must set before you the complete facts of the case that you may be able to act in full knowledge of the truth."

Eleanor was writing not from Canterbury House at Evanston, but from her mother's house in New York, where she had fled with her children to the psychiatric care of Charlie Taylor and the spiritual care of Father Taber.

"During the first two years of my marriage I became aware that Alan's preoccupation with sexual matters was extreme," Eleanor went on, "but as his 'demands' on me were not frequent I considered it highly probable that my lack of understanding of such things was coloring my view. His 'demands,' however, were of a type that made intimate relations most uncomfortable to me and

I also discovered that he was a frequent masturbator, although I did not draw any inference from this knowledge at that time."[1]

The bishop may not have known of Eleanor's depression, frigidity, and invalidism, but he must have wondered at this point in the letter whether Watts's "demands" were unreasonable, or whether he was dealing with a prudish woman who was repulsed by her husband's normal expectations.

Most bishops then, and perhaps now, were accustomed to a situation in which clergy gave so much of their time to caring for their parishioners that they often had very little energy left over for their wives and families. Clergy wives, he would know, were often seething with rage that they received very little of their husbands' love and attention. Yet it was difficult for them to get sympathy if they complained, since their husbands were dedicated to God, and God was an impossible rival, worse than another woman. Watts had certainly worked unceasingly since he arrived in Evanston, and Eleanor had watched him become an important figure on campus, with students flocking to services and later into her home to carry on conversations with him. Once vivacious and attracting attention herself, Eleanor was depressed by her present contrasting role as housewife and mother, and took out some of her temper on the children, particularly on Ann.

Eleanor did not tell the bishop of the boredom and frustration of being the chaplain's wife, however. On the contrary she describes how she had dutifully cherished Alan's vocation to the priesthood in the hope that the discipline and ideals of the church would make him steady and responsible. But, she complains,

> So far, i.e., before his ordination, I had had the entire responsibility for the home upon my shoulders both financially and socially, as well as the upbringing of our daughter. Alan lived in his own particular "ivory tower" and the practical world seemed to have no reality for him. To my surprise and concern the change to a lovely

> home, another child, and a new career did nothing to help this state of mind, in fact he retreated further than ever from his family and his responsibilities as the head of the family. Our intimate relations became more infrequent, another matter of concern which I put down to "consideration" on his part.[2]

Eleanor's tone, if somewhat self-righteous, nevertheless suggests what a miserable married life they had been pursuing.

"In May, 1944," Eleanor goes on, "we moved into Canterbury House. Here again I was left with the full responsibility for the home and the rearing of the children. Our intimate relations were few but as his attitude towards me in this sphere was increasingly distasteful to me, and as I was not well, this state of affairs, although unhappy, seemed all that could be expected."

The strains between the Wattses, still unnoticeable when Joy Buchan visited, began to be apparent even to casual visitors. Jean McDermid, Alan's cousin from Minneapolis, was out motoring one day with her new husband Malcolm, whom Watts had never met, and they stopped in to pay a call on the Wattses. Watts answered the door, but was not his old jolly self, nor did he seem pleased to see them. He showed them into his study and made polite conversation for a bit. Lunch time came, but the half-expected invitation did not come with it. All of a sudden the door shot open, Eleanor marched furiously in, placed a tray with one plate on it in front of Watts and went out without speaking to them. Watts uneasily ate his pork chop. Shocked by this scene, the McDermids went angrily away, swearing that they would never call on the Wattses again.

Eleanor went on:

> In the early summer of 1946 Alan came to me with the story that one of his students was desirous of having relations with him and asked my advice as to how to handle it. He had visited her in her

> rooms on several occasions and had indulged in "necking parties" with her. This announcement came as a complete surprise. I tried my best to point out to him the incongruity of such a relationship for one in his position and how it endangered both his vows as a priest and as a husband. After much argument and discussion we *seemed* to come to an agreement as to principles.[3]

Watts's misery in his marriage and his guilt about his sexual longings had become too much for him. Later he was to say that he thought that he and Eleanor had clung together so hard in the beginning that "mutual strangulation" had taken place. This made each of them the other's "chattel," and with hindsight he thought this a hopeless kind of relationship: "You must so trust your partners as to allow full freedom to be the being that he or she is."[4] There seemed to be no freedom between him and Eleanor, and each was exasperated at the other, Watts seeing a frigid invalid, too depressed to care for her children, and Eleanor a man whose sexual desires frightened and disgusted her. She makes it clear to the bishop just what the euphemism, "uncomfortable," which she had used in her letter, meant to her:

> Alan at last confided to me the whole story of his sexual difficulties. I can only repeat his story to you to the best of my ability.
>
> He had been sent to boarding school at the age of seven and there had been introduced to certain sexual practices by older boys and even a master. In his Preparatory school [she means King's School, Canterbury] this early start was nourished further. Apparently sex in all its forms was a constant topic of interest and experimentation and added to that was the type of discipline administered there [flagellation] which set the pattern for Alan's sex life. He told me that he had practiced masturbation more than once daily from his schooldays to the present and that as the phantasy life which accompanied this practice grew more compelling he spent hours in drawing pornographic pictures and reading pornographic

literature to excite his interest. He also inflicted various tortures upon himself in order to achieve orgasm. [It is interesting in this connection to recall his suggestion to his headmaster that beating be abolished at the school.]

At the time that he married he had hopes that a normal sexual relationship would prove to be a settling influence but he found to his dismay that it became increasingly difficult for him to complete such a normal relationship without some extraordinary stimulus.

Over the years of his marriage pornographic interests and phantasy, while more attractive to him than the normal marriage relationship, lost some of their power to stimulate him and he began to seek stimulation from women outside his marriage.[5]

It is not difficult to imagine how shocked the prudish young Eleanor must have been as her husband tried to tell her what he needed from her. Without experience, maturity, or even enough love for him to try to imagine his feelings, she was left feeling "uncomfortable" and with the conviction that her husband was incurably "abnormal."

"On hearing this story," she tells Conkling, "I was horrified but, at the same time, sympathetic. I could not see wherein he was to *blame* and after much discussion I agreed to do my best as a wife to try to help him overcome his difficulties. I urged him to see a psychiatrist which he refused to do."

It is easy to imagine the couple talking far into the night, Watts, having begun to speak freely of his sexual distress, almost unable to stop talking, Eleanor too taken up with her own generosity to take in fully what he was trying to tell her. At one point he openly invited her to beat him, but she indignantly refused. He began to consider finding a woman who might respond to his needs, but the image most people had of the clergy made such requests difficult.

By this stage Watts had had enough of being humbled and told he was in the wrong. He went over to the attack.

> [He] began seriously to question *my* state of mind and I discovered that he considered monogamous marriage to be quite out of date and unable to fulfill the "natural needs of the male." He then attacked me for my lack of understanding of "male nature" as well as what he chose to call my frigidity and prudishness. He assured me that he had never had any intention of remaining "true" to me and that my "ideals" were merely the produce of my own psychotic mind and that I was merely taking refuge in ancient codes to "excuse" my inability to adapt to modern ways. He was not the slightest bit repentant and absolutely refused to discuss his affairs with an older priest as he said that such a priest "could not be honest as he would have vested interests" to consider.

Watts by now felt certain that Eleanor could not help him, that the only way he could cope with his sexual needs was to look outside his marriage, a fairly desperate situation for someone whose job demanded monogamy and sexual circumspection. He began to nag Eleanor ceaselessly to change her "ideals" and Eleanor, in despair, consulted a priest herself, a Father Duncan. Father Duncan asked Watts to visit him, but Watts refused, and Duncan's recommendation to Eleanor was that she leave him. Explaining to Bishop Conkling why she did not do that, Eleanor remarked, piously, that

> I believed in his religious teaching and felt bound to save that at any cost. I was sure his priesthood would suffer if I left him and besides I considered myself a married woman and did not wish to run away from what I considered to be my responsibility to Alan. I realize now that I was quite wrong to attempt to protect him in this way. It was not honest, but the summer I had lived through with the pressure from Alan had so confused me that I thought

perhaps he *was* right and that my "Ideals" might be as foolish and unreal as he considered them to be.

In fact during 1947 Eleanor had become friends with a music student, Carlton Gamer, ten years younger than herself. They had arranged that he would give her a weekly piano lesson in return for a Sunday dinner at the Wattses' house. Gradually Eleanor and Carlton discovered many tastes in common, she confided her unhappy marital situation to him, and before long the two of them had fallen in love. Eleanor reported this new development to Watts, obviously expecting him to behave like an outraged husband, only to discover that he seemed rather to like the idea. He even read her a little lecture about getting it right. "He hoped I would not make life miserable for Carlton by my frigidity and prudery and that as long as I gave up any idea of divorce, he could see no hindrance to an affair for us. . . . To my horror I discovered that he still expected me to fulfil my 'wifely obligations' to him, the fact that I was loved by another man being very stimulating to him."[6]

At Watts's suggestion Carlton moved into Canterbury House. It was a bizarre arrangement for any household, but particularly so for a clerical family in the 1940s. Joan still remembers trying to puzzle out why their home life seemed so different from other people's. Eleanor undoubtedly had a greater enthusiasm for this arrangement than appears in her disingenuous letter to Bishop Conkling in which she suggests that she only put up with it for the sake of helping Watts keep his job. In fact she and Watts went on a long motoring holiday to California with Carlton during the summer of 1948, and soon after that she became pregnant by Carlton. Watts cannot have been as content with the arrangement as Eleanor makes him appear. He knew that campus gossip, or Eleanor's growing bitterness, could destroy him.

In June 1948 Eleanor flew to New York to consult Ruth, who suggested that she pay another visit to the psychiatrist, Charles Taylor, who had helped her in the past. Taylor, Eleanor claimed, urged her to leave Alan and to remove the children from his influence.

She returned home with a challenge. Either Watts must receive psychiatric treatment, or she would leave him. Well aware that refusal meant that he would lose his job, since he was required to appear happily married, Watts did visit a psychiatrist, but soon showed that he had no intention of changing. He refused once again to accept the help of a fellow priest.

Michael, Eleanor's son by Carlton, was born in June 1949, an event both the Wattses' daughters remember with pain. Always ambivalent in her feelings about her daughters, particularly Ann, Eleanor suddenly switched all attention away from the two little girls and concentrated it on the longed-for son, perhaps in part to teach her husband that she no longer cared for him at all. Joan and Ann, already suffering in a difficult and bewildering situation, felt this loss of affection very acutely. Joan went away to boarding school at Versailles, Kentucky, while Ann continued unhappily with her mother.

Finally, in July 1949, Eleanor set off once again for New York to consult Ruth, Ruth's lawyer, and Dr. Taylor. All three of them recommended a divorce, and in September Eleanor finally left Watts, taking the three children with her to settle in New York with Ruth. She was in a dilemma. She wished to be free to marry Carlton and wanted the sort of divorce that proved the matrimonial fault to be Alan's, yet the birth of a child by another man made her seem other than the innocent victim she pretended to be. She could only vindicate her own actions by exaggerating the oddness of Watts's behavior. Father Taber, who, only a few years before, had encouraged Watts to become a priest, now thought that an annulment was the answer, so early in 1950 Eleanor went off to Reno and secured her annulment on the grounds that at the time of her marriage her husband had concealed from her that he was a "sexual pervert." (Alan's version of this in his autobiography was that the Nevada annulment was obtained on the grounds that he believed in "free love.") Anxious to absolve herself in Bishop Conkling's eyes Eleanor wrote,

> As far as I myself am concerned I can only say that throughout this affair I have acted in the only way I saw possible, wrong as that has been. I have constantly had the good of the Church in my mind although I have made dreadful mistakes in endeavoring to accomplish that good, nor have I understood in what that good consisted. However, I have made my peace with the Church and perhaps my honesty with my advisors here has been an important factor in the mercy and consideration they have shown me, and the faith they have that I am ready for a "Christian marriage."[7]

Bishop Conkling had every faith in Father Taber's assessment of the situation. He was deeply touched at the thought of all that this wealthy penitent had endured and sent a sympathetic reply.

Unfortunately, Carl Wesley Gamer, Carlton's father, saw it all very differently, and he in his turn wrote to the bishop. The Gamers had slowly become aware that their son did not wish to come home for vacations, that he preferred to spend his summers in Evanston, and in 1948 he announced that he was to go on a car trip through the western states with the Wattses, with all expenses paid by them. Only gradually did his parents discover the arrangement in which Carlton was living, and at last they learned with horror that he had had a child with a married woman, ten years older than himself and the wife of a minister. Not unreasonably Carl Gamer felt that the Wattses had exploited his son while he was under 21, that Eleanor had seduced him, and her husband had connived at the fact. He considered bringing charges against Watts, especially after hearing from Carlton that in view of Eleanor's annulment there would now be no objection to a marriage, either civil or ecclesiastical. Father Taber had even pointed out the relevant canon to the couple that would allow them a church marriage.

Sickened by this piece of casuistry and determined to impede an unpromising marriage, Gamer senior attacked the church for its apparent complacency in Eleanor's conduct and suggested that even under the lenient law of Nevada, Eleanor could not have obtained an annulment if the full facts had been known to the court. In a letter to Bishop Conkling he writes, "Her annulment was a case of 'clear fraud' perpetrated upon a court. In addition to that, Eleanor by her affaire with Carlton, appears to have violated the criminal statutes of both Illinois and New York State and furthermore a federal statute which carries with it confinement in the penitentiary."[8]

Bishop Conkling was able to sidestep the issue of Eleanor's remarriage since it came under the jurisdiction of the bishop of New York, but Watts, on the other hand, was his concern.

As the situation worsened between him and Eleanor during 1949, Watts knew that it was only a matter of time before his private life was public knowledge. He had worked well and enthusiastically at his chaplain's job, and he dreaded the thought of the gossip and rumor, knowing it would destroy his career and uncover his private wounds. The humiliation of being the object of sexual gossip, the shock and disappointment of his parents, the surprise of friends and relatives who had believed the two of them to be happily married, the loss of his children, the bitter return to unemployment all made the future look hopeless. He continued alone at Canterbury House knowing that sooner or later the blow would fall.

Even before he received Eleanor's letter, Bishop Conkling had begun to hear rumors that the Wattses' marriage was breaking up, and he wrote to Watts in May of 1950 to ask for information. Was it true that Eleanor was divorcing him? He asked Watts to come to see him.

Watts, just back from a trip to Kentucky, to see Joan at boarding school, wrote that he hoped divorce would be avoidable. When he went to see the bishop, Watts managed to suggest that he and Eleanor were having a temporary separation, and that the marriage would continue.

By the end of June, when Eleanor wrote her long letter to Bishop Conkling, she had already secured her Reno annulment. Her letter blackened Watts successfully in the bishop's eyes, and he was touched by the picture of the suffering woman — until a few weeks later when he heard the Gamers' side of the story.

Regardless of who was to blame for what, it was plain enough to Watts that it was all up so far as his career in the church was concerned. His pride was badly hurt, and rather than waiting for processes of dismissal or even working out his resignation, he left Canterbury House for Thornecrest Farmhouse in Millbrook, New York, where a friend lent him a house. All the hard work and enthusiasm he had put into his work as chaplain was destroyed.

He was in no mood for penitence. Furious over what had happened, he wrote the bishop a long letter full of abrasive criticism of the church and its hypocrisy. He said that he had now decided to abandon not only the priesthood, but also the communion of the Episcopal church: "Part of the reason is that, having in mind both the proper care of my two girls and my own essential needs, I am quite sure that I must marry again."[9]

His original attraction to the priesthood, he says, had really been one of nostalgia, part of the common tendency to yearn for the securities of the past. Gradually, he had come to feel that the ancient forms of ritual, beautiful and profound as they were, no longer spoke effectively to modern men and women. His own ministry had enjoyed a kind of success because he had tried some original approaches, some of them borrowed from other spiritual traditions. Yet he was full of doubt about Christianity. "Somehow or other the language, the forms, of the Church are ceasing to be either relevant or communicative. Forms lose their power, perhaps because all material things die, or because the Spirit within them is breaking them as a bird breaks from its shell."

Spiritual life, he thought, now depended upon ceasing to cling to any form of security. "Forms are not contrary to the Spirit," he lectures his bishop, "but it is their nature to perish. I wish I could take this step without hurting the Church. For the Church is people — people whom I have learned to love. Yet for that very love, I cannot be a party to their hurting themselves and others by seeking security from forms which, if understood aright, are crying, 'Do not cling to us!' "

It is difficult to take these high-minded reasons for leaving the church at their face value when Watts had shown no signs of wishing to leave until his position became impossible — he had taken the church's money and preached its accepted wisdom fairly uncritically. Whatever truth in his observations, it seems too striking a coincidence that the church's value in general seemed to decline in Watts's eyes just at the moment that it rejected him.

The church's mistake, he said, was to insist that it was the "best of all ways to God." "Obviously one who has found a great truth is eager to share it with others. But to insist — often in ignorance of other revelations — that one's own is supreme argues a certain inferiority complex characteristic of all imperialisms." This claim to supremacy, anxiety for certainty, and wish to proselytize, seemed to him a tragic form of "self-strangulation."

In the letter he also returned to the idea that there was something strange and absurd about treating a clergyman as a "moral exemplar." It was "an aspect of that unfortunate moral self-consciousness which has so long afflicted our civilization."

It was no good telling people they ought to love and then blaming them if they couldn't do it, he added with feeling. "The moralism which condemns a man for not loving is simply adding strength to that sense of fear and insecurity which prevents him from loving. You may help him to love neither by condemning nor consoling, but by encouraging him to understand and accept the fear and insecurity which he feels." Instead of this healing acceptance he felt that Christian attitudes to sex had aggravated people's fear, had taught many to "foster a simulated love which is fear in disguise." This approach made the church's dealings with marriage clumsy and inept, more concerned with protecting a social institution than helping people to love.

He is not, he says, an antinomian.

> What I see is what life has shown me: that in fear I cling to myself, and that such clinging is quite futile. I have found that trying to stop this self-strangulation through discipline, belief in God, prayer, resort to authority and all the rest, is likewise futile. For trying not to be selfish, trying to realize an ideal, is simply the original selfishness in another form. I can understand worship as an act of thanksgiving for God's love, but the formularies of the

Church make it all too plain that it is likewise to be understood as a means of spiritual self-advancement.

The more clearly I see the futility of trying to raise myself by my own spiritual boot-straps (of which asking the grace to be raised is but an indirect form), the less choice I have in the matter: I cannot go on doing it. At a yet deeper level—the more I am aware of the futility of clinging to self. I have no choice but to stop clinging. And I find that in this choiceless bondage one is miraculously free. . . .

I have no thought of trying to persuade anyone to "follow my example" and leave the Church likewise. You cannot act rightly by imitating the actions of another, for this is to act without understanding, and where there is no understanding the vicious circle continues. I have no wish to lead a movement away from the Church, or any such nonsense. If any leave, as I do, I trust they will do so on their own account, not from choice, not because they feel they "should," but only if, as in my own case, understanding makes it clear that, for them, there is no other alternative.

Watts continues by saying that he has no intention of joining any other religious body. He expects to devote his working time to writing and talking "because I love this work more than any other, and believe I have something to say which is worth saying."[10]

It was a startling letter for Bishop Conkling to receive. He must have felt rather as a judge might if he were to receive a moral lecture from a prisoner on whom he was about to pass sentence. Here was Watts, having committed adultery and encouraged his wife to commit adultery, causing a public scandal to the church, and running away from his job without asking leave, telling his bishop in no uncertain terms that the whole thing was the church's fault. Whether or not one agrees with his strictures, some of Watts's statements are movingly self-revelatory. If nothing else, he deserves top marks for cheek. With an amusing effrontery that Coyote might have affected, he appeared to saunter away from the encounter with the air of one who thinks he is the victor. Bishop Conkling was left to fret and fume, writing strong expressions in the margin of Watts's letter: "What conceit!!" "This is *not* true," "What does he mean by love?" "rationalizing for his own desire," and "a perverted man's perverted sight!" Surprisingly, in the end he wrote Watts a rather courteous letter.

My dear Alan,

Though your letter grieves me yet it is not a surprise. I do not believe there is any need for comment on your position. When an individual moves as far as you have from the group, words have little avail. Sometimes the individual proves to be a leader and to have a genius for truth; more often he shows himself in a much less complimentary position. . . . I am grateful for all you tried to do for good in your ministry and I commend you to the justice and mercy of God.

Sincerely yours, Wallace E. Conkling, The Bishop of Chicago.
Chicago, Illinois, July 5, 1950.[11]

Watts had robbed Bishop Conkling of any chance to dismiss him. He had already written his letter of resignation to the appropriate committee and had married Dorothy De Witt, the graduate student who had been the babysitter of his two daughters. This action automatically secured excommunication, since in the eyes of the Church he was still married.

Seven

A Priest Inhibited

1950-1951

WATTS AND HIS NEW WIFE moved to a temporary home, Thornecrest Farmhouse, in Millbrook, New York, in July 1950, "one of those archaic rural structures whose rooms are severe closetless boxes with small window-frames decaying from much painting."[1] It was bitterly cold that winter, and they found themselves spending much of their time in the kitchen to keep warm. Watts spent a lot of his day writing — letters to his friends and to others explaining or justifying the turn his life had taken, and a new book, to be called, appropriately enough, *The Wisdom of Insecurity*.

His financial situation seemed, at first, rather desperate. From being a rising young priest-theologian who had written a very good book about Christianity and was enormously in demand as a lecturer, he had suddenly become a pariah within the Christian community. He had lost his job and his income and the riches that accompanied life with Eleanor — after their annulment he had felt bound to return the stock she had made over to him. His studies and his natural inclination only fitted him for one thing: "to wonder . . . at the nature of the universe," as he put it. The difficulty was to see how to make a living at it. Very fortunately the writer Joseph Campbell intervened for Watts and got him a grant from the Bollingen Foundation, an institution founded on Lake Zurich by a wealthy patient of C. G. Jung, which was prepared to finance research in myth, psychology, Oriental philosophy, and many other subjects that interested Watts. The theme of his new book qualified for enough money to keep the Watts household for six months.

The new situation might have been easier if Watts had been deeply in love with Dorothy, but love was not one of his main reasons for marrying her. Spared as he had been by Eleanor's money and by the care of his parents from any real need to come to terms with the more humdrum details of life, he felt dependent on Dorothy's sheer practicality to help him through this difficult phase. Each of them, it seemed to him later, had hopes of "making over" the other into the person each *really* wanted to be married to. Finally, and most important, he believed that marriage gave him the opportunity to offer a home to Joan and Ann, whom he deeply loved.

Dorothy, for her part, found herself in a most painful position. Whether or not she believed that Watts loved her, the glamorous young priest who had been so much admired at Northwestern was suddenly a disgraced man without job or income. During the holidays she was saddled with Joan. (Ann had gone to New York to live with Eleanor and her grandmother.) She had had to give up her own graduate work in mathematics and was stuck in a bleak farmhouse with an unhappy man uncertain of the future.

Even in adversity, however, Watts was good at enjoying whatever was to be enjoyed. During evenings and weekends he set himself to learn cooking, a skill he would be proud of all his life. He and Dorothy began to cook ambitious meals together to such an extent that they were able to serve an elegant Christmas feast of *pâté de veau en croûte* and turkey with chestnut stuffing to such house guests as the Campbells, their benefactors, Ananda Coomaraswamy's widow Luisa, and the composer John Cage.

Not a bitter man by nature, Watts was, however, angry about what he felt as his public disgrace, endlessly going over it all in his mind, explaining and justifying it all to others. Even when he came to write about it in his autobiography, over twenty years later, the details still rankled. He published the circular letter he had sent to his friends, itself a working over of the long exculpatory and critical letter he had sent to Bishop Conkling. The responses were various. The one he found most unforgettable, because of its tone of moral superiority, was from Canon Iddings Bell, the reviewer who had thought *Behold the Spirit* one of the half dozen most significant books of the century.

Canon Bell wrote reproachfully:

> It is not easy, not possible, to undo spiritual commitments. You are a priest forever—and a priest inhibited. You think you can wipe our your ordination, restore that which was before your ordination, start all over. You can't. Life is not like that. What has been, still is.
>
> I remain your friend, but I see no good in our seeing one another, nor in correspondence, at least for as long as you are able to persuade yourself that you are content. If ever this becomes no longer possible, call on me and count on an understanding response.[2]

Penitence was a price Watts had no intention of paying. He replied, saying that he knew perfectly well that he was always a priest, but "I have no thought whatever of going back to a former state, or making a fresh start." There is an insecurity, he suggests, to be welcomed by those who will not use religion as a guarantee of safety: "One may embrace this kind of insecurity as a gesture of adolescent bravado. One may also embrace it, because, having seen the futility of other courses, there is nothing else to do. As a result I feel my priesthood to be uninhibited rather than, as formerly, inhibited."[3]

Other clerical friends were shocked at his suggestion that Christianity might have anything to learn from other religions. "There are many religions. There is but one gospel," wrote one of them. "Religions are man's search for God; the gospel is God's search for men." To which Watts replied that he believed Christ was not the only incarnation of God: "The identical theme of God's search for man is the essence of the Hindu doctrine of the Avatars, and the Buddhist Bodhisattvas. For me they are all incarnations of 'the only begotten Son'."[4]

Another correspondent, Theodore Green, wrote warmly of Watts's new position, a letter without judgment or criticism, which Watts quoted in his autobiography.

> As a layman in the church I have been in doubt again and again as to whether my proper course should be to remain in the church, and, in all humility, try to fight its multiple failures and abuses, or whether I should leave it and join the vast army of the unchurched. Rightly or wrongly I still feel that I should take the first course and that is what I am doing, although with great misgivings at times. Meanwhile, you have a tremendous contribution to make as a scholar and teacher from your new vantage point.[5]

Depressed as he was, and disillusioned both about himself and the world that had rejected him so resoundingly, Watts began to think more about God and about the God-filled person "wholly free from fear and attachment." Such a person was to be envied, he thought.

> We, too, would like to be one of those, but as we start to meditate and look into ourselves we find mostly a quaking and palpitating mess of anxiety which lusts and loathes, needs love and attention,

> and lives in terror of death putting an end to its misery. So we despise that mess, and put "how the true mystic feels" in its place, not realizing that this ambition is simply one of the lusts of the quaking mess, and that this, in turn, is a natural form of the universe like rain and frost, slugs and snails.[6]

The blessing that came to him in his distress was the realization that his own "quaking mess," as he called it, was natural, even a part of the divine. What he needed to do was live it, not fight against it. Eleanor's departure had released him forever from the need to pretend to be something he wasn't, a "respectable" person as defined by the mores of his time. "I am a mystic in spite of myself," he wrote, "remaining as much of an irreducible rascal as I am, as a standing example of God's continuing compassion for sinners or, if you will, of Buddha-nature in a dog, or light shining in darkness. Come to think of it, in what else could it shine?"[7]

It was this new insight that Watts explored movingly in his new book, which was dedicated to Dorothy, his partner in insecurity. Swinging sharply away from Christianity he suggests that it is not dogma but wonder that is the window on life. Writing out of his own uncertainty he says that "salvation and sanity consist in the most radical recognition that we have no way of saving ourselves."[8] Instead of the pitiful human tricks to avoid insecurity by clinging to one idol or another, and in particular to the idols buried in the heart of religion, the answer is to embrace insecurity by living each moment intensely as it happens.

In a desperate attempt to avoid the moments of pain and to know only pleasure, the Western mind had fallen into a tragic duality in which body and mind were dangerously split. Body, with its fine instinctual wisdom, had become the enemy of "will," the device with which we fondly imagine insecurity can be defeated. The body became both feared and despised, "Brother Ass," as Saint Francis dubbed it and as many Christian saints had experienced it. But to lose touch with the body, said Watts, is to lose touch with our real feelings and emotions, and to sink into an "insatiable hunger" for possessions, food, drink, sexuality without tenderness, and crude sensation of all kinds. The answer is to rediscover the rhythms and wisdom of the body, to help it to live naturally and spontaneously. Aiming at security "means to isolate and fortify the 'I,' but it is just the feeling of being an isolated I which makes me feel lonely and afraid."[9]

Watts was beginning to speak in the voice that would become famous in the sixties, a voice that would speak for the loneliness and alienation of many. The loss of his clerical career was pushing Watts back to a rediscovery of his old Buddhist beliefs.

Eight

The Wisdom of Insecurity

1951-1960

IN FEBRUARY 1951 Alan Watts and Dorothy drove westward, away from the harsh winter of the East, heading for Los Angeles and eventually San Francisco. On the earlier visit, with Eleanor and Carlton, Watts had been captivated by California. Now it delighted him all over again as he came upon the Mojave desert, the palm trees and dates of Indio, the misty San Bernardino range, finally Los Angeles itself. There Aldous Huxley and Christopher Isherwood had set up a meeting for him with Isherwood's guru Swami Prabhavananda and his Vedantist followers. Predictably Watts disagreed with the swami's emphasis on asceticism, sexual continence, and will power, and he mischievously let it drop that he thought orgasm was analogous, if not in some sense identical with, *samadhi,* or mystical experience. The swami's response was equally predictable; he was dismayed at the idea that enlightenment might come without effort and discipline.

In early March the Wattses passed through the country between Los Angeles and San Francisco, where Watts was overwhelmed by the beauty of the Santa Lucia range of mountains. At Big Sur he stopped to call on Henry Miller (who was away), but he fell in love with Partington Ridge, with its waterfalls, aromatic herbs and hay — "sage, wild thyme, sorrel, Indian Paintbrush, and acres of dangerous fire-prone golden grass three to four feet high, amidst which one can sometimes discover rattlesnake grass with its light, fragile, and airy heads designed like the rattlesnake's tail, or like those Japanese fish ornaments."[1]

From there they continued on to San Francisco itself, where an old London acquaintance, Frederic Spiegelberg, had had the idea of setting up what he called the American Academy of Asian Studies and had invited Watts to join him. The plan, as understood by the backers, was that the academy should be an information service at graduate level, an independent school granting master's and doctor's degrees, that would meet the new American interest in all things Asian. Its offerings would include Asian languages, art, histories, politics, and religion taught at a more practical level than the more formal Oriental departments at existing universities. Businessmen, government officials, teachers, and interested travelers would, it was thought, benefit from such courses, and initially funds came from such business, which set the academy up in the financial district of San Francisco.

At heart, however, both Spiegelberg and Watts had a more ambitious plan, nothing less, in Watts's words, than "the practical transformation of human consciousness."[2]

With the latter rather than the former plan secretly in mind they built up the staff of the new academy. Prof. Haridas Chaudhuri came from the University of Calcutta. Sir C. P. Ramaswamy Aiyar, previously dewan of the state of Travancore, was another recruit, "a princely man, close to seventy, who somehow reminded one of the elephant god Ganesha."[3] Judith Tyberg, who came to teach Sanskrit and yoga, a Japanese lama, Tokwan Tada, the Polish/English writer Rom Landau, who taught Islamic studies, and a Thai scholar who was also a princess — Poon Pismai Diskul — made up the rest of the staff.

Watts, for whom six months previously life had looked so grim, had found himself a paying job that couldn't have been more congenial to him in a climate and part of the world that he found a joy to live in. He, Dorothy, Joan (during her school vacations), and Ann moved briefly to Palo Alto, and then to a house on Woodside Drive off Skyline Boulevard. When the children first saw it they loved it; it was a log cabin surrounded by woods where they could play at tracking and camping, a magical place where their imaginations could run free.

In other ways the children's lives were not so happy. The two of them, ten and six years old, while visiting Ruth's house in New York, had been summoned separately to the library of the brownstone and asked to choose which parent they wanted to live with. The pain was acute. Joan described it this way:

> It was like being asked to choose between the devil and the deep blue sea. We loved our father; he had been most caring towards us during the difficult times at Evanston. If ever our parents were going anywhere, Eleanor was always the one who didn't let us come; basically she didn't want us around. Whereas Alan always said, "Sure, come along." Even though we disliked Dorothy we still had this tremendous feeling of our father loving us, and I am sure that colored our choice — we both chose to live with him.

Both Ann and Joan were already very unhappy at their parents' divorce, and Ann had spent some wretched months with Eleanor and Michael at Ruth's house. Eleanor continued to ignore her in favor of Michael and to find her naughtiness intolerable. When Dorothy gave birth to a daughter, Tia, the situation felt to Ann and Joan like a repetition of Michael's birth.

Joan went off to boarding school and Ann found comfort in the blessed world of school, partly, as she began to read, into the fantasy world of books. She had some children's books with beautiful illustrations given her by Ruth and by her parents, and alone in her room, or late at night in bed, she would pore over them for hours.

In addition, sometimes Watts, who knew how to set up a treat, would take her alone with him to a restaurant, usually where the cooking was exotic, and feeling very grown-up and proud to be out with him, she would loyally develop tastes for strange kinds of food. When she was ill her father could be very kind to her, bringing her hot toddies, reading to her, playing with her. As a result she longed to be ill and tried to bring it about by standing out in the rain without a coat. Sometimes he would take her with him to the academy where she wandered about happily, talking to faculty and students while Watts lectured or went to meetings. Maybe people at the academy perceived something about her unchildlike sadness and her need for love. In particular, Watts's secretary Lois became a friend and used to take her out on expeditions, treating her, to her delight, as if she were grown up. She received the love and attention eagerly, drawing from it an element of sanity that seemed missing from her family life.

But despite Watts's loving ways, he could let Ann down by not giving her the real help and understanding that she wanted and needed from her father.

Joan too was having problems with her father at the time. She remembers waiting at school with other girls to be fetched for a half-term vacation. One by one the others disappeared with relatives, until it gradually became obvious that no one was coming to fetch her. Out of kindness a teacher offered to take her home for the holiday.

Watts, we may feel, hated himself at this period of his life, mainly because, in his longing to "belong," he conformed to a conventional middle-class pattern that he despised. In his long hours at the academy he was as much a workaholic as any successful businessman, he had little time to spare for his wife and children, he was habitually unfaithful with various young women. As so often in his life, he had a taste for the good things money could buy — a very pleasant house, books, Oriental objects, a relaxed style of entertaining — yet he resented the cost to himself of the pressures and claims of a growing family, and felt no compunction in dodging the chores and responsibilities. His hard work, his wit and charm, were reserved for his students and colleagues, for the women he easily attracted.

Slowly, he came to feel that the price paid for the comfort of his present life was too high, and perhaps that the life itself — that of an absentee husband and father — was not a good or dignified one. He was searching for a way out.

The academy was attracting students. It was a simple building of classrooms and offices, with a library largely stocked with books from Watts's huge collection. Many of the pupils who came were artists or poets, and once a week Spiegelberg held a colloquium in which there was intense discussion about the contributions of East and West, the nature of the self, methods of meditation, and other such ideas that had interested Watts for years. Watts pushed the idea, which some of his Asian colleagues already believed, that "the egocentric predicament was not a moral fault to be corrected by willpower, but a conceptual hallucination requiring some basic alterations of common sense." Chaudhuri said that the illusion of the isolated, separate ego could only be overcome by yoga and meditation. Watts replied that to try to unseat the ego by summoning up its own strength and resources to help you to do it was like trying to lift yourself off the ground; it couldn't be done. Methods of meditation, he said, only worked if they showed the ego and its will to be unreal. Fellow members of the faculty affectionately accused him of laziness.

The school was turning out to be a wonderful meeting ground for unusual and interesting people. A group of artists, including Jean Varda and the surrealist Gordon Onslow-Ford, attended the academy, and so later on did Michael Murphy and Richard Price, the founders of Esalen. The poet Gary Snyder was among the pupils. Snyder was later described by Watts as "a wiry sage with high cheek-bones, twinkling eyes, and a thin beard, and the recipe for his character requires a mixture of Oregon woodsman, seaman, Amerindian shaman, Oriental scholar, San Francisco hippie, and swinging monk, who takes tough discipline with a light heart. He seems to be gently keen about almost everything, and needs no affectation to make himself interesting."[4] He had read the prospectus of the academy in a journal of Asian studies and thought it seemed worth looking at. He had studied anthropology and linguistics in Indiana and had decided to attend the University of California for graduate studies in classical Chinese and contemporary Japanese. He went to hear Watts lecture, got talking to another man in the audience, Claud Dahlenberg, who later joined the San Francisco Zen Center, and as a result got taken along to the academy and began to attend Watts's lectures.

From the beginning Watts and Snyder got on very well. Because there were still few students, Watts had plenty of time to talk and to enjoy informal meetings. He was, at this stage, Snyder remembers, "very straight, very British, short hair, necktie." On Friday nights the two of them started going to a study group at the Berkeley British Church; one night Watts drove Snyder home from a meeting and they finished a bottle of wine together and talked deeply about Buddhism. The friendship really took off, however, when Snyder sent Watts a letter on some points of discussion between them and wrote it in italic calligraphy. Calligraphy, one of Watts's great enthusiasms, became another shared pleasure between them like their interest in classical Chinese. Details of translation and interpretation became a running topic between them, and at Watts's invitation, Snyder gave readings of his Chinese translations at the academy. His relationship with Watts at this time, he remembers, was comfortable, respectful on his part, the relationship of a pupil with a good teacher.

Another of Watts's students at this time was Lock McCorkle, later to be a key man in est. McCorkle, like a number of other students at the academy, was a pacifist; he was fighting a jail sentence for resisting the draft, and Watts gave evidence in his defense in court.

Watts was excited by the originality and intellectual vitality of his students. One of them, Leo Johnson,

> had been haunting the University of California in Berkeley as a voracious reader and auditor of courses without the slightest interest in credits, examinations or degrees. . . . He was . . . simply interested in knowledge. His material ambitions were minimal; he lived in extreme simplicity; such money as he had went mostly for books, which he gave away; he had a ribald, bawdy, belly-laugh attitude to life which came out at unexpected moments, and was so informed

> with intellectual expertise that it was a real risk to expose him to scholarly company. . . Leo impressed upon me the important idea that the ego was neither a spiritual, psychological, or biological reality but a social institution of the same order as the monogamous family, the calendar, the clock, the metric system, and the agreement to drive on the right or left of the road. He pointed out that at such times such social institutions became obsolete . . . and that the "Christian ego" was now plainly inappropriate to the ecological situation into which we were moving.[5]

Another student, Pierre Grimes, had been "nurtured on Plato," but in working with Watts

> he had graduated to Nagarjuna and began very practical experiments with that great Mahayanist's philosophy. He saw that Nagarjuna's method was a dialectical process that went far beyond sophistry and intellectual acrobatics, and could be used as a very powerful instrument for what I had in mind—namely, the dissolution of erroneous concepts felt as precepts. Pierre devised an encounter group on the metaphysical level. That is to say, he worked out a situation in which the participants would probe for each other's basic assumptions, or axioms, about life, and then demonstrate that they were no more than assumptions; not truths, but arbitrary game-rules. This dialectic was as traumatic for a logical positivist as for a Hegelian, for as basic assumptions crumbled, members of the group would begin to show intense anxiety. He would then probe for still deeper assumptions underlying the anxiety until he could bring the group to a state of consciousness in which they could happily relax, and abandon the frustrating and futile project of trying to make a false hypothesis called "I," on the one hand, get mastery over another false hypothesis called "experience" or "the world," on the other. The process seemed extraordinarily therapeutic both for Pierre himself and for those who worked with him. I had feared that he would become a scornful, prickly

intellectual, but he turned out to be a man of singular compassion and humor, as well as of good sense in the practical matters of life.[6]

The academy was an arena in which people asked the hardest questions about living; it was a long way from the "information service" it had once purported to be. But its success in touching spiritual and philosophical depths did not help it financially. In the autumn of 1952 the "angel" who had maintained it thus far ran out of funds and could no longer pay the salaries. Frederic Spiegelberg resigned as director and went to teach at Stanford. But Watts, "having nothing else to do, decided that the Academy was an adventure too interesting to be abandoned, and slipped by default into the position of its administrator." The academy moved from the financial district to a rambling old mansion on Broadway in Pacific Heights. For another four years Watts managed to keep this offbeat and exciting project alive. He invited many interesting people to lecture, among them D. T. Suzuki, G. P. Malalaskera, Buddhist scholar and diplomat, Bhikku Pannananda from Thailand, the Zen master Asahina Sogen, the Thera Dharmawara from Cambodia, and his ex-mother-in-law, Ruth Fuller Sasaki, "who entranced the whole student body with her formal and definitive lecture on the use of koan in Zen meditation." It was as a result of Ruth's visit, and Watts's introduction of Gary Snyder to her, that Snyder was later given a scholarship grant to take him to Japan.

San Francisco was, in many ways, an ideal setting for the academy. Faculty and students visited, on the warmest terms, with the Chinese Buddhist community of San Francisco. Japanese Buddhists in the city also became deeply involved with the academy. Hodo Tobase, a Zen master at the Soto Zen temple on Bush Street, taught calligraphy at the academy, his assistant priest gave Watts lessons on Zen texts, and another Zen master, Shunryu Suzuki, saw the possibilities of developing "Western Zen" on the West Coast and went on to found San Francisco Zen Center. On one occasion Watts took a whole party of students on a "joy ride" to visit Krishnamurti at Ojai, camping at night on a beach at Carpinteria, with fires of driftwood.

In 1952 Laurence and Emily visited Alan and Dorothy and were distressed at Ann's state of physical and psychological health. Ann, at ten years old, was afflicted with gastric ulcers. Gently, Laurence and Emily suggested a way out — that Ann might come to live with them in England — and so Ann returned with them to Rowan Cottage. This was the beginning of a much happier time for Ann. Emily, who had so longed for a daughter, poured love and care on the little girl, who felt as if she was allowed to be a child for the first time in her life. She stayed with her grandparents for the next eight years, going to school at Farrington's, behind the garden at Rowan Cottage.

In 1953 Watts, Dorothy, Joan, and Tia moved to Mill Valley in Marin County. There was a big garden — a former garden nursery — with a big lawn, four great pine trees, twenty-seven fruit trees, a stream, cats and chickens, nice neighbors, a Volkswagen bus in which to transport the children, and a big library.

Dorothy, according to Watts, had very much wanted the suburban life, and it may be that he relished its comforts more than he later cared to remember. In any case the move to new surroundings was a distraction from the real difficulties of the marriage, from Dorothy's resentment that Watts was away for most waking hours and for some of the sleeping ones too. He was at the academy, or he was out with friends, or he was broadcasting on the Berkeley radio station KPFA or appearing on the educational television station KQED. In addition, Dorothy was suspicious, with good cause, that he was unfaithful to her with other women. She had reason to be bitter, not least because she was expecting another child, Mark, and she enjoyed very little of her husband's care and attention.

In 1954 the Japanese artist and printmaker Sabro Hasegawa visited the academy, and Watts was so delighted by his personality and his skills as a lecturer and teacher that he immediately invited him to join the staff. Not only was he a fine teacher of *sumi-e* (spontaneous ink painting derived from Zen practice), but he also became a kind of informal therapist for the faculty. He was, among other things, a tea master, and when Watts and Lois were becoming intolerably harassed by administrative problems he would wander into their office and suggest that they take time out for tea. Then in Hasegawa's room, "where the enshrined image of the Buddha was a piece of driftwood that had originally been the lathe-turned leg of a very ordinary wooden chair," the three of them would sit on the floor, and "with easy conversation, watch him spoon powdered green tea into a primitive Korean rice-bowl, cover it with boiling water from a bamboo ladle, and then whisk it into a potion which has been called 'the froth of the liquid jade'."[7] Lois used to say that one tea with Hasegawa was worth fifteen visits to a psychiatrist.

The friendship between Watts and Hasegawa went deep. When, a few years later, Hasegawa died of cancer, Watts unofficially became guardian to his daughter Sumire, acting as confidant and adviser. Because of the calm and wisdom of Hasegawa, Watts also took to wearing a kimono and found it much more comfortable than formal Western clothing.

The influence of the academy had brought Watts full circle back to his early passion for Zen. In 1956 he wrote *The Way of Zen* (published the next year), perhaps his most famous book, and dedicated it to "Tia, Mark and Richard who will understand it all the better for not being able to read it." (Richard was the Watts's newborn baby.) It covered some of the same ground as *The Spirit of Zen*, written twenty years before, but it had the benefit of all the Chinese studies he had worked at since.

In his preface he says firmly that he does not want to get himself labeled as a "Zenist or even as a Buddhist, for this seems to me to be like trying to wrap up and label the sky."[8] It is more that he wants Western readers to take pleasure in Zen, to enjoy its art and its literature, and to borrow any ideas that might be of service to them in leading their own lives. He longs to see Westerners give the same respect to the "peripheral mind" as they do to conscious intelligence, and part of that process is to go back to the Taoist beliefs, which preceded Zen Buddhism, with their clear certainty that "the natural man is to be trusted."

The freedom that lies in Zen is the discovery that we deny our own freedom by determinedly manufacturing our own ego, with all its attendant problems, from moment to moment. "Man is involved in karma when he interferes with the world in such a way that he is compelled to go on interfering, when the solution of a problem creates still more problems to be solved, when the control of one thing creates the need to control several others." The remedy is an "insight and awakening" that suggests an alternative, a way to get off the roundabout. "Sitting" meditation is not a spiritual exercise, it is simply "the proper way to sit," a method without ulterior motive, an action performed, like all Zen actions — like eating, or walking, or shitting, or yawning — for its own sake. As always with Watts, the thing that matters most is getting rid of the subjective distinction between "me" and "my experience," the painful dualistic split: "The individual, on the one hand, and the world, on the other, are simply the abstract limits or terms of a concrete reality which is 'between' them, as the coin is 'between' the surface of its two sides."[9]

By 1956 Watts realized that he could not make the academy work financially and that he was becoming bored with academic and administrative life. Dorothy was perpetually angry with him, with good reason, and with some idea of making a fresh start with her he decided to take up the free-lance life. Although she supported him in his resolve to work independently, he felt that she was putting pressure on him "to suburbanize myself, to live a more ordinary life, to mow the lawn, play baseball with the children, and abandon my far-out bohemian friends." The return to the job wilderness was not without pain. There was again the sense of failure, "voices from the past echoing in my skull: Alan, why can't you be like everyone else? Why are you so weird? Why don't you come down to earth and face reality?"[10] But all the same, in the spring of 1957 he resigned from the academy (which tottered on for a year or two before collapsing) and thenceforward would earn his living as a writer and as a peripatetic teacher, lecturer, broadcaster, philosopher, and entertainer. Meanwhile, Dorothy had given birth to another child, Richard.

The longing to write that had helped precipitate Watts's resignation from the academy soon found expression in a new book —

Nature, Man and Woman. It discussed the duality of mind and body that Christian spirituality had so often unconsciously encouraged. In the Western tradition woman was often depicted as "Eve," the temptress leading men away from God into sin; by projection she had become synonymous with "the flesh" or "the body," and sexuality itself was seen as a regrettable lapse into weakness for those who had not the strength and determination to be celibate.

Watts believed that a new approach to sexuality could transform it. Neither man nor woman had to be seen as a lonely abstract entity wandering like an orphan through the world. Rather, each should be considered part of the very fabric or expression of the world, so love-making becomes one part of nature recognizing another part, while also recognizing that other part as itself.

One problem, he said, was that we are afraid to let go of the "chronic cramp of consciousness," the narrowed, serial thinking, the memory-stored stream of impressions that give us a sense of "ego," which gives us the feeling that we are, as it were, the driver of the machine. But the same ego inflicts upon us an awkward loneliness, a self-consciousness, a separateness that inhibits joy. We need, Watts thinks, to recognize that the ego is no more than a convenient fiction, to learn an awareness that is diffuse and comprehensive rather than sharp and selective, and to discover that there is no longer the "duality of subject and object, experiencer and experience. There would simply be a continuous, self-moving stream of experiencing, without the sense either of an active subject who controls it or of a passive subject who suffers it. The thinker would be seen to be no more than the series of thoughts, and the feeler no more than the feelings."[11]

Such an outlook makes possible a spontaneity of feeling, where the "organism is no longer split into the natural animal and the controlling ego. The whole being is one with its own spontaneity and feels free to let go with utmost abandon. Pain, which we have been taught to avoid, and pleasure, which we have learned to seek, become indistinguishable in orgiastic response. Shame, on the other hand, is part of the frightened opposition of the conscious will, the ego, to that which it cannot control."[12]

After writing at length of the release of feeling and of ecstasy, Watts goes on to look at the relation between man and woman.

For Watts the union of two lovers is the overcoming of *maya*, the illusion of duality and separateness. Without fear, shame, or desperate need for gratification, the two gain a glimpse of a real, rather than an ideal, vision of how things are. Their vision, not just of each other, but of the world, can be transformed: "Sexual contact irradiates every aspect of the encounter, spreading its warmth into work and conversation outside the bounds of actual 'love-making'." Within love-making duality may be overcome: "At a particular but unpredetermined moment they may take off their clothes as if the hands of each belonged to the other. The gesture is neither awkward nor bold; it is the simultaneous expression of a unit beneath the masks of social roles and proprieties. . . . There is not the slightest compulsion to assume a pretended character."[13]

In the spring of 1958 Watts was invited to Zurich to give lectures at the C. G. Jung Institute. It was his first visit to Europe since he had left England as a young man twenty years before. Photographs show him still slim and youthful looking at forty-three, with a short haircut.

En route he went back to Chislehurst. He enjoyed visiting the cottage with the enormous garden he had loved as a little boy, and Chislehurst itself was still the same small country town surrounded by woods, ponds, and common land. There were still the same advertisements printed on sheets of metal at Chislehurst station — for Stephens' ink and Palethorpe's sausages — the old high street contained the same sweet shop, the chemist's shop still run by the same owners, and he could still walk across the green and round by the ancient church for a drink with his father at the Tiger's Head. Even the vegetables grown by his parents had the same delicious taste that he remembered from the past — twenty years of heavy smoking had not completely spoiled his taste buds.

Despite the delights he had mixed feelings about being back in England. He had always enjoyed the company of Laurence, now retired from business. But Emily, despite her love and care for him, still filled him with ambivalence, the more distressing since most of his relatives considered her very lovable and could not understand the emotions she aroused in him. He could only reflect that he had always felt that she hated her own body, felt cold to him, and had seemed physically unattractive for as far back as he could remember; he felt a fear in her presence and a sense of the impossibility of living up to her expectations.

England itself, after so long an absence, also felt like a chilly mother. It was peaceful, but weary, obsessed with its imperial past. He spoke in Cambridge at the invitation of the Departments of Theology, Anthropology and Oriental Studies and found them a dull and unimaginative audience. He felt hurt that none of his books seemed to be read much in his native country.

He went to London and lunched with Christmas Humphreys and D. T. Suzuki, both of them his boyhood mentors at the Buddhist Society, and he had his photograph taken with the pair of them, looking, beside the patrician High Court judge and the twinkling little Japanese, a rather ambiguous figure not quite at his ease, neither solidly British anymore, nor unequivocally American.

Zurich, somewhat to his surprise, turned out to be much more fun. Watts talked about the Hindu doctrine of *maya*, suggesting that the illusion of duality arose not from the evidence of the senses but from our mistaken concepts. The mystic, or enlightened person, lived in the same natural world as everyone else but saw it differently. He had got past the riddle of duality and regarded himself not as separate from the rest of the world but as part of it.

Watts enjoyed the audience, composed partly of the young studying to be psychotherapists and partly the company of "elderly, refined, and extremely well-educated ladies of formidable appearance who set the tone of the Institute."[14] He felt, however, that he rather blotted his copybook by going about Zurich with a young woman, called Sonya, a former patient who had been abandoned by the Jungians as hopelessly psychotic.

The high spot of his visit was the trip out to Jung's lakeside home at Küsnacht. The old man began with one of his favorite gambits, assuring Watts that he himself was not a Jungian, and then the two of them got down to a subject of mutual interest—Oriental philosophy. They discussed the concept of the unconscious, Watts suggesting its similarity to the Mahayana Buddhist term *alaya-vijnana*, the "store consciousness," which, like Jung's "collective unconscious," was the origin of archetypal forms or images. Watts also remembered how Suzuki had sometimes translated the Japanese term *mushin* (*no mind*) as *the unconscious*, meaning by it a sort of aware unselfconsciousness.

They went on to talk of the effects computers might have on

human psychology and finished by discussing a pair of swans they could see on the lake.

"Isn't it true," Watts asked, "that swans are monogamous?" Jung said that yes they were, but the odd thing about their first mating was that they invariably began by picking a fight, which was resolved when they worked out the method of mating.[15]

Watts found Jung open, eager, without conceit, full of humor and intellectual curiosity.

When Watts returned to the United States *Nature, Man and Woman* had just come out, and it was enthusiastically reviewed. There was, however, a sad irony in his publishing a book about sexual intimacy and the union of lovers. He and Dorothy were by now barely on speaking terms; the experiences that had begun to release him from his old sexual fears had mostly been with other women. He had discovered that many desirable women found him attractive and lovable and that he could be a successful lover, neither awkward nor frightened, nor ashamed. Only at home did he feel captive and wretched, emotions that he chose to blame more and more on the suburban atmosphere of Mill Valley, where he had taken on the expenses of luxurious family life. Bitter that he was not free to do as he wished, he complained that life at home was like something out of *Sunset* magazine: "picture windows of the ranch-type house, the outdoor barbecue, the children playing ball on the lawn, the do-it-yourself projects of tiling the bathroom and putting up shelves, and the station-wagoning of loads of sun-browned and quarrelsome papooses and brats to picnics on the beaches or marshmallow roasts in state parks."[16]

In 1959 Gary Snyder returned from Kyoto and borrowed a log cabin from a friend in Homestead Valley, in walking distance of

Watts's home. At once the two men resumed the friendship begun at the academy. Snyder took out one of the walls of his cabin, put in an altar stone, and made a small *zendo*. Watts, with other friends, came over two or three nights a week to sit *zazen*. From December 1 to 8 they sat *rohatsu sesshin* (a winter marathon of *zazen*) together.

On New Year's Eve, Snyder was invited to a party at Mill Valley given by Watts and Dorothy. Snyder liked Dorothy — he thought her intelligent, clear, and cool; she ran the household on orderly and immaculate lines and seemed a good mother. He observed, however, that she and Alan did not behave like a couple. Watts was out most evenings at parties alone and seemed detached from home and family. It struck him that Watts was still very much part of the affluent bourgeois life, often formally dressed, refusing marijuana when it was passed to him at parties. "He had not yet," Snyder decided, "shifted gears into counterculture."

Watts was, in fact, in the agonizing dilemma of those who know that their marriage is a disaster, but who have not quite summoned the courage and strength needed for separation and divorce. Watts now had four children by Dorothy — Tia, Mark, Richard, and Lila — in addition to Joan and Ann. He knew that his income was and would remain uncertain, that Dorothy would, naturally enough, expect substantial financial guarantees in the event of a divorce, and that would mean that, however hard he worked, he would be a poor man. As painful as any of these worries was the sense of being once again a failure. "He was one," Snyder remarks mildly, "who sowed problems wherever he went."

Watts wrote about the problem later, in self-justifying terms:

> It is well known that — for men especially — the forties are a "dangerous" decade, because if they have been well brought up, it

takes them this long to realize that one sometimes owes it to other people to be selfish. . . . Dutiful love is invariably, if secretly, resented by both partners to the arrangement, and children raised in so false an atmosphere are done no service. . . . Permanence may fairly be expected of marriages contracted and families raised under the ancient system of parental arrangements for then the partners are not required to feel romantic love for each other. But modern marriage involves the impossible anomaly, the contradiction in terms of basing a legal and social contract on the essentially mystical and spontaneous act of falling in love. The partners to such folly are sometimes lucky, and that is the best that can be said for it. They may sometimes become wise in the ways of the human heart by suffering each other, but such wisdom may also be learned in a concentration camp.[17]

Watts was spending nearly all of his time away from home and was drinking heavily, vodka mostly. In *The Wisdom of Insecurity* he had written poignantly of the plight of the alcoholic:

In very many cases he knows quite clearly that he is destroying himself, that for him, liquor is poison, that he actually hates being drunk, and even dislikes the taste of liquor. And yet he drinks. For, dislike it as he may, the experience of not being drunk is worse. It gives him the "horrors" for he stands face to face with the unveiled, basic insecurity of the world. Herein lies the crux of the matter. To stand face to face with insecurity is still not to understand it. To understand it, you must not face it but *be it.*[18]

The "horror" had moved closer to Watts since he had written those words, nearly ten years before.

Ironically he was increasingly in demand as a broadcaster, seminar speaker, and lecturer, gaining a reputation all over the country as someone who could tell people how to live. He tried to insist that he was a "philosophical entertainer," "in show biz," "a genuine fake," and an "irreducible rascal," perhaps to help him endure the sense of hypocrisy that his fame gave him, but most of his listeners were no more than mildly puzzled by such statements, perhaps thinking them a sign of a rare sort of humility.

Watts was doing a lot of teaching in New York. In the late fifties Charlotte Selver was giving remarkable seminars there on bodily awareness, using techniques to teach people to notice their own bodies and to be more acutely aware of the world around them, and she and Watts began to teach together in a particularly lively series of seminars. One student at these seminars in 1960, a woman of around Watts's own age, was Mary Jane Yates—Jano, as she liked to be called—and gradually she and Watts started to see a lot of one another. Together they drank and dined in Greenwich Village, exploring the small shops that then housed a number of craftsmen selling their wares. Before long Watts began to fall in love with her.

Jano hailed originally from Wyoming. She had been the first woman reporter on the *Kansas City Star* and had worked for some years in New York as Mobil's chief public relations officer. She was interested in many things that interested Watts, particularly in Taoism and Zen. He was, he says, fascinated by

> her voice, her gestures, the humor of her eyes, her knowledge of painting, of music, of colors and textures, her skill in the art of the loveletter and her general embodiment of something I had been looking for all down my ages to be my chief travelling companion. . . . My first idea was to whisk her off to a lonely shack by the Pacific, where we could sit on foggy nights by a log fire and talk over a bottle of red wine.[19]

So Watts left his family. The saddest feature of this desertion was that Dorothy was once again pregnant; in one of those painful episodes of attempted reconciliation or seduction that sometimes come right at the end of an unhappy marriage, she had again conceived. So Watts was leaving the comfortable suburban house, a pregnant wife, and four children. "At the age of forty-five I broke out of . . . this wall-to-wall trap, even though it was a hard shock to myself and all concerned. But I did it with a will and thus discovered who were my real friends."[20]

Among those who experienced the "hard shock" were Watts's parents in England. Brought up in a very different age, they had been shocked enough when Alan and Eleanor parted. They found the circumstances of this second failure deeply distressing; Laurence, usually a rather overadmiring father, wrote a sympathetic letter to Dorothy when she gave birth to her youngest child, Diane, after Watts had left, saying that he regarded Alan as a failure as a husband and father.

Watts's justification for his "breaking out" was that he felt himself stifled emotionally: "I had been slipping into the emotional constipation peculiarly characteristic of genteel academia — the mock modesty, the studied objectivity, the cautious opinion, and the horror of enthusiasm."[21]

Not only with Jano but also with one or two close friends Watts began to enjoy an emotional warmth of which he had not believed himself capable. Two of these friends were Roger Somers and Elsa Gidlow. Somers was a jazz musician and an architect-carpenter of great brilliance and originality, who had come to the Bay Area from a puritanical Midwest background and had gradually discovered himself as a joyful pagan. "He is an incarnation of the Greek god Pan," Watts wrote of him enthusiastically, "if you can imagine Pan based on a bull instead of a goat. . . . For his physique is formidable, his grizzly hair sticks out like short horns, and his energy is endless. He plays the saxophone, the oboe and all kinds of drums.

He dances — free form — like a maniac, and his shrieks of delight can be heard all over the hill."[22] Elsa Gidlow was a gifted landscape gardener and a poet who made no secret of the fact that she loved women more than men.

In the late 1950s, Elsa, Roger, and Roger's wife found a beautiful and secluded site in a eucalyptus grove on Mount Tamalpais, and they planned to build houses and landscaped gardens there for themselves and for a few friends. They called it Druid Heights and had already invited Watts and his family to join them there. Only Dorothy's disapproval and dislike of Elsa had prevented this from happening.

Now, with his new sense of freedom, Watts found himself frequently visiting them. Perhaps because Elsa offered no sexual challenge, Watts enjoyed her as a comforting and sympathetic elder sister, or maybe as a sort of white witch, practicing her good magic. He liked watching her choosing herbs from her garden or talking to her cats. Roger encouraged a kind of freedom and unselfconsciousness Watts had never known before. In Somers's beautiful Japanese-style room, with its Buddhist household shrine and its gold and redwood walls, the two men played drums, or practiced a sort of freedom singing, or chanted, or danced. Watts remembers it as the discovering of a *yoga*, a joining with the energy of the universe, and as such, a sort of religious exercise.

In New York, too, in the Greenwich Village loft of jazz musician Charlie Brooks (soon to be the husband of Charlotte Selver) Watts found himself breaking free of his old inhibitions. "So it was," he says simply, "that I found a new self." It was as if he had learned something quite new about being close to people. "I found myself among people who were not embarrassed to express their feelings, who were not ashamed to show warmth, exuberance and earthy *joie de vivre*. . . . I found too that these friends had always considered me a little distant and difficult to know, and had charitably put it down to British reserve."[23]

Elsa made it possible for Watts to realize his fantasy of an idyll with Jano. She owned a lonely cottage on another part of Mount Tamalpais, which she lent to them. In the cottage and in the garden that Elsa had made they rediscovered a childhood world lost by adult busyness and responsibility. They looked together at

> the convolution of a leaf, the light in a drop of water, the shadows of a glass in the sun, patterns of smoke, grain in wood, mottle in polished stone . . . we slowed down time. We watched the sun blazing from a glass of white wine and watered the garden at sunset, when the slanting light turns flowers and leaves into bloodstone and jade. We studied the forms of shells and ferns, crystals and teazels, water-flow, galaxies, radiolaria, and each other's eyes, and looked down through those jewels to the god and the goddess that may be seen within even when the doubting expression on the face is saying "What, *me?*" We danced to Bach and Vivaldi and listened to Ravi Shankar taking hold of the primordial sound of the universe and rippling it with his fingers into all the shapes, patterns and rhythms of nature.[24]

Going down to the sea and hunting for sand dollars at Stinson Beach, wandering the lonelier paths of Mount Tamalpais, looking and talking and making love in Elsa's cottage, they were slowly discovering each other and themselves.

Nine

Counterculture

1960-1968

CALIFORNIA. San Francisco. 1960. Something new could be felt in the air. Later, journalists and social commentators found words for it. *Utopianism, radical divergence, revolution, religious revival, San Francisco Renaissance, counterculture* — each caught a bit of the action, without successfully describing the whole.

Looking back, a decade later, Alan Watts perceived that "something was on the way, in religion, in music, in ethics and sexuality, in our attitudes to nature, and in our whole style of life. We took courage and we began to swing."[1]

The roots of the counterculture were Eastern religion — particularly Buddhism — jazz, poetry, the "alternative reality" of psychedelic drugs, and perhaps behind that the transcendental tradition. A major preoccupation was the relation of the individual self to his or her surroundings; how was the lonely and alienated self to find release? Gestalt therapy, owing a great deal to Buddhist insights, and other kinds of therapy, such as the encounter group, vied with various religious disciplines to offer an answer.

The swift movement towards counterculture coincided with the radical change in Watts's private life when he left Dorothy. Watts had a new sense of hope, as did many in the counterculture, that these social changes would bring a new freedom. The first step toward this freedom was going with Jano to live on an old ferry-boat called the *Vallejo* ("a dilapidated old hulk") moored at gate 5 in Sausalito in 1961. Nothing could have plunged Watts so successfully into a new bohemian world. The boat was owned by a painter, Gordon Onslow-Ford, who had already let half of it to another painter, Jean Varda, one of the most colorful characters of the waterfront. Instead of becoming exasperated by Varda or envying the ease of his social contacts, particularly with women, Watts in fact admired and enjoyed him immensely, using him, as he had used other admired friends, as a model of the sort of person he would like to be himself. Varda seemed to him to be "a marvellous amalgamation of exuberation, sensuality, culture, and literacy, salted with that essential recognition of one's own rascality which is the perfect preservation against stuffiness and lack of humanity."[2]

One of the things Watts admired about Varda was that he was poor and preferred it that way — he said it led to less bother with the tax people. (Struggling to pay alimony on a free-lance income Watts needed the example of someone who seemed to meet poverty with a light heart.) With Varda, or Yanko, as he was always known (the Greek word for uncle), there was always wine, good food, and marvellous company. Yanko held court in his big peacock chair "at the end of a long table scratched and stained with the memories of innumerable banquets of minced lamb in vine-leaves, stuffed peppers, and fish cooked in herbs and wine."[3]

Varda had arrived in California from Greece in 1940 and settled first at Big Sur. A painter by training, he was already less interested in painting than in mosaics, collages, and sculpture made out of whatever material came to hand — pipes, bottles, cans. His favorite subjects were women and "The Celestial City," visions of which ran through all his work.

He lived with enormous joie de vivre, a joy that attracted all kinds of visitors to the *Vallejo*. "In the fifties," said the *Pacific Sun*, "Varda was sporting strawberry-colored pants and driving through Sausalito in a purple car. He would sometimes wear mismatched socks. 'Why limit yourself?' he would say in his high-pitched Greek-accented voice. And people loved him. He was always surrounded by young, desirable women. All who knew him swear he was a romantic, not a lecher. Each person who entered his life felt beautiful, wanted, special."[4] Varda's pleasure in living was derived from his gift for living in the moment.

On Sundays there were wonderful sailing trips on board the *Perfidia*, Yanko's lateen-sailed dhow, which often had a crew of women and was "supplied with loaves and cold chicken and gallons of wine."[5] The boat had no engine and was often in danger of running aground because of the insobriety of the crew, but it survived, maybe because of the great eye on the prow, put there, Greek fashion, to avert the "evil eye." There were parties on neighboring beaches or aboard the *Vallejo* itself.

On weekdays both Watts and Varda rose and began work early. "As I sat at my typewriter," wrote Watts,

> I would hear him hammering and rustling about in the studio. A little after eight I would often light a cigar and wander over for coffee with him. . . . Even at this hour there would be others at the table — his current mistresses, or young men helping him with boat construction; and as the day wore on a stream of visitors would be in and out — diplomats, professors, ballerinas, fishermen, pirates and models — for hour after hour of multilingual badinage. By lunchtime there were jugs of wine, jack cheese, and sourdough bread on the table, and towards evening Yanko would get together lamb or fish with olive and peppers, vine leaves and lemons, egg-

> plant and onions . . . mixing salad in an immense wooden bowl. . . . All the while he would regale us with anecdotes, real and imaginary, and outrageous commentaries on art, women, nautical adventures.[6]

What Yanko so effortlessly lived, Watts had spent years trying to understand, to explain, in books, articles, and talks on radio station KQED. His quarrel with Christianity was that it did not believe that "the natural man is to be trusted." Its emphasis on the will, together with the continual need to watch oneself and to curb the lusts of the flesh, seemed to him to heighten the human predicament, the "hard knot" of the mind seeking to know the mind, or the self seeking to control the self. Continually watching oneself made one lonely and also encouraged a kind of hallucination—that the self was real. "When that tense knot vanishes there is no more sense of a hard core of selfhood standing over against the rest of the world."[7]

Watts had explored this idea at length in *Nature, Man and Woman* (1958), suggesting that the split between mind and body that Christianity inherited from Greek dualism, had affected all subsequent attitudes toward women, since fears about the wayward flesh or body were often projected upon women. With both tenderness and realism Watts was trying to explore new ways in which men and women might relate to one another.

Many of these ideas about Zen Buddhism and about sensuality had been explored before Watts by the group known as the beats, or the beat generation. The poets of North Beach, San Francisco, had often gathered in the early 1950s to drink and read poetry. In the spring of 1955, many of them met at the Six Gallery—Gary Snyder, Kenneth Rexroth, Philip Whalen, Michael McLure, Lawrence Ferlinghetti, and others—and there Allen Ginsberg read his poem *Howl*, a devastating attack on contemporary society delivered by a man with the temperament of an Old Testament prophet. Jack Kerouac sat on the side of the tiny platform, drinking wine, and "giving out little wows and yesses of approval and even whole sentences of comment with nobody's invitation but in the general gaiety nobody's disapproval either."[8]

There was a lot of interest in Zen Buddhism among the beats, the most enthusiastic exponent being Gary Snyder, already a close friend of Watts.

Jack Kerouac, who had written the influential book *On the Road*, a beat generation odyssey that had sent many young people traveling around the country on freight trains, fell under Snyder's spell and wrote a new book about their friendship and about Buddhism titled *The Dharma Bums* (1958). The two main characters in the novel, Ray Smith and Japhy Ryder, take part in wild, wonderful, drunken parties round bonfires, in which many of the guests take off their clothes for the pleasure of walking around naked. They believe that to live in poverty, religious belief, and joyful sexuality is the way to overcome the consumer society.

The Dharma Bums and *On the Road*, along with Watts's writing, gave the young a new ideal, as well as the ideas and words of a religion that seemed more exotic and exciting than their native Christianity.

Watts observed Kerouac's brand of Zen with a certain amount of doubt and suspicion, feeling that it mistook sloppy, undisciplined art, selfishness of all kinds, and idleness for spontaneity. Watts was, however, careful to exempt Snyder from his strictures.

Kerouac, for his part, obliquely mocked Watts, whom he knew from parties and poetry readings as well as in print. Watts appears in *The Dharma Bums* as Arthur Whane. He arrives at a party at which most of the guests have chosen to be naked.

> Whane stands there in the firelight, smartly dressed in suit and necktie, having a perfectly serious discussion about world affairs with two naked men.
>
> "Well, what is Buddhism?" someone asks him. "Is it fantastic

imagination, magic of the lightning flash, is it plays, dreams, not even plays, dreams?"

"No, to me Buddhism is getting to know as many people as possible." And there he was going round the party real affable shaking hands with everybody and chatting, a regular cocktail party.[9]

The vision that Watts, Snyder, and Kerouac shared was the renunciation of the values of bourgeois and suburban life. In 1962 Herbert Marcuse was to claim in the preface to *Eros and Civilization* that there is a kind of revolution that breaks out not in hopeless poverty, but at the very heart of affluence. Freed from acute anxiety about survival, human beings begin to ask more of life, and in particular they ask about meaning, in work, in relationships, in society, and in religion. It was to the search for this kind of meaning that the contemporary historian Theodore Roszak applied the term *counterculture* in 1968, a word that was widely taken up and used.

In 1960, when Watts and his contemporaries "began to swing," Kennedy had just been elected president and there was a feeling of hope and newness in the air, of the possibility of new moves toward peace and racial integration, an intoxicating sense that things could be different. Kennedy championed civil rights, had talks with Martin Luther King about racial problems, seemed to show a new initiative toward the Soviet Union, enjoyed and encouraged the arts. Idealism with style offered a way forward.

On the college campuses this idealism took the form of a radical activism that seemed more colorful and less grim than the old-style Marxism; students rather than the working classes were to be the new agents of change. Folk music, hitherto associated with rural settings and traditional themes of love and death, began to be adopted by urban idealists who gradually adapted it to express other passionately held sentiments about brotherly love, peace, and racial equality.

One of the most profound differences between the college generation of the sixties and their parents' generation had to do with sexuality. The earlier generation, lacking effective contraceptives and still firmly in the grip of a Christian ethic that believed "fornication" to be a sin, had officially held to the ideal of sexuality expressed only within monogamous marriage. The young, however, took their models from such books as *The Dharma Bums*, in which, for example, Japhy Ryder and a friend, sharing the delectable girl they call Princess in what she calls *yabyum*, roll delightedly on the floor in sexual ecstasy. They were repudiating the America that Japhy Ryder remembered from when he was a "kid," the America of the Protestant work ethic, of nervous liquor laws, of censorious attitudes toward sensual experience, and of devotion to the ideal of the family.

Watts was speaking — about sexuality, about sensuality, about religion, about psychedelics, about food, about clothing, about how to live — on campuses all over the United States, and weekly on the radio. In 1961 he spoke at Columbia, Harvard, the Yale Medical School, Cornell, Chicago, and at other schools, and gave seminars on the *Vallejo* and elsewhere. He was the sort of speaker who used his voice as consciously as a pianist uses his fingers. Sandy Jacobs, who was later to record Watts extensively on tape, remembers the way he captured an audience and how effortless it seemed.

> He didn't *prepare*. He had a fine library, of course, and he did extensive research for his books, but for his lectures? No way. He would just wander into an auditorium someplace — some college town. He'd walk up on the stage, and he'd say, "Let's see, today we were going to discuss, say, Ramakrishna." Right away, some totally brilliant opening would suggest itself to him, he'd gather up the audience with some incredible beginning which would draw people in. There'd be this long, rambling middle, which would keep peo-

ple's interest — jokes, laughs. He had a mental watch which said, "Hey! It's fifty minutes," and he'd draw it all in, and come up with this cliffhanger, a conclusion, but it was a pregnant moment where everybody would say, "God, that's fantastic!"

In 1962 Watts received a two-year travel and study fellowship from Harvard University's Department of Social Relations, and he began a series of visits to Harvard. Here he began to see quite a lot of Timothy Leary, whom he already knew slightly. Leary had turned his house into a sort of commune, in which all kinds of people gathered in the kitchen for meals and conversation. Watts, always fastidious in his personal habits, said later that he could not understand how anyone who had had his or her consciousness raised by psychedelic drugs could tolerate the squalor of the Leary household — the unswept floors and the unmade beds. Messiness apart, though, he liked Leary; later he was surprised when Leary proved to have a genius for getting into trouble that even exceeded his own.

Leary too remembered the evenings in his kitchen when

> the wizard held court, drinking heavily, spinning out tales of fabled consciousness expanders of the past. [Watts talked of Madame Blavatsky, Annie Besant, Krishnamurti, and Gurdjieff.] . . . He gave us a model of the gentleman-philosopher who belonged to no bureaucracy or academic institution. He had published more influential books than any Orientalist of our time. Although he could teach rings round any tenured professor, he had avoided faculty status, remaining a wandering independent sage, supporting himself with the immediate fruits of his plentiful brain. . . . Watts taught us to divide mystics into two groups — the lugubrious and the witty.[10]

Watts was to participate in Leary's life at intervals thereafter, once coming to a pagan festival Leary held to celebrate the vernal equinox at Millbrook. There was a huge bonfire, and the congregation sat in a candlelit circle while Watts consulted the *I Ching*. Watts, Leary says, probably admiringly, "whose orientation was past and Eastern rather than scientific and Western, used the *I Ching* as an elegant mumbo-jumbo tea ceremony, which raised the esthetic level of our gathering and made us feel part of an ancient tradition."[11]

Leary and Watts were each, in different ways, to affect people's use and understanding of drugs, but ahead of either of them in exploring this territory was Aldous Huxley. In 1953, at the invitation of a psychologist conducting research, Huxley took mescalin, a natural drug that, like the synthetic drug lysergic acid, has chemical similarities to human adrenalin.

"One bright May morning," wrote Huxley in *The Doors of Perception*, "I swallowed four-tenths of a gram of mescalin dissolved in half a glass of water and sat down to wait for results." Within an hour Huxley, a man who on his own admission had a poor visual imagination, was looking at something utterly extraordinary. A flower vase on the table containing a rose, a carnation, and an iris, which had interested him briefly at breakfast, became the focus of his attention: "I was not looking now at an unusual flower arrangement. I was seeing what Adam had seen on the morning of his creation—the miracle, moment by moment, of naked existence.

'Is it agreeable?' somebody asked. . . .

'Neither agreeable nor disagreeable' I answered. 'It just *is*.' "

The "Is-ness" (*Istigkeit*) of which Meister Eckhart had spoken—the Being of Plato—suddenly Huxley saw it in the flowers. "A transience that was yet eternal life, a perpetual perishing that was at the same time pure Being, a bundle of minute, unique particulars in which, by some unspeakable and yet self-evident paradox, was to be seen the divine source of all existence."[12]

All the hints and painful attempts at explanation that Huxley had read in the mystical literature suddenly made sense. This was what the beatific vision was like, or *Sat Chit Ananda* (Being–Awareness–Bliss). And when the Zen novice asked his master what the dharma-body of the Buddha was like (dharma is the doctrine or method by which freedom is attained), he got the baffling answer "The hedge at the bottom of the garden." This was what the master saw.

It began to seem to Huxley that the function of the human senses and nervous system was to filter out the extraordinary wealth of information constantly available to it in order to enable the individual to deal with simpler necessities. But potentially, and in our earliest baby awareness of the world, each of us is, has been, Mind at Large, aware of everything, remembering everything. Mystics, schizophrenics, and those under the influence of such drugs as mescalin, see life without the filter. Painters, Huxley thought, see that life in part.

He emerged from this profound experience feeling that he had seen into the deeps of contemplation and could at least imagine the deeps of madness. He felt that contemplation demanded that something be added to it (as the saints and bodhisattvas believed), some effort of active compassion that could release others from suffering. In Eckhart's phrase they should be ready to "come down from the seventh heaven in order to bring a cup of water to a sick brother."

Partly because of Huxley's experiment and his vivid description of it, a wider group of people became interested in hallucinogens, such as mescalin, lysergic acid, psilocybin, and peyote. Anthropologists who had long known about the tradition of taking cactus buds (peyote) and "the mushroom" (psilocybin) in Mexico and in some countries of South America among the Indian populations were interested in the effect of drugs that had previously been used primarily as part of religious rituals. Psychologists were interested in the drugs for any light they might throw on the subject of perception and for revelations they might produce about schizophrenia. Religious people were interested in the information they might offer about mystical experience. Painters and musicians were after new perceptions of light, color, form, and sound.

In 1958 Watts, who, unlike the beats, had always been wary of drugs, was invited to take part in an experiment by Keith Ditman, the psychiatrist in charge of LSD (lysergic acid diethylamide) research in the Department of Neuropsychiatry at the University of California, Los Angeles. One of the things that encouraged him to do so was the way he thought that the mescalin experience had made the ascetic Aldous Huxley warmer, more human. So he went along to Ditman's office and took one hundred micrograms of LSD. Perception was changed in a fascinating way: time was slowed down, plants and grass and a church across the road were all great marvels, and a book of *sumi-e* paintings was a revelation; yet he was faintly disappointed. It seemed to him that he had had a wonderful aesthetic experience, but one that did not approach the mystical unity that Huxley had described. Later he was to believe that the clinical/laboratory atmosphere of a formal test in a hospital had itself imposed certain limitations on his response, though it is also true that the dose is a small one.

He let a year go by and then tried a series of five experiments with the drug, varying the dosage from seventy-five to one hundred micrograms. These trips were extraordinarily rewarding. Perhaps the most remarkable effect had to do with time, what Watts called "a profound relaxation combined with an abandonment of purposes and goals. . . . I have felt, in other words, endowed with all the time in the world, free to look about me as if I were living in eternity without a single problem to be solved." Within this freedom was another astonishing freedom: "I was no longer a detached observer, a little man inside my own head, *having* sensations. I *was* the sensations. . . . It is like, not watching, but being, a coiling arabesque of smoke patterns in the air, or of ink dropped in water."[13] An irresistible feeling of beauty and wonder, absent from his first experiment with the drug, took over.

Watts writes of one experiment conducted late at night at his house in Millbrook:

> Some five or six hours from its start the doctor had to go home, and I was left alone in the garden. For me, this stage of the experiment is always the most rewarding in terms of insight, after some of the more unusual and bizarre sensory effects have worn off. The garden was a lawn surrounded by shrubs and high trees—pine and eucalyptus—and floodlit from the house which enclosed it on one side. As I stood on the lawn I noticed that the rough patches where the grass was thin or mottled with weeds no longer seemed to be blemishes. Scattered at random as they were, they appeared to constitute an ordered design, giving the whole area the texture of velvet damask, the rough patches being the parts where the pile of the velvet is cut. In sheer delight I began to dance on this enchanted carpet, and through the thin soles of my moccasins I could feel the ground becoming alive under my feet, connecting me with the earth and the trees and the sky in such a way that I seemed to become one body with my whole surroundings.
>
> Looking up, I saw that the stars were colored with the same reds, greens and blues that one sees in iridescent glass, and passing across them was the single light of a jet plane taking forever to streak over the sky. At the same time, the trees, shrubs, and flowers seemed to be living jewelry, inwardly luminous like intricate structures of jade, alabaster, or coral, and yet breathing and flowering with the same life that was in me. Every plant became a kind of musical utterance, a play of variations on a theme repeated from the main branches, through the stalks and twigs, to the leaves, the veins in the leaves, and to the fine capillary network between the veins. Each

> new bursting of growth from a center repeated or amplified the basic design with increasing complexity and delight, finally exulting in a flower.[14]

The beauty of the experience reminded Watts insistently of something, and he realized that the garden had the kind of exotic beauty of the pictures in the *Arabian Nights*, of scenes in Persian miniatures or in Chinese and Japanese paintings. Those artists too had seen the world like this. Was that because they too were drugged and seeing therefore a strangely heightened and beautified version of the world, or was it that the effect of LSD was "to remove certain habitual and normal inhibitions of the mind and senses, enabling us to see things as they would appear to us if we were not so chronically repressed?"[15] What the Oriental artists saw in their health and wisdom, Watts is saying, he could see with the help of LSD.

Inevitably Watts wondered about the possibilities of a drug so potent. Writing in 1960 he says that "the record of catastrophes from the use of LSD is extremely low, and there is no evidence at all that it is either habit-forming or physically deleterious. . . . I find that I have no inclination to use LSD in the same way as tobacco or wines and liquors. On the contrary, the experience is always so fruitful that I feel I must digest it for some months before entering into it again."[16] It was a drug, he goes on to say, to be approached with the care and dedication with which one might approach a sacrament.

He continued to experiment with it throughout the next couple of years and achieved, in an experience with his friends at Druid Heights, a piercing sense of how very lonely he had felt all his life, "a bag of skin," chronically and hopelessly cut off from all other "bags of skin" — "the quaking vortex of defended defensiveness which is my conventional self." Sitting up on the ridgepole of the barn with Roger and his friends, laughing helplessly with them at the sight of a broken car standing in Elsa's garden, sitting round a table on the terrace, sharing homemade bread and wine, he had the most extraordinary intimation of peace, of having "returned to the home behind home."[17]

This sense of being loved and cared for, of a place of deep trust, made it possible for him to know what he called the "helpless crying of the baby." The confident talker and performer and entertainer suddenly knew himself as an infinitely needy and sensitive self, "a blithering, terrified idiot, who managed temporarily to put on an act of being self-possessed. I began to see my whole life as an act of duplicity — the confused, helpless, hungry and hideously sensitive little embryo at the root of me having learned, step by step, to comply, placate, bully, wheedle, flatter, bluff and cheat my way into being taken for a person of competence and reliability."[18]

It was both a wonderful and an agonizing discovery, one that raised even more interesting questions as to what this amazing drug could achieve. Writing *The Joyous Cosmology* in 1962 Watts had come to see drugs like LSD and mescalin as a kind of medicine for sick modern men that would give them the experience of being "temporarily integrated." Like medicine, transforming drugs were not, in his view, a way of life. You took them if you needed them, you deepened the experience "by the various ways of meditation in which drugs are no longer necessary or useful."

In 1961 LSD was only just beginning to become available outside the medical world. Watts shared Huxley's feeling that it might be shared by minds already developed by aesthetic, philosophical, and religious ideas and practices. Unlike Huxley he guessed at the danger of a widespread availability of LSD, fearing that it would produce the chemical equivalent of bathtub gin. One of the reasons for writing *The Joyous Cosmology*, Watts claimed, was to inform people about the drug while there was still time, to encourage them to approach it with a kind of reverence, rather than with a desire simply for "kicks."

In this he was entirely opposed by Timothy Leary. Leary came relatively late to LSD, not actually trying it until 1962. But for several years before that he and Richard Alpert (a psychologist, who later became Ram Dass) had experimented extensively with psilocybin and had tried unsuccessfully to persuade the psychology faculty at Harvard to set up a series of systematic drug experiments there. So instead Leary and Alpert worked with university staff members and volunteer students and their families. There were a lot of volunteers.

Partly because of a series of experiments involving use of psilocybin by prisoners in the Massachusetts prison system, in which he found that he could make prisoners less depressed and hostile and more responsible and cooperative, Leary began to feel that psychedelic drugs might have something to offer everyone, and he developed a kind of evangelical zeal to share his discoveries. He gave out mushroom pills freely, particularly to writers; Robert Lowell, William Burroughs, Gregory Corso, Jack Kerouac, Arthur Koestler, and Allen Ginsberg all "took the mushroom" with Leary.

He was following a tradition that the British philosopher Gerald Heard and the psychologist Oscar Janiger had begun in the 1950s of deliberately initiating people into LSD, believing that it was God's way of giving the twentieth century the gift of consciousness and saving it from Armageddon. "When you made contact, it was like two people looking at each other across the room, and with a sort of nod of the head that acknowledged that you 'too!' "[19] wrote Leary. Janiger had turned on a number of Hollywood film stars and directors, Cary Grant, Jack Nicholson, and Stanley Kubrick among them. He had also run tests with people from many walks of life, a number of whom had felt illuminated and changed by the LSD experience, and he had had some encouraging results working with depressed patients.

The rumors of the effects of psychedelic drugs began to cause a kind of excitement that boded ill for the sort of controlled initiation Huxley or Watts or Janiger favored. At Harvard Leary was continually being approached by students who wanted to try LSD. When he obeyed college rules and refused to oblige them, they got supplies in Boston or New York. The chemistry students synthesized their own. Leary described it this way: "In this the third year of our research the Yard was seething with drug consciousness." Dozens of Harvard students had visions. Some dropped out and went to the East. "Not necessarily a bad development from our point of view," Leary wrote with his usual insouciance, "but understandably upsetting to parents, who did not send their kids to Harvard to become Buddhas." Worse still, "dozens of bright youths phoned home to announce that they'd found God and discovered the secret of the universe."[20]

In California, LSD, not yet illegal, was being widely distributed, much of it synthesized by an entrepreneur named Stanley Owsley. Leary's *Psychedelic Review* disseminated information about methods of taking it. Braver or wilder souls, like Ken Kesey, author of *One Flew over the Cuckoo's Nest*, held rock-and-roll dances in which the place of honor in the middle of the floor was given to a baby's bathtub full of punch spiked with lysergic acid.

The words *hipster* and *hippie* were coming into the language and were applied to the new "far-out" crowd by the beats. By the end of 1965, in the words of a harassed police captain, "the word is out that San Francisco is the place for the far-out crowd," and within San Francisco the old student neighborhood of Haight-Ashbury had become the most far-out, both because of its cheapness and because of the attractiveness of its Edwardian houses. As if to fit in with the landscape many of the hippies started wearing Edwardian and Victorian clothes — they were cheap and good to look at during LSD trips or when stoned on marijuana.

Golden Gate Park became a sort of extension of the neighborhood, together with a handful of favorite stores and coffee houses that stayed open all night. A professor opened an experimental college in the Haight in which students could decide what they wanted to study, outline a course, get a faculty sponsor, and hire a teacher. There was a preponderance of people wanting to study art, psychology, and occult religion.

Street theatre became a common sight, and it mostly reflected antiwar or antiracist sentiments. The new rock-and-roll, which, to begin with, was not interested in much besides "love," was gradually adopting antiestablishment ideas. Already by 1965 many folkies were turning to the electric guitar and were singing songs, like Dylan's "Subterranean Homesick Blues," that caught the new mood. The hippies listened to the new bands, like the Jefferson Airplane, the Grateful Dead, and the Byrds, and to new singers, like Janis Joplin and Jimi Hendrix. They admired the Beatles, but began by thinking them a bit "cozy." The bands played against and within light shows in which their audience danced in the light of strobes, ultraviolet light, and overhead projectors. Charles Perry describes a message displayed by projector at one light show that went: "Anybody who knows he is God go up onstage!"

The Haight was beginning to get into the drug market. By the early sixties marijuana (once enjoyed mostly by Latins and working-class blacks) had become popular on campuses, and by 1963 people were smuggling it from Mexico. Most of the selling was done by hippies who found it a way of making a living. Ounces ("lids") sold for eight to ten dollars, a kilogram at around sixty dollars. The hippies broke up the kilos and sold smaller amounts at a good profit.

LSD was still legal (until October 1966), and the extraordinary perceptions and fantasies, images and colors associated with it began to influence pop art, clothes, and songs. The Beatles' new album *Revolver* gave broad hints that the Beatles themselves were "turning on," while a new paper, the *Oracle*, with an amazing use of colored inks, exploded in a vast rainbow that included all hippie preoccupations in one great Whitmanesque blaze of light and camaraderie. American Indians, Shiva, Kali, the Buddha, tarot, astrology, Saint Francis, Zen, and tantra all rubbed shoulders in one edition, one that sold fifty thousand copies on the streets. When the *Oracle* printed the *Heart Sutra*, it devoted a double spread to the Zen Center version, complete with Chinese characters.

There was, briefly, a touching kind of innocence about the hippie movement. In the early days of Haight-Ashbury there was a café on Eighth Street where people threw their spare change into a tray so that those who could not afford the price of a cup of coffee or a meal could eat. There was a movement of people called "the Diggers," who handed out free meals to all who came, an action based on the ideology that food belonged to the people. Young people from all over the United States regarded San Francisco and the Haight as a mecca to be reached at all costs, and many of them received a free meal and a free bed before either returning to home and school or joining the growing population around the Panhandle, the handle-shaped extension of Golden Gate Park.

During the years 1960 to 1965, Alan Watts visited Japan two or three times a year, escorting tourists to Kyoto. He was helped with the practical chores of tour guiding by Gary Snyder, who had extensive knowledge of the country; installed in his monastery, Snyder sorted out accommodation and currency problems for Watts and gave him a welcome bolt-hole from the responsibilities of looking after his charges. Snyder was by this time advanced enough in Zen studies to be able to discuss some of the things Watts was curious about, such as what actually went on in the silence of a Zen monastery, for example, and how the system was structured. Snyder introduced Watts to his *roshi* and to some of the head priests, and arranged for him to attend lectures at the monastery, as well as some of the ceremonies, which Watts enjoyed tremendously.

"I got to like him more and more, even though I realized he was getting naughtier and naughtier," says Snyder. "Which was all right because I was naughty too. So we enjoyed each other's company."

Watts's spoken Japanese was poor —"only enough to direct taxis and order food in restaurants, helped out with Chinese characters on a scratch-pad"—but he felt very at home in Japan, particularly in Kyoto. He visited temples and gardens, filled with wonder and joy, and was fascinated by all the rituals of tea, and by the shops with materials for "ink-and-brush meditation," a pastime he had long enjoyed. One day he and Jano

> took a day off for meditation at Nanzenji, not in the temple itself, but on the forested hillside behind it, where we sat on the steps of some ancient nobleman's tomb, supplying ourselves with the kit for ceremonial tea and a thermos bottle of hot saké. Zen meditation is a trickily simple affair, for it consists only in watching everything that is happening, including your own thoughts and your breathing, without comment. After a while, thinking, or talking to yourself, drops away and you find that there is no "yourself" other than everything which is going on, both inside and outside the skin. Your consciousness, your breathing, and your feelings are all the same process as the wind, the trees growing, the insects buzzing,

> the water flowing, and the distant prattle of the city. . . . The trick, which cannot be forced — is to be in this state of consciousness all the time, even when you are filling out tax forms or being angry.[21]

In the grounds of one of the ruined temples, Jano and Watts, by now married, served each other LSD, each pouring the liquid into the other's tiny cup, as the Japanese serve sake.

Watts's repeated visits to Kyoto brought an old acquaintance back into his life, Ruth Sasaki, by now the abbess in the Rinzai sect of Zen. He and Ruth at this stage in their lives had a sort of amused respect for one another.

Watts's writing and speaking about Zen at public lectures and seminars, on tape and television, in books, and above all on public radio, gave him a strong influence on the hippie culture. He talked of what interested him — mystical experience, drugs, food, clothes, lifestyle, poverty and wealth, pacifism — and he did it brilliantly. Theodore Roszak remembers the fascination these broadcasts held for all sorts of people, and the way conversation with friends the next morning often turned on "what Alan Watts said last night." He was struck by Watts's deep scholarship and by the courage of his efforts to translate the insights of Zen and Taoism into the language of Western science and psychology.

> He has approached his task with an impish willingness to be catchy and cute, and to play at philosophy as if it were an enjoyable game. It is a style easily mistaken for flippancy, and it has exposed him to a deal of rather arrogant criticism: on the one hand from elitist Zen devotees who have found him too discursive for their mystic tastes (I recall one such telling me smugly, "Watts has never experienced satori"), and on the other hand from professional philosophers who have been inclined to ridicule him for his popularizing bent as being, in the words of one academic, "The Norman Vincent Peale of Zen."[22]

Roszak believed that, on the contrary, Watts's intellectual grasp and achievement was real and solid; he was more interested in sharing his ideas with the world at large than in reserving them for a small academic circle.

The charisma of Watts began to make him a revered figure in the whole Bay Area. People who wanted to be his disciples or to have their problems straightened out by him turned up unannounced at the *Vallejo* or insisted on telephoning him at all hours of the day and night. There was a woman who came and knelt at his feet on one occasion when he was dining out at a San Francisco restaurant. As a man who seemed to have answers, to know something others didn't, he drew the lost, the worried, the depressed, and the seeking like a magnet. Watts's cheerful talks often began from the proposition that his listener was in a sort of trap:

> You feel the world outside your body is an awful trap, full of . . . people, who are sometimes nice to you but mostly aren't. They're all out for themselves like you are and therefore there's one hell of a conflict going on. The rest of it, aside from people, is absolutely dumb—animals, plants, vegetables and rocks. Finally, behind the whole thing there are blazing centers of radioactivity called stars, and out there there's no air, there's no place for a person to live. . . . We have come to feel ourselves as centers of very, very tender, sensitive, vulnerable consciousness, confronted with a world that doesn't give a damn about us. And therefore, we have to pick a fight with this external world and beat it into submission to our wills. We talk about the conquest of nature; we conquer everything. We talk about the conquest of mountains, the conquest of space, the conquest of cancer, etc., etc. We're at war. And it's because we feel ourselves to be lonely ego principles, trapped in, somebody inextricably bound up with a world that doesn't go our way unless somehow we can manage to force it to do so.[23]

This way of looking at ourselves, Watts said, this view of the world about us over against our own ego, is hallucinatory, a completely false conception of ourselves as (a favorite expression of his) "an ego inside a bag of skin."

A truer way of looking at things, according to Watts, is to see our own body, along with animal and plant life and everything else, as part of a natural environment in which we are all intimately connected, human beings depending on air that is within a certain range of temperatures, and on the nutrition that natural life provides. People "go with" their environment, exactly as a bee goes with a flower — neither bee nor flower could exist without the other.

Watts regarded the ego, the need to think of ourselves obsessively as "I" and to build elaborate images about that persona, as an illusion — "an illusion married to a futility." The trouble is, in his view, you can't get rid of such a powerful illusion just by trying; conscious effort, even effort aimed at losing the ego, only reinforces the condition. So what is the answer?

> You find that you can't really control your thoughts, your feelings, your emotions, all the processes going on inside you and outside you that are happening — there's nothing you can do about it. So then, what follows? Well, there's only one thing that follows: You watch what's going on. You see, feel, this whole thing happening and then suddenly you find, to your amazement, that you can perfectly well get up, walk over to a table, pick up a glass of milk and drink it. . . . You can still act, you can still move, you can still go on in a rational way, but you've suddenly discovered that you're not what you thought you were. You're not this ego, pushing and shoving things inside a bag of skin. You feel yourself now in a new way as the whole world, which includes your body and everything that you experience, going along. It's intelligent. Trust it.[24]

This way of looking at the ego, compounded with the insights gained from taking LSD, chimed perfectly with the spirit of the counterculture. The passion for transformation, for inner change, that was a central feature of the movement, had found a quasi-religious leader in Alan Watts. Describing himself as a "philosophical entertainer" and a "genuine fake," he had clearly and well thought out things to say about many of the traditional constituents of religion — about God, about the self, and about the self's relationship to God and to fellow creatures.

At the time some theologians were discussing the idea of the "death of God." It was not, Watts suggested, God who was dying, but a particular way of thinking and talking about him that had died "by becoming implausible." Watts suggested a return to the God of the Theologia Mystica of Saint Dionysius, a God not limited by our concepts, or our pitiful need for security. "The highest image of God is the unseen behind the eyes — the blank space, the unknown, the intangible and the invisible. That is God! We have no image of that. We do not know what that is, but we have to trust it. There's no alternative. . . . That trust in a God whom one cannot conceive in any way is a far higher form of faith than fervent clinging to a God of whom you have a definite conception."[25]

Watts put some of his thinking about God into a new book, *The Two Hands of God* (1963). It was a book about overcoming the Western obsession with duality, the duality that separated the ego so painfully from its environment; it explored the themes of light and dark, life and death, good and evil, as well as Oriental imagery — the Cosmic Dance, the Primordial Pair, and legends of dismemberment and resurrection.

Next came *Beyond Theology* (subtitled *The Art of Godmanship*; 1964), a cheerfully naughty but carefully argued book that approaches Christianity with determined irreverence.

> Perhaps I can best indicate the spirit and approach of this book by asking you to imagine that you are attending a solemn service in a great cathedral, complete with candles, incense, chanting monks,

> and priests in vestments of white, scarlet and shimmering gold. Suddenly someone pulls you by the sleeve and says, "Psst! Come out back. I've got something to show you." You follow him out by the west door, and then go around the building . . . into the sacristy or vestry. This is the ecclesiastical equivalent of the green room in the theater, and you are about to enter by what, in a worldly setting, would be called the stage door. However, just outside you notice a couple of clerics — in their vestments — lighting up cigarettes.[26]

Watts then transposed this scene to heaven and himself to the role of a kind of jester or fool at court, unmasking the solemnity that surrounds the idea of God, debunking the crushing reverence that makes it impossible to reason about some of the more baffling statements of Christianity. Watts returns to some favorite targets.

How can an all-powerful God permit the Devil, or evil, to be at work in the world, unless he has somehow planted him there to heighten the drama? Watts imagines God playing hide-and-seek with himself in the world, then forgetting that it is a game and losing himself (in the person of his creatures) in scenes in which the drama gets altogether out of hand.

Why are Christians sometimes declaring themselves to be gods and sometimes insisting that they are terribly sinful? Why can they not see that asceticism and eroticism are two sides of the same coin? Their unwillingness to see this, Watts suggests, exacts a terrible price in prudery, misery, and warped lives: "The game is just too far-out."[27]

Two years later, in a book called *The Book: On the Taboo Against Knowing Who You Are*, Watts went back to his favorite themes of ego and non-ego, of living in the moment, of spontaneity, of ecstasy and the importance of living fully in the body, to repeat his favorite message — You are It. He was now moving into Vedanta with Hindu concepts to make his points, but the points were much the same.

Since his early experiments with LSD, his shared life with Varda and Jano, his friendships at Druid Heights and elsewhere, and his involvement with the counterculture as articulator and charismatic leader, Watts had changed a good deal. According to Gary Snyder, by about 1967, the summer of love as it was called, Watts had become a full-scale flower child, as committed to the colorful, the experimental, the provisional, and the original as any campus dropout or high school runaway. His shyness, primness, and correctness, eased by the warmth of the sixties climate, gave way to confidence, pleasure in acclaim, flowing hair, and a wonderful range of garments, including a sort of chasuble made from hairy material which kept him warm in cooler weather, a Philippine sarong ("the most comfortable garment ever invented"), and the Japanese *yucata* in which he liked to work. (He was particularly opposed to trousers for men, regarding them as "castrative.")

Waves of counterculture, often carrying Watts's messages with them, were washing around most of the Western world. Experimentation with psychedelics was widespread, not infrequently producing the sequence Timothy Leary had advised—"Turn On, Tune In, Drop Out"—and thousands of young people did just that, abandoning study or regular employment, giving themselves up to drugs or meditation, living as beggars. Others, not prepared to go to such extremes, nevertheless found their habits and outlook changed. When he came to look back on this period some years later Watts still felt astonished at what had happened.

> I could not have believed—even in 1960—that, say, Richard Hittleman, who studied with me at the Academy, would be conducting a national television program on yoga, that numerous colleges would be giving courses on meditation and Oriental philosophy for undergraduates, that this country would be supporting thriving Zen monasteries and Hindu ashrams, that the *I Ching* would be selling in hundreds of thousands, and that—wonder of

wonders — sections of the Episcopal Church would be consulting me about contemplative retreats and the use of mantras in liturgy.

It was not only the young who were affected. "One by one," says Watts of his middle-aged friends, "I watched this change coming over my friends as if they had been initiated into a mystery and were suddenly 'in the know' about something not expressly defined."[28]

A strongly pacifist mood was growing; horror as the details of the Vietnam War became better known, resentment at the draft, and the newfound wonder at the natural world, all made war seem deeply repulsive and produced the slogan "Make love not war." "Flower power" gradually hardened into a more overt kind. Theodore Roszak describes "the troubles" at Berkeley in 1966:

> A group of undergraduates stages a sit-in against naval recruiters at the Student Union. They are soon joined by a contingent of nonstudents whom the administrators then martyr by selective arrest. . . . Finally, the teaching assistants call a strike in support of the menaced demonstration. When at last the agitation comes to its ambiguous conclusion, a rally of thousands gathers outside Sproul Hall, the central administration building, to sing the Beatles' "Yellow Submarine" — which happens to be the current hit on all the local high-school campuses.[29]

In October 1966, it became a misdemeanor to possess LSD or DMT in the state of California and a felony to sell them. They were widely available, however, and the ban on them only increased the interest in the drugs and their effects. In Berkeley a hillside that high school students had been in the habit of painting with the name of their school and their class year now bore the legend in huge letters, LSD. The initials were also spelled out in a song,

"Lucy in the Sky with Diamonds," in the Beatles' new album *Sgt. Pepper's Lonely Hearts Club Band* (1967).

Life in the Haight had taken on a psychedelic quality in itself, as Charles Perry says, "like a running Beaux Arts Ball. . . . People brought things to share, such as food or Day-Glo paints with which to decorate each other's bodies or paint designs on the floor [the dance halls all had ultraviolet lights to make Day-Glo fluoresce more brilliantly]. Or little toys: soap-bubble blowers, bells, convex mirrors, . . . sparklers, yo-yos or pens that glowed in the dark."[30] Stores flourished that had caught the new mood, with names like Wild Colors, the Psychedelic Shop, Far Fetched Foods, the I/Thou Coffee Shop.

In January 1967 the counterculture staged what was to be its biggest show, the "Be-In," or "Human Be-In." It was held in the polo field in the Park Stadium of San Francisco, and the day, January 14, was decided through consultation with an astrologer. "Jerry Rubin told reporters the Be-In would show that hippies and radicals were one, their common aim being to drop out of 'games and institutions that oppress and dehumanize' such as napalm, the Pentagon, Governor Reagan and the rat race, and to create communities where 'new values and new human relations can grow.' "[31]

The *Berkeley Barb* said about the Be-In, "The spiritual revolution will be manifest and proven. In unity we shall shower the country with waves of ecstasy and purification. Fear will be washed away; ignorance will be exposed to sunlight; profits and empire will lie drying on desert beaches; violence will be submerged and transmuted to rhythm and dancing."[32]

On the morning of January 14, Snyder, Ginsberg, Watts, and others performed *pradakshina*, a Hindu rite of circumambulation at the polo field. It was a fine day, and from early in the morning people began walking from all over the city toward the meadow. Tens of thousands were there, some with banners, some in robes and exotic clothing, others in denims. "The proper ecstatic note in dress was usually provided by a bright shirt or scarf, or a string or two of beads or buttons with drug or peace messages. But many people brought fruit, flowers, incense, cymbals and tambourines, . . . bells, mirrors, feathers or bits of fur, the kind of thing people had long carried on Haight Street to blow the mind of a passing tripper."[33]

Speakers, rock bands, and Shunryu Suzuki-roshi of the San Francisco Zen Temple meditating on the platform and holding up a flower passed the afternoon. According to Charles Perry, some people hoped a flying saucer "with good news" might come down. In the event what came down was a parachutist said to be Owsley. At sunset Gary Snyder blew on a conch shell, Allen Ginsberg led a chant, and the crowd drifted away, some of them to build fires, chant, and pray on Ocean Beach. An unexpected spin-off from the Be-In was the comment of Police Chief Thomas Cahill.

"You're sort of the love generation, aren't you?" he asked a delighted group from the Haight, a title which was instantly claimed.

For all the love, ecstasy, religious devotion, and peaceful aims of the love generation, there were signs that the wave had reached its crest and was beginning to crash. One of the major problems was in the Haight itself. So well publicized was it that it became a mecca for teenagers from all over the country, some who came for a weekend, some who had the idea of dropping out of school and staying permanently. Along with this crusade of the innocents came the drug pushers and a world of criminality.

As early as 1967 Nicholas Von Hoffman noted in the *Wash-*

ington Post how the flower child world of Haight-Ashbury had disintegrated into a nightmare of murderous criminality, as the drug entrepreneurs, interested not in expanded consciousness but in money, fought for territory. Unintentionally, Von Hoffman said, the hippies had come to constitute "the biggest crime story since prohibition."

The money tray no longer waited in the café on Eighth Street. Too many people had come to Haight-Ashbury looking for an easy buck. A doctor who ran a "radical clinic" for hippies spoke about the downfall of the neighborhood like this:

> I think the mass media were primarily responsible for the destruction of HA; they had for three, four years a quite interesting social experiment and with some health problems, but in general we were all doing a good job and then all of a sudden hippies became publicity material, the word had spread throughout the United States, and every disturbed kid, runaway teenager, ambulatory schizophrenic, drug addict, knew about HA and they knew that if they came to HA or at least they thought, there would be love and peace and people sharing, which is exactly what happened about three or four years ago, but you can't share items that are necessary for three hundred people with three hundred thousand, you know, and the community just became destroyed as a result of this mass influx, also the media publicized the hippies so much that it aroused the anger of the dominant culture and it was declared a Communist conspiracy or un-American and it's amazing the hostility that mystical, non-violent, long-haired youth can evoke in the conservative element in the United States.[84]

There *was* a growing anger against the "love generation." Clergy began to preach sermons against it, and police opposition hardened. Leary was deported, first from Mexico because of pressure by the CIA, then from Dominica. Some of the hostility was richly deserved. There were groups like that around Andy Warhol in New York, indifferent to vision and spiritual experience, but unashamedly into "booze, speed, downers, . . . drugs that provide escape, that turn off, toughen, and callous the nerve endings."[35]

Leary's original hope (never fully shared by Watts), that if people could experience the sense of meaning, unity, and wonder given by LSD, then social problems would be solved, began to look very naive. Mental hospitals bore pathetic witness of practical "jokes" played on unsuspecting victims who had drunk a soft drink or a cup of coffee containing the drug, and were full of people who could not "come down" after one or more trips.

The more idealistic among the young had begun to think in terms of moving into the country, of growing their own food, of starting their own farms, and a number moved out into Marin County, California, and beyond.

Others, influenced initially by Watts and Snyder, moved on from drugs to Zen. Snyder quoted D. T. Suzuki as saying that people who came to the *zendo* from LSD experiences showed an ability to get into good *zazen* very rapidly. Snyder told the English Benedictine monk Dom Aelred Graham in 1967 that "LSD has been a real social catalyst and amounts to a genuine historical unpredictable. It's changing the lives of all sorts of people. It's remarkable and effective and it works in terms of forms, devotions, personal deities, appearances of bodhisattvas, Buddhas and gods to your eyes. It doesn't work in terms of non-forms, emptiness. ("This isn't form is the same as emptiness," one Zen teacher who tried it reported, "this is emptiness is the same as form.")

"In several American cities," Snyder also observed, "traditional meditation halls of both Rinzai and Soto are flourishing. Many of the newcomers turned to traditional meditation after an initial acid experience. The two types of experience seem to inform each other."[36] (D. T. Suzuki later appeared to go back on the qualified respect he had shown for the LSD experience and announced that the meditation experience was quite distinct from Zen.)

Many who had used LSD as an opening to the inner world were attracted to formal meditation. By the fall of 1966, according to Rick Fields, "close to a hundred and fifty people were sitting zazen and attending lectures at the San Francisco Zen Center; fifty or sixty sat at least once a day, and eighty people, twice as many as the previous year, had attended the seven day sesshin. . . . As Zen Center itself grew, it naturally spawned a number of satellite centers run by senior students . . . in Berkeley, Mill Valley and Los Altos."[37]

San Francisco Zen Center raised a large sum of money to buy land at Tassajara Hot Springs in the Los Padres National Forest, and the Tassajara Zen Mountain Center was founded. More than a thousand people contributed money.

"It is for us in America," wrote Watts, "to realize that the goal of action is contemplation. Otherwise we are caught up in mock progress, which is just going on toward going on, what Buddhists call samsara — the squirrel cage of birth and death. That people are getting together to acquire this property for meditation is one of the most hopeful signs of our times."[38]

So the counterculture had moved by way of color, free sex, civil rights, rock music, brotherly love, LSD and other psychedelics, and innovative lifestyles toward — at least for some people — a serious interest in meditation. A few years later Watts was to say that people who had experimented with psychedelic chemicals might find that they had left them behind, "like the raft which you use to cross a river, and have found growing interest and even pleasure in the simplest practice of zazen, which we perform like idiots, without any special purpose."[39]

Ten

The Home Behind Home

1969-1973

IN 1969 WATTS AND JANO moved to Druid Heights. The *Vallejo* had become so well known from films and photographs that Watts had begun to be pestered by disciples on the Sausalito waterfront, and he badly needed a place where he could not easily be found. He continued to use the boat for seminars and meetings of the Society for Comparative Philosophy, the organization he and Jano had founded in 1961 to promote ways of understanding drawn from many religions and cultures. But henceforward home was on Mount Tamalpais.

Ever since his sequence of LSD experiences Watts had seen Druid Heights as "home" and "the home behind home." Now he and Jano lived in their circular house, built by Roger Somers, high up over a valley with a view of great beauty. It was a kitchen, sitting room, and bedroom all in one. The bed disappeared out of sight during the day, so that Watts did not have to retire to a separate bedroom in the way that he hated, and there was a sun deck for outdoor living.

The house "is hidden in a grove of high eucalyptus trees," wrote Watts, "and overlooks a long valley whose far side is covered with a dense forest of bay, oak, and madrone so even in height that from a distance it looks like brush. No human dwelling is in view, and the principal inhabitant of the forest is a wild she-goat who has been there for at least nine years. Every now and then she comes out and dances upon the crown of an immense rock which rises far out of the forest."[1]

In 1968 Watts lost his earliest home: Rowan Cottage. In 1961 Emily died, and Watts, somewhat to the shock of his relatives, did not return to England for the funeral. Now Laurence had grown too frail to live on his own and had moved to an old people's home called Merevale. (It was pronounced Merryvale, but Laurence, with contempt, took pleasure in calling it Mere Vale.) Watts had gone to England to help him with the sad task of going through his possessions and getting rid of them — the legacies of many years of happy marriage.

Watts sadly put Rowan Cottage up for sale, having offered it to Joy Buchan, who declined the offer. One day as he was clearing the house he came upon "the Housetop," the enormous bureau that in his childhood had seemed to contain an arcane secret; he found himself going through its contents almost feverishly. "There were lots of interesting treasures and trinkets — but in all such quests and searches, as also in my pull to the West, it keeps coming back to me that the secret is in the seeker."[2] He was looking, he thought, for a jewel. Just as he had often searched Persian miniatures with a magnifying glass, losing himself in their tiny mystical worlds, he thought that the concentration on a tiny perfect whole — a dewdrop, a jewel, a snowflake, a flower — was an image of the universal of which we ourselves are a part. Looking for the jewel in the Housetop was his search for the universal and eternal, for the energy that had formed him, but from which he had so often felt cut off.

His years of fame had not in a sense helped him to find the

jewel. Film taken of Watts in 1969 shows him looking seedy, ill, and older than his fifty-four years; friends were concerned about his obvious fatigue and about his heavy drinking.

Gary Snyder, who had just returned to California from one of his periods of study in Japan, this time with his wife Masa and his son, Kai, began to notice that drinking had become a serious problem for Watts. Watts had arranged to rent Gary and Masa a house at Druid Heights, so the two men saw a good deal of one another. In Kyoto, Snyder had noticed that Watts drank more than was necessary, but now he had moved into a phase of heavier drinking.

> I told him as best as I could to get off it, but by this time he was stuck with an enormous alimony payment, and he was having to take far more gigs than anybody in their right mind would want to do just earning money, and he was also spending more money than he had to. He lived very well, and he was also supporting lots of people, including a full-time secretary. So he had to keep working, and as you keep working, you know, you got to play these roles, and you also keep drinking 'cause there's always these parties and so forth, so that doesn't help you slow it down. So he just wore himself out. It was out of his control, that was my feeling. The dynamics of his life had gotten beyond his control, and he didn't know what to do about it.
>
> The amazing thing was that he kept such expansiveness, such good humor, you know, with that great big laugh. . . . He never showed a waver or a wobble in his self-esteem, in his confidence. He never let a little crack open that "I'm having trouble." But he was putting away a bottle of vodka a day—I saw those bottles under the sink.

Roger Somers believed that the "tragic flaw" in Watts was that he suffered a deep neurotic shyness when it came to small groups, as for example at the sort of cocktail party that was usually given before or after one of his lectures:

> He would sweat blood before these events and was quite uncomfortable in them. Then one day he discovered that if he had two, maybe three martinis, he was not only comfortable, but the life of the party. He could not have gone on with his lecture tours and the cocktail parties that went with them with any ease at all without that lubrication. . . . He could talk to people one to one, or a hundred to one, but cocktail party banter had him trembling and perspiring.

Paula McGuire, his editor at Pantheon Books, remembers Watts's telling her in 1968 that he was suffering from an enlarged liver, and that his doctor had warned him that he must give up drinking. For some months he did so, to the relief of his family and friends. Elsa Gidlow remembers the disappointment of sitting beside him at a Druid Heights lunch party and noticing that he was drinking again.

"Oh *Alan!*" she said, as he reached for the brandy.

"If I don't drink, I don't feel sexy," he growled in reply.

Perhaps the drinking came from a deep sense of loneliness that he had so often written about, a loneliness that increased with the cocktail parties and the fame. Considering Watts's lifelong interest in psychotherapy it seems odd that some wise and clever therapist could not help him; the trouble was that though Watts seemed to think psychoanalysis a good idea for other people, he could no more undertake and sustain it himself than he had been able to sustain *sanzen* with Sokei-an. He recounted how, at his one attempt, he felt that the analyst had turned the tables and was asking him for help. Jano, he claimed, had had the same experience, and she had cheekily suggested that she and her analyst adjourn to the nearest bar where he could buy her a drink and talk about *his* problems. The comment is scathing, superior, and is meant to suggest that Watts and Jano knew so much about themselves that no analyst could help them — a somewhat unlikely state of affairs. It also might be a defense against painful revelations. If there was a choice between maintaining the precarious self-control of the "know-it-all" adult and the humble discipline of trying to rediscover the lost child in himself, Watts was not prepared to make it.

Another kind of therapy comes to many people through love affairs or marriage. Perhaps Watts never quite despaired of this sort of healing, although his attempts at loving had often brought down storms of accusation on his head. By the time he married Jano he knew that he was incapable of monogamy. What he offered her instead was public loyalty and private devotion that was unswerving.

Life with Watts was hard for Jano, though. An intelligent woman, well-fitted to be his intellectual companion, she soon found when she traveled with him or sat in on his seminars that people sat spellbound at the feet of her guru-husband and had little interest in her ideas, even when they were just as good as his. She was too blunt, too honest, too little in awe of Watts, too human, not to be exasperated by this. As time went on she got into the habit of arguing with him or contradicting him in public. Sandy Jacobs, who first recorded Watts on tape, remembered how often on recordings you could hear the guru laying down the law as the awestruck pupils lapped up his pronouncements. Then Jano's voice chipped in with "No, Alan, you've got it wrong. . . ." Watts seemed to accept this correction meekly, as if he felt he needed it.

If she undermined him at his seminars, he had subtle ways of undermining her elsewhere. Joan and Ann, who were fond of her, noticed how when Jano started to cook a meal, Watts would gradually take over from her, leaving her with nothing to do. Even in small areas of life, he "knew better," needed to be in control.

Early in the marriage he was already having affairs, usually with very bright, attractive, younger women he met on his travels.

He used to say to friends, though not to Jano, that he "could not bear to sleep alone." So he would pick up a pretty girl on a university campus and take her to bed with him. There were many women who were happy to accommodate him; he was reputed to be an accomplished lover, and fame was a predictable aphrodisiac. He was a fine lover so long as he did not feel there was any attempt to hold him or trap him into marriage, and there were deeper, more lasting relationships with women friends with whom he could relax. He made it clear that there was no question of his ever leaving Jano.

Roger Somers thought that Watts might have made a better job of marriage if he had married women with whom he did not feel the need to play the Pygmalion role.

> He would have felt insecure if he'd been with some really heavy, finger-popping, laughing, gay woman, yet that was the kind of woman he sought in extracurricular ways. He saw them freely, was quite effective with them, and loved them, but to *live* with one of those—here was the crack in the vase: his unwillingness to accept joy. Instead his self-importance was demonstrated by their inability to cope—he would take over from them—and of course, they would end up morbidly dependent upon him. This was not like the man who was talking to us about Zen. That's not Zen—that's Zen backwards.

Watts refused to acknowledge any of this when Roger brought it up in conversation. "He would be a little awkward about it, and it was not easy as a rule for me to make him feel awkward."

Jano, as well as Watts, was drinking a good deal—the strains of their life together, as well as the mutual example of heavy drinking, exacerbated the problem for both of them.

Paula McGuire remembers an evening when she and the writer Joseph Campbell were to dine out with the Wattses in New York. Instead of accompanying them Jano was sent home in a taxi, suffering, according to Watts, from hypoglycemia. "We just thought she was drunk," says McGuire. Whether or not she was drunk on that occasion, Jano did suffer from a blood sugar problem that affected her health and was not helped by her heavy drinking.

Quite apart from his marriage, Watts was living under considerable tension. There was Dorothy's alimony and the cost of maintaining her five children and paying their medical expenses, in addition to the living expenses of Jano and himself (and Jano, on occasion, was given to wild bursts of spending). The life of a freelance writer is a notoriously anxious one, even for those with a modest number of dependents; for Watts to meet his financial commitments meant a life of almost unceasing industry: writing, lecturing, broadcasting, appearing on television, traveling to speak on university campuses, or going abroad to take part in other talks and television appearances. The periods of idleness, which for Watts permitted inner development and change, became fewer and fewer. Though his writing was always professional, competent, and often brilliant in its perception and exposition, Watts began to repeat himself and covered his lack of energy with a self-assurance that some found very irritating. From clothes, to food, to lifestyle, to sex — Watts knew best how it should be managed.

Many people, however, were fascinated by the "know-it-all" touch, perhaps interpreting it as an authentic bit of British arrogance, perhaps merely liking to be told what to do by someone who had interesting and original ideas. They allowed Watts to tell them to sleep on mattresses on the floor of the living room, to wear loose Oriental clothes, to cook with fresh, natural ingredients, to dance, to chant, to make love freely and joyfully, and to despise chairs and plastics, both of which he disliked. What he wanted, he told his readers, was that they should "come to their senses." The advice was good, and many people were probably the better for following it.

Watts did try to insist that he was a fake, a rascal, and, primarily, an entertainer, but that only added to his fame and his following. The tragic underside of this fame could be seen in the furious and bitter letters from Dorothy complaining that he did not send enough money (though he was faithful in keeping up his commitment), in an unhappy Jano who only stopped drinking when he went away on his travels, and in his own desperate dependence on vodka.

Fame did at least put Watts in touch with a kind of international brotherhood of people interested in the same sets of ideas. He knew scientists and priests, Buddhist monks and artists, psychotherapists and craftsmen, academics and doctors. It seemed to him that the ideas of people from disparate disciplines were converging in important areas. By listening to theologians, religious thinkers from East and West, anthropologists, psychiatrists, psychotherapists of many schools, and neurologists, Watts might begin to try to join together ideas derived from different experiences of the human body, mind, and spirit. He knew, or corresponded with, Thomas Merton; Dom Aelred Graham; Shunryu Suzuki and his successor at San Francisco Zen Center, Richard Baker-roshi; Lama Govinda; Lama Chogyam Trungpa; anthropologist Gregory Bateson; scientist John Lilly, the Zurich Jungians; a group of Stanford neurologists working on the human brain; R. D. Laing, Fritz Perls, and Abraham Maslow; and the Esalen people.

Snyder observed that Watts moved from Zen to social and psychological concerns, then to visionary concerns, and finally, late in the sixties, to an interest in Taoism. Snyder saw Watts as part of a group of visionaries helping to give birth to a new consciousness. Much of the time, Snyder felt, Watts was right on top of what was going on, understanding it, and helping it on its way. And by about 1967 Watts had turned into a full-scale flower child.

Once or twice Snyder challenged Watts about the sort of popular books he was writing, wondering if they were worthy of the ideas he was trying to expound.

> I was beginning to question what seemed to me the easiness of his books — but his argument was that these ideas needed a skillful and popular exponent. As I got a chance to browse in his library, I was very impressed and convinced that perhaps he knew what he was doing; obviously this was no lightweight thinker. . . . He had really done his homework, and that deepened my respect for the kind of work he was trying to do.

Christians and Christianity still interested Watts a good deal. When Dom Aelred Graham, the author of *Zen Catholicism* and a Benedictine monk from Ampleforth Abbey in England, wanted to visit Kyoto to hold lengthy conversations with the *roshis* and monks at the Zen temples there, Watts seemed a natural adviser and guide. The conversations were later published in book form.

Considering that Watts was not an official participant in the conversations, he recurs surprisingly often in the text. One of the Zen exponents, Prof. Maseo Abe, commented a little severely on Watts:

> *M.A.*: I think he's a very clever man, clever interpreter of Zen, but I don't know how much he has practised Zen meditation.
> *Graham*: Not much, I don't think; but one can't be sure.
> *M.A.*: Maybe not.[8]

Watts had given Dom Aelred two fans, on one of which he had drawn the calligraphic characters for "Form is emptiness" and on the other the circle representing *sunyata, ku*, roughly translated as "emptiness." They became a focal point in several of the interviews. The Rev. Kobori Sohaku at his subtemple at Daitoku-ji Monastery was scarcely more enthusiastic than Professor Abe, once the Japanese interpreter had explained the origin of the fans. He dealt with the situation by using the Zen trick of disclaiming all understanding.

> *K.S.*: I hope you will explain the meaning. I don't know!
> *Graham*: I have come all the way to Japan to find out.
> *K.S.*: I don't know the meaning. It is taken from scripture, a very famous saying. He is quite good at calligraphy, Mr. Watts. The fan is too little for you — you need a much bigger one.[4]

Dom Aelred also interviewed Gary Snyder about his beat background, and about how Snyder would compare the insight given by LSD and similar drugs to the insight acquired through sitting in *zazen*. Snyder saw the grave dangers of such drugs, but also believed that the insights they gave were real. Watts came into this conversation too, in a joking way.

> *Graham*: Alan's going to found a new religion in San Francisco, I understand.
> *G.S.*: Which Alan?
> *Graham*: Alan Watts.
> *G.S.*: Is he going to start a new religion?
> *Graham*: Called Hum. On September fifteenth in San Francisco.
> *H.T.* [Harold Talbot]: He's not founding it; he's drawing attention to it.
> *G.S.*: That's nice.[5]

Dom Aelred was, in fact, having a wonderful time in Watts's company, accompanying him to parties of hippies and on all sorts of interesting trips in Japan. On one occasion they took LSD together. "I think there was a touch of genius about him," Dom

Aelred says, "and that he did much good for lots of people, especially perhaps in California. Like the rest of us, of course, he had his weaknesses. He could lift the elbow regularly and frequently, but he was generous and kind, and I never heard him speak harshly of anyone."

Watts's private expeditions in Kyoto were a source of great pleasure. His favorite haunt was Tera-machi Street where, in the tiny shops, he could buy implements for the tea ceremony, wonderful tea, ancient pottery, rosaries, books, incense that smelled of aloeswood (the essential smell of Buddhism, according to Dr. Suzuki), writing brushes, paper, and fine ink. One of his finds was a small stick of vermilion ink covered with gold leaf. He said that to use it he rubbed it on a windowsill, early in the morning, using a drop of dew for water.[6]

On that same trip Gary Snyder remembers Watts's pleasure in a big party at Kyoto, which was full of congenial guests: Japanese poets and artists, priests from the Jodo Shin sect in California who were particularly fond of jazz, and Hindu visitors. The party seemed to catch the worldwide, cosmopolitan nature of the counterculture.

Then, as so often, Watts's extraordinary capacity to enjoy himself came to the fore. It was his gift for play that his friends enjoyed most.

Roger Somers, who had noticed a similar quality in some of the great black jazz musicians he had met, felt that Watts had the greatest quality of play of anyone he had ever known. Living close to Watts allowed him to know and appreciate the small details of Watts's life and habits that most people did not know about. He remembered how, when the two of them sat together out-of-doors, butterflies would come and settle all over Watts, while scarcely one would settle on him. He remembered Watts's taste for shooting arrows straight up into the air above his own head. (Jano once saw one of the arrows come down to land, quivering, between his feet.) He remembered Watts's awkwardness in handyman tasks around Druid Heights; the Brahmin education had spoiled him for those sorts of skills.

Jano's niece, Kathleen, herself now part of the boat community of Sausalito and an artist and craftswoman, remembers the extraordinary way Watts played with her and her brother when she was still a child. Once in New York he took them to the zoo and bought helium balloons for all three of them. While the children happily clutched theirs, Watts deliberately released the string of his and watched it float up into the sky — an act that made a deep impression on the children.

In 1964 Watts met the Jungian analyst June Singer at a cocktail party. June Singer had recently become a widow after a long marriage and was suffering from depression. At the party, given in Watts's honor, a sense of sympathy and recognition passed between them. She had just moved into a new apartment, and the next morning, a beautiful sunny day, she was sitting staring at a row of paint pots and thinking that she should begin work on repainting when she decided on an impulse to call Watts at his hotel and find out how he was getting along. He was delighted to hear her voice and suggested that they spend the afternoon on the beach, a meeting that was the beginning of a long and happy, though intermittent, love affair.

Watts would stay with her whenever he found himself in Chicago, and little by little she came out of her depression. Shaped by an "uptight" Jewish background and a rather correct Jewish marriage, she was surprised and delighted by Watts's attitude to life and to sex. His extraordinary energy, his readiness to dance or to sing or to make love, his pleasure in all the sensual joys of life deepened her own capacity for happiness. She was amazed at Watts's ability to unwind; after a grueling evening as a speaker in which he had been giving out for hours, he would curl up like a cat, utterly relaxed.

She knew also that Watts's pleasure in the relationship came partly from the absence of demands, and she did not make them upon him. From the beginning she was aware of his intense devotion to Jano. He seemed to her responsible but not guilty in his attitude to his marriage.

She found the public aspect of Watts difficult, the act of what she called "I am Alan Watts" when they went to a restaurant together. After a year or two their friendship temporarily foundered. She was working hard at her doctoral dissertation and told Watts to keep away since she did not want to be distracted. Hurt by what he felt as rejection Watts did not come back, and it was only after they met by chance on an airplane runway that their relationship continued.

Watts helped her with her writing and suggested the title for her book *Boundaries of the Soul*. Throughout much of their time together Dr. Singer was working on an idea that she later expressed in her book *Androgyny*; her theory was that human beings were developing in the direction of psychological androgyny, and that the more advanced people among us, in evolutionary terms, already showed marked characteristics of both masculine and feminine in their make-up. Watts seemed to her the perfect androgyne, active in his masculine aspect, receptive in his feminine. Besides this, she felt he had a gift of seeing the spark in people, in knowing where life and growth lay.

But like many of his friends she was saddened to see how heavily he was drinking. On one occasion she visited him in the hospital, where he was suffering from delirium tremens, and she realized that he knew how destructive the habit had become.

"That's how I am," he said to her sadly. "I can't change."

By 1970 his other friends were growing more concerned about his obvious fatigue and the effects of his drinking. Robert Shapiro, who thought he was being "eaten alive" by his many dependents, discussed the problem with him. The strain of making enough money to keep everybody and of living out his extraordinary role in the counterculture was slowly killing him. The solution, Shapiro said, was for him to get out of it all for a bit. It was absurd that a man of his interests had never been to China. What he should do was to go away to China for a year, giving no address, and leaving Robert to handle the claims and complaints of his relatives. It was a gesture of friendship and seemed to offer real hope for Watts to get his health and his energy back. He set off on the first leg of his journey, but then Robert received a telephone call. The guilt was too great; he could not abandon Jano, even temporarily.

Despite failing health Watts continued to lead the bohemian life, going to parties, staying up late, drinking and smoking heavily. Yet even for a bohemian and a drinker, he was very disciplined, rising early to write, coping well with business and with his vast correspondence, never missing an airplane or a deadline. His publishers always received meticulously typed manuscripts on time.

He never admitted in public to making very serious attempts at meditation, implying that the closest he came to *zazen* was going for a walk. Gary Snyder, however, believed that he sat in *zazen* more and more often in the last years of his life — they talked a lot about *zazen* together and Gary noticed the well-worn meditation cushion in front of the altar in Watts's house.

In a growing number of incidents the public facade almost cracked. Joan and her husband Tim remember going to collect Watts when he was due to give a public lecture — as his drinking had grown worse he had given up driving — and finding him heavily drunk. They drove a few blocks, and Watts insisted that they stop at a liquor store, where he bought a bottle of vodka. He put it on the back seat, and they drove off with Watts sitting between them in the front, but soon he had to turn round and take a swig out of the bottle. Joan was amused at the sight of the famous Alan Watts with his bottom in the air drinking neat vodka; she was also fully aware of the tragic implications. When they arrived at the lecture hall Watts walked onto the podium and gave his usual admirable lecture. (This was a miracle frequently repeated.) Only those who knew him very well could have guessed that he was very drunk indeed. Questions from the floor were more difficult. Watts seemed not to be able to make sense of what he was being asked, or to be answering some other question altogether. Occasionally he appeared to have gone to sleep between the asking of the question and his answering of it. Such was the awe in which he was held in the Bay Area, or such was people's readiness to attribute any eccentricity to some rare piece of Zen insight, that groups continued to ask him to speak; he gave good value. He no longer thought in terms of giving up drinking. He knew now that he was riding a tiger and that it was too late to get down.

It was ironic that his reputation, which had declined slightly at one point in the sixties when he did not involve himself with civil rights or with the peace movement, seemed to be rising again as his own grasp on life was failing. Apocryphal legends about him abounded, many of them absurd, though he did seem to have unusual perceptions and intuitions. For instance, Joan remembers talking to a woman who had gone to Watts for counseling. He interrupted her in midsentence and told her to stand up. He placed a steadying hand on her shoulder and at that moment there was quite a severe earthquake shock. Watts had been aware of the coming shock waves several minutes before she was.

Watts's relations with his older children were good. Joan and Ann and eventually Mark and Ricky, his two sons by Dorothy, were all fond of him and saw a good deal of him; the daughters of his marriage to Dorothy, on the other hand, never overcame the distance set up by his desertion in 1960 and were perhaps strongly influenced by Dorothy's bitterness toward him. On occasions when he tried to visit the family there were verbal attacks on him, and he used to take Joan or Ann with him to try to forestall these outbursts.

He gave each of his children a particular legacy. At the age of eighteen or so he would offer them LSD and care for them most lovingly through the trip, a remarkable memory for each of them. (Others, such as the friend Ruth Costello, who first took acid with Watts also remember how careful and helpful he was.)

Mark, who was parted from his father at the age of thirteen when Watts left Mill Valley, got to know him again in New York just before his eighteenth birthday. It was a happy reunion; they had a great time together. Watts arranged for him to take a photography course in the East Village, and Mark remembers with pleasure a visit by Watts to New York when Watts took him to visit friends at the Chelsea Hotel. Up in the penthouse suite of the hotel they played a wicked game on the passersby with a tiny laser beam device that they shone down upon the baffled people below.

"There was this wino," Mark remembers, "who was convinced he had seen Jesus."

Later on, at Druid Heights, Watts would take his vodka and Mark would take a joint, and they would go and sit up on the hills together and talk about things. Mark, like the others, was troubled by his drinking: "I'd say to him, 'Dad, don't you want to live?' and he would say, 'Yes, but it's not worth holding onto.' "

In 1971 was Laurence Watts's ninetieth birthday, and Watts and Jano returned to Chislehurst to hold a celebration for the old man. They gave a big family party at the pub by Saint Nicholas's Church, the Tiger's Head, and after dinner Watts sang the Pete Seeger song "Little Boxes" as part of the entertainment. His cousins formed the impression that both Alan and Jano were a little strange, that they were "on" something. Believing the wild rumors of life in California the cousins assumed it must be drugs rather than alcohol.

Watts also made such a long after-dinner speech to wind up the evening that the waiters, wanting to clear up and go off duty, were visibly impatient. Visible, that is, to everyone except Watts who went on talking.

"If Confucius here would just stop talking we could go home," one of the waiters was heard to remark. When Watts eventually realized their irritation he was surprised and concerned. He had not meant to be arrogant; he was just absorbed in the pleasure of talking to his friends and relatives.

On that same trip Watts and Laurence motored up to Cambridge, at the invitation of Bishop John Robinson, to conduct a "liturgy of contemplation" at Trinity. The chapel was packed with undergraduates. Watts had sent his usual meticulous instructions to Bishop Robinson before the service, and the occasion had a moving and simple drama about it. A chair had been set in the middle of the altar steps with a candle alight on a chair beside it. Many who came to the service sat on cushions on the floor in front of the speaker with a half circle of chairs behind them. Watts came in wearing a cassock, sat down, and talked about contemplation: "Man discovers himself as inseparable from the cosmos in both its positive and negative aspects, its appearances and disappearances."[7] Then he intoned the first line of "Veni Creator," the ancient hymn that invokes the action of the Holy Spirit, while the lights dimmed overhead. He conducted a meditation, with long periods of silence. Then they sang the Nunc Dimittis and a litany, after which Watts gave a benediction and the choir sang a long Gregorian amen. Watts could still orchestrate a moving and beautiful service.

This liturgical experiment was not an isolated occasion. Licensed by Bishop James Pike in San Francisco, Watts had held similar services in Grace Cathedral, which were enthusiastically attended. News of his involvement with the church caused rumors that he was thinking of asking to have Anglican orders restored to him, but rumors were all they were. Far from returning to the church, he still managed to offend Episcopal high-church sensibilities on occasion.

On one such occasion, entertained by senior clergy in New York, he had been drawn into discussion of the Anglican Holy Communion service as compared with the Catholic Mass. The complacency of his companions over the rather sober rite used at the time pushed him into his now famous outrageousness.

"Holy Communion?" he was heard to remark. "Why, it's like fucking a plastic woman!" In the silence that followed the only sound to be heard was the bishop's wife biting nervously and noisily into an apple.

More seriously, he had written about "the problem" of the churches. "What are we going to do with an enormous amount of valuable real estate known, not quite correctly, as the Church — whether it be Catholic, Episcopalian, Presbyterian, Lutheran, Methodist, Congregational, or Unitarian?"[8] Strip them of pews, was his suggestion, leaving only a few chairs for the sick and elderly, and putting carpets and cushions down for the rest. Abandon the "interminable chatter" of sermons and petitions, and substitute instead a liturgy that helped the worshippers into mystical contemplation and silence — by way of chanting, singing, dancing, meditative rituals, and dramatic enactments of the Mass.

For Christmas 1971 Laurence made a tape wishing Alan and his grandchildren well and reciting the Kipling poems that he loved. Watts played it during Christmas dinner at Joan's house in Bolinas, and then one by one Watts's grandchildren, Joan's husband, Tim, Elsa Gidlow, Jano, and finally Watts himself, sent their good wishes to "Granddaddy." On the tape Watts described the turkey lunch, complete with *pâté en croûte* made by him, and Joan's daughter Elizabeth described how Joan had just given her a doll that had once belonged to her, together with a four-poster bed and a doll's wardrobe made by Laurence and a quilt and an embroidered stool made by Emily. Jano described how, as soon as Christmas was over, she and Alan were to go off on vacation to Mexico "away from mails, the telephone, and family." In fact, they went on this rare vacation before Watts finished the tape. Completing the recording in May Watts described how, in the first few months of 1972, he had given lectures all over New Mexico and in Boulder, Colorado, and how he had spoken in Vancouver and on Cortes Island and then in Chicago. He had, he added laughingly, been obliged to pay a tax bill of ten thousand dollars in April, so he had had no choice but to work hard.

And work hard he did, for despite the alcoholism, his energy for his projects had not diminished. He had gone to Esalen to work with Army officers on the drug problem in the U.S. Army. The formal meetings had not yielded much, since the officers would talk in "memorandese," but the informal conversations had made him feel more hopeful and had given him insight about official attitudes. In addition, he, Mark, and Sandy Jacobs were making a series of half-hour video cassettes in preparation for the growing video market. Up at Druid Heights Elsa Gidlow and Roger Somers were considering selling land to the government on a one-hundred-year lease and building a Japanese-style library for Watts's books.

Another significant publication was in the works, Watts's autobiography. In 1970 Paula McGuire had suggested to Alan that he might like to write an autobiography, which he did, and in 1972 Pantheon published *In My Own Way*. Mrs. McGuire remembers her disappointment when the manuscript came in. Though an interesting book in many ways and one that was bound to sell, there was something too coy, too knowing about it, an infuriating air of effortless ease. It was honest as far as it went, but it hardly went far enough, in her opinion. "I sensed he had not really written about his mother at all," she says. There was something thin and unsatisfying about it, a lot of name dropping, perhaps to make up for the other omissions of the book, and it had the air of having been dictated rather carelessly. The material was haphazard in its order; Watts repeatedly returned to discussing his childhood and his schooldays long after he had passed on to later stages of his life.

It is easy to guess at some of the difficulties that Watts had as he approached this task. The book was a guaranteed seller in advance, and he needed the money, but a truthful autobiography would have imposed impossible conditions upon him.

He could not write easily of his feelings about his mother without causing great distress to his father (though within strict limits he made a brave attempt). In fact, other interesting omissions may have occurred, in part, from Watts's attempt to spare his father's feelings. There is no account of his parents' removal from Rowan Cottage when economic hardship overwhelmed them, nor does he mention the pain of Laurence's unemployment. Not only did Laurence write the foreword, but he also read the book in draft, suggesting many omissions.

Watts also could not write truthfully of the sexual difficulties that had gradually destroyed his marriage to Eleanor and had lost him his job in the Episcopal priesthood without alienating most of his admirers. He could not write of his present marital difficulties; in fact, he gives Jano a slightly patronizing pat on the head whenever he mentions her, as if, like a sulky child, she will become difficult if not publicly noticed. He is, however, generous to both his other wives in the book, probably because it was not in his nature to be bitter. Eleanor was deeply touched by the book when she read it and felt largely reconciled to Watts because of the way he described their marriage.

In the early seventies Watts paid a couple of visits to the Sierra Nevada, where Gary and Masa Snyder had built Kitkitdizze, a Japanese-style house and a *zendo* deep in the woods. Watts admired the house; lying on his back on the floor and looking up into the pitched ceiling he said that it was "a very noble view." Gary remembers their shooting arrows together and sitting outside peeling apples, preparing to dry them. They had "lots of sake and gossip" and talked, among other things, about whether LSD was a good idea or not.

Their feeling by this time was that "letting it loose in the society" had done harm. The first people to experiment with peyote, LSD, and similar drugs had been artists, poets, psychologists, and students of religion, and most of them had handled it well, finding it an interesting and creative experience. Consequently, no one was prepared to see that when LSD became more widely used in society the results would be bizarre indeed, with people who were not in any way ready for the experience becoming monomaniacs and self-appointed messiahs. It was just too potent for those who were psychologically, aesthetically, or spiritually unprepared for it.

Watts's own religious interest was now centered on Taoism. In a journal he wrote during 1971–72, *Cloud-hidden, Whereabouts Unknown*, he describes his feelings on watching the mountain stream after the rains on Mount Tamalpais:

> When I stand by the stream and watch it, I am relatively still, and the flowing water makes a path across my memory so that I realize its transience in comparison with my stability. This is, of course, an illusion in the sense that I, too, am in flow and likewise have no final destination — for can anyone imagine finality as a form of life? My death will be the disappearance of a particular pattern in the water.[9]

The human problem, as Watts sees it, is the attempt to gain control of the "streaming," a habitual tension that sets up a chronic frustration, the belief that force or effort or will can solve our difficulties.

In contrast to this Western approach to "how things are" is the Chinese concept of the Tao, the course of nature, that which flows of its own accord, says Watts: "You can get the feel of it by breathing without doing anything to help your breath along. Let the breath out, and then let it come back by itself, when it feels like it." Once the breather has "let go" of the breath and allowed it to go its own way, it becomes slower and stronger. "This happens because you are now 'with' the breath and no longer 'outside it' as controller." In the same way, thoughts, feelings, and all experiences may be allowed to follow their own course, watched detachedly by the one who has them. "If you find yourself asking who is watching and why, take it as simply another wiggle of the stream."[10]

Our fear, says Watts, is that if we don't control everything, events will run wild — our suspicion of what is natural and spontaneous is deep. Letting go is an experiment few are prepared to make. Letting go works in the paradoxical sense that creative and constructive action comes from a knowledge that

> every willful effort to improve the world or oneself is futile, and so long as one can be beguiled by any political or spiritual scheme for molding things nearer to the heart's desire one will be frustrated, angry or depressed — that is, unless the first step in any such scheme is to see that nothing can be done. This is not because you are a victim of fate, but becaue there is no "you" to be fated, no observing self apart from the stream.[11]

Once the illusion of the separate self is dissipated, then, he says, it is like restoring balance in dancing or in judo; once the "you" knows itself as part of the stream, then the true energy or power works through it.

Watts began a book developing these ideas: *Tao: The Watercourse Way*, continuing with his image of the stream. He had been teaching, both at Esalen and at Sausalito, with the tai chi master Al Chung-liang Huang. A friendship quickly grew between them as they worked over Chinese texts together, trying out various translations, trying to decipher all the possible meanings.

In their last teaching session together at Esalen Al Chung-liang Huang remembered a joyful afternoon session in which their pupils ended up dancing and rolling down the grassy slopes:

> Alan and I started to walk back to the lodge, feeling exuberant, arms around each other, hands sliding along one another's spine. Alan turned to me and started to speak, ready to impress me with

> his usual eloquence about our successful week together. I noticed a sudden breakthrough in his expression; a look of lightness and glow appeared all around him. Alan had discovered a different way to tell me of his feelings: "Yah . . . Ha . . . Ho . . . Ha! Ho . . . . . ." We gibbered and danced all the way up the hill.[12]

Watts finished five chapters of the new book, one on the Chinese use of ideograms and the difference such a language makes to the understanding of those who use it. By contrast the linear language of the West has resulted in an emphasis on progress and thus on control, as opposed to the cyclic Chinese view of time and history.

The next chapter described the two poles of cosmic energy, the yang and the yin, otherwise thought of as the light and the dark, the firm and the yielding, the strong and the weak, the rising and the falling, the masculine and the feminine—the complementarity that is the key to harmonious existence.

In the third chapter he repeats the image of the stream, the watercourse way from which you cannot really deviate even if you wish; you can only fight against it like a swimmer exhausting himself by trying to swim against the tide. Next, Watts discusses *wu-wei*, the famous principle of nonaction, the refusal of counterfeit action, meddling, forcing, working against the grain of things.

Finally, he writes about *Te*—virtue—a way of contemplation, of "being aware of life without thinking about it," the expression of the Tao in actual living.

When these five chapters were completed Watts told Al Chungliang Huang with glee, "I have now satisfied myself and my readers in scholarship and intellect. The rest of this book will be all fun and surprises!"[13]

Before he could get on with the fun and surprises, however, he had another exhausting lecture tour to Europe planned. He wrote to Laurence on September 5, 1973:

Dear Daddy,

I have made arrangements for Jano and I to arrive in London on the morning of September 25th and to stay at the Charing Cross Hotel until about October 4th, when we have to go to the Continent — Frankfurt, Heidelberg, Amsterdam and Geneva.

In the meantime, I have opened a London bank account. This is at Barclays, 27 Regent Street, SW1 and the number is 20–71–64 20048305. I can't imagine that they have more than 20 million clients, but that is it!

During the visit to England I shall need to take two days out to go to Cambridge and York — to see Joseph Needham and John Robinson, and to confer with the Benedictine fathers at Ampleforth. I have a date with Toby [Christmas Humphreys] on the 29th.

Otherwise, take it that we shall come down to Chislehurst on the afternoon of the 25th and have dinner together at the Tiger, and make up our plans from there on. Will you let Joy know that we are coming. We would also very much like to see Leslie and Peggy.

I am more than halfway through my next book — a rather scholarly though simply written study of Taoism.

Much love from us both,

As ever, Alan.

The eve of the trip, however, found both Watts and Jano in poor shape for such a demanding undertaking. Early in September Jano's twenty-one-year-old niece Kathleen came over from Europe for a holiday at Druid Heights. The plan was for her to spend a few weeks with Watts and Jano and then accompany them back to Europe when they went on the trip. When she arrived, full of excitement and enthusiasm, she found Jano far too ill as a result of drinking to go anywhere at all, and Watts in only marginally better shape. Having admired this unusual couple from afar for most of her youth she felt very shocked and let down.

"Uncle Alan, *why?*" she asked him, as his children had so often done.

"When I drink I don't feel so alone," he told her.

Kathleen offered to stay behind and look after Jano while Watts was away in Europe; in his absence, as on other occasions, Jano stopped drinking.

Watts's trip to Europe included a trip to the Benedictine Abbey at Ampleforth at the invitation of Dom Aelred Graham and the then abbot, Basil Hume (now cardinal). The previous year Watts had been to a conference held by the Benedictine monastery of Mount Savior, in New York,

> to which the good fathers invited a whole gaggle of gurus for a five-day contemplative retreat. It was a marvellous and most encouraging experience. For . . . we found that any real opposition between the I–Thou [devotional or bhakti] attitude and the All-is-One attitude could be transcended in a silence of the mind in which we all stopped verbalizing. It was fascinating to take part with Hindu swamis and Trappist monks in 4:30 A.M. sessions for Zen meditation where we all seemed to get into a state of consciousness in which there was nothing left to argue about — as well as to attend sessions for the Hesychast Jesus prayer conducted by an Archimandrite whose theological views were extremely conservative. It all ended up with everyone dancing on the green to the guitar music of a Hassidic rabbi! Lex orandi lex credendi.[14]

The visit to England included taking part in a television program about drugs called "The Timeless Moment." Other participants ranged from a simple-minded acidhead at one end of the scale to a disapproving clergyman at the other. Watts took a moderate line on taking drugs: "I don't exactly advocate it. I say it's a very useful adjunct to human knowledge to have these drugs, just as microscopes and telescopes are, but they have to be used with greatest care because all investigation into these realms is dangerous." But he thought the changed perception that found the world so amazingly beautiful, the sudden understanding about how foolishly we rush and worry in the world, and the sense of unity between the individual and the universe was valuable. "It teaches you — it teaches you to feel, not merely just to know intellectually, but to feel in your bones that you are one with the whole natural environment, and therefore you respect it as you respect your own body."[15]

After England there were to be trips to Germany, Holland, and Switzerland, and more public appearances. First there were occasions for family meetings, however. There was a visit to his cousins Leslie and Peggy in Kingston Vale. Peggy remembered waiting an hour and a half to pick up Watts and Laurence at the Putney tube station. Then Watts arrived, happily oblivious of any offense caused.

On another evening he met them for dinner at Simpson's in the Strand, a very traditional and sober restaurant. He was wearing a turtleneck shirt and sandals, and the doorman politely declined to let him in.

"You don't like my wear?" asked Watts in amusement. He went back to the Charing Cross Hotel to change and reappeared, still wearing his sandals, but in a necktie and jacket.

"Are you happy now I look like all the other undertakers?" he asked.

His relatives found him warm, loving, fun to be with, generous. He dominated the conversation, but was well worth listening to. He seemed to them, however, always "in a world of his own."

In October Watts returned from his visit to Europe exhausted and lay on the couch "jet-lagged." A friend brought him a red balloon to play with, and as he watched it float away from him he said, "This is just like my spirit leaving my body." He had spoken of death a good deal in the previous year or so, telling Baker-roshi on a long motor ride just what kind of funeral he would like to have. When someone made a joke about the telephones at Druid Heights being tapped, he said that after his death he would watch the situation, and if the phones were tapped he would come in a lightning flash and knock out the underground cable. He had made his will, and he had told Sandy Jacobs and his son Mark, who had both worked on his tapes and videocassettes, that now he would be able to communicate "without carrying this body around."

Gradually Watts had been overtaken by the sense that living was a burden. His strength was clearly declining, yet the financial demands on him grew no less. As for his marriage, far from re-energizing and comforting one another, he and Jano seemed to aggravate each other's problems; something in the chemistry of life between them was decidedly destructive to Jano.

On the morning of November 16 Jano tried to wake Watts but found him "strangely unmoveable." With deep shock she realized he was dead. When the doctor came he certified that Watts had died of heart failure. In Joan's words he had "checked out." He was fifty-eight.

There were strange stories surrounding Watts's death: that the great gong on the terrace of Druid Heights sounded when there was no one there to strike it. That on December 21 of that year, the winter solstice, a lightning flash knocked out the underground cable at the top of the lane that led to Druid Heights, and that this must be Watts fulfilling his promise.

Jano believed, and said as much in a letter to Laurence Watts, that Watts had been experimenting with breathing techniques to reach *samadhi*, had somehow left his body, and had been unable to get back into it again.

. . .

As the news of Watts's death was announced, messages poured into Druid Heights, and Jano and the Druid Heights community sent out a letter of reply with a circle drawn on it in Watts's calligraphy and stamped with his Chinese seal. "Alan joins us," it read, "in thanking you for your farewell message. Listen, and rejoice, as his laughter circles the universe."

In her letter to Laurence, Jano wrote of her grief and of his.

> Besides the "this isn't so" feeling I get often when coming out of sleep, and it's often dreadful, there are all those "reality" tasks, thank heavens. Things that must be done, and things that I get excited about in planning projects for my own life, and to keep Alan's life-after-death name alive. Both with objectives in mind—financial and idealistic. Alan left me everything—all loose ends to tie up, if possible: the chance to make my own way: the decisions related to the "health, education and welfare" of his children and other heirs. Wow!

Jano went on to speak of the rites of Alan's death and her disappointment that her mother, who had loved Alan, was too ill to attend. She felt she now understood better her mother's grief at the death of Jano's father.

> Excuse me, a few tears. It happens several times a day, and I recover. And it's so odd that from the time of Alan's death until after midnight on the Winter Solstice, when I spent the night before his altar and ashes in the library, I had not shed one tear. I was nowhere. Then I had a dialogue with him, a long one, and he said, in short, "Do it, baby, while it lasts. Have a ball; I toss it to you." And I really cried—endlessly that night.
>
> Oh Daddy, there is so much I want to discuss with you, not practical details, which can be handled by correspondence, but about why, maybe, and how, maybe, this fantastic event, Alan's death, occurred. And I just can't say this or that was the reason, although I suspect that he knew he would not last too long, with

> all that mental and psychic strength carried by a not-so-strong body. And he refused to care for his physical being, anything said by me or Joan or anyone being considered an interference to his own responsibility.

She writes of the various hints there had been that he expected to die before long.

> Anyway, Daddy, with all that seems to have been lost so early with Alan's death, I sometimes wonder. His very last lecture was a string of pearls — of all the best things he had said many, many times, word for word: his unfinished book on Taoism isn't really unfinished: it's perfect. It only needs a summation as to how such a philosophy can be applied today, and he had prepared several persons to do that. [Al Chung-liang Huang actually did it.] All is being considered. Alan did fantastic things in his lifetime. With his resting, all he said may become, oh dear, gospel. Maybe. Alan's statement, one that sticks with me: The secret of life is knowing when to stop. That's like opening a fortune cookie, only more profound.[16]

There was a requiem mass in February at Druid Heights, the scattering of ashes there in front of Watts's library, and the interment of ashes beneath the stone stupa on the hillside behind the Zen Center's Green Gulch Farm. It was the one-hundredth day in the Buddhist calendar. Full honor was given to Watts as an "ancestor" by the abbot of the San Francisco Zen Center.

> At the Crossing Over ceremony Zentatsu Baker-roshi — carrying the monk's staff Alan Watts had once given Suzuki-roshi at Tassajara — gave Watts a Buddhist name, Yu Zen Myo Ko — Profound Mountain, Subtle Light — to which he added the title Dai Yu Jo Mon — Great Founder, Opener of the Great Zen Samadhi Gate — a title, he said, "given very rarely, once a generation or a century."

Gary Snyder wrote:

> He blazed out the new path for all of us and came back and made it clear. Explored the side canyons and deer trails, and investigated cliffs and thickets. Many guides would have us travel single file, like mules in a pack train, and never leave the trail. *Alan* taught us to move forward like the breeze, tasting the berries, greeting the blue jays, learning and loving the whole terrain.[17]

In the last year of Watts's life, his daughter Joan had told him of her unfulfilled wish to conceive another child.

"After I'm dead," Watts told her, "I'm coming back as your child. Next time round I'm going to be a beautiful red-haired woman." He had written in *Cloud-hidden, Whereabouts Unknown* of the "completely rational" belief in reincarnation that he held. He thought that the energy that had made him in the first place was bound to do it again in some other form. "After I die I will again awake as a baby."

Joan was not sure how lighthearted he was being in his promise to return as her child, but not long after his death she did conceive and eventually gave birth to a very pretty red-haired daughter, Laura, whose character sometimes reminded Joan of her father. Once, when Laura was a tiny girl, she and Joan visited a friend's house, and Laura went to the cupboard where the liquor was kept, pushed a number of bottles out of the way, reached in, and removed a bottle of vodka from the back of the cupboard. Joan laughs as she tells this story, neither quite believing nor disbelieving her father's promise.

Notes

All quotations for which references are not given are taken from conversations I have had with Alan Watts's relatives and friends. The context makes it clear who these are.

1. The Paradise Garden, 1915–1920

1. Emily Watts to William Buchan, December 25, 1912.
2. Alan Watts, *In My Own Way: An Autobiography* (New York: Random House, Pantheon Books, 1972), p. 22.
3. Ibid., p. 15.
4. Ibid.
5. Emily Watts to William Buchan, March 17, 1918.
6. Laurence Wilson Watts, foreword to Watts, *In My Own Way*, p. vi.
7. Watts, *In My Own Way*, p. 13.
8. Ibid., p. 35.
9. Ibid., pp. 30–31.
10. Ibid., p. 8.
11. Ibid., p. 9.

12. Ibid., p. 38:

> Il y avait un jeune homme de Dijon
> Qui n'aimait pas la religion.
> Il dit, "O ma foi,
> Comme drôle sont ces trois:
> Le Père, et le Fils, et le Pigeon."

Which Watts translated as:

> There was a young fellow of Dijon,
> Who took a dislike to religion.
> He said, "Oh my God,
> These three are so odd —
> The Father, the Son, and the Pigeon."

In ruder vein is a limerick Watts taught to Gary Snyder:

> There once was a Bishop of Buckingham,
> Who took out his thumbs and was sucking 'em,
> At the sight of the stunts
> Of the cunts in the punts
> And the tricks of the pricks who were fucking 'em.

2. The Education of a Brahmin, 1920–1932

1. Alan Watts, "Clothes — On and Off," *Does It Matter? Essays on Man's Relation to Materiality* (New York: Random House, Pantheon Books, 1970), p. 57.
2. Watts, *In My Own Way: An Autobiography* (New York: Random House, Pantheon Books, 1972), p. 89.
3. Ibid., p. 89.
4. Ibid., p. 93.
5. Ibid., p. 44.
6. Ibid., p. 14.
7. Ibid., p. 69.
8. Ibid., p. 68.
9. Ibid., p. 69.
10. Ibid., p. 66.
11. Ibid., p. 26.

12. Patrick Leigh Fermor, *A Time of Gifts* (London: John Murray, 1977), p. 15.
13. Watts, *In My Own Way*, p. 98.
14. Ibid., p. 54.
15. Leigh Fermor, *A Time of Gifts*, p. 17.
16. Watts, *In My Own Way*, p. 91.
17. Ibid., p. 99.
18. Leigh Fermor to the author, December 18, 1983.
19. Watts, *In My Own Way*, pp. 103–4.
20. Ibid., p. 61.
21. Leigh Fermor to the author, December 18, 1983.
22. Watts, *In My Own Way*, p. 57.
23. Ibid., p. 71.
24. Laurence Watts to William Buchan, May 25, 1929.
25. Watts, *In My Own Way*, p. 76.
26. Ibid.
27. Watts to Gertrude Buchan, c. 1931.
28. Ibid.
29. Watts, *In My Own Way*, p. 83.
30. Ibid., p. 86.

3. Christmas Zen, 1932–1938

1. Editorial, *The Middle Way: Journal of the Buddhist Society* (August 1983). Memorial issue on Christmas Humphreys.
2. Alan Watts, *In My Own Way: An Autobiography* (New York: Random House, Pantheon Books, 1972), p. 77.
3. Ibid., p. 113.
4. Ibid., p. 106.
5. Ibid.
6. Ibid., p. 107.
7. Ibid., p. 116.
8. Rick Fields, *How the Swans Came to the Lake: A Narrative History of Buddhism in America* (Boulder, Colo.: Shambhala, 1981), p. 137.

9. Watts, *The Spirit of Zen: A Way of Life, Work, and Art in the Far East* (New York: Grove Press, 1958), p. 26.
10. Ibid., pp. 27–28.
11. Ibid., p. 75.
12. Watts, *In My Own Way*, p. 121.
13. Fields, *How the Swans Came to the Lake*, p. 189.
14. Watts, *In My Own Way*, p. 127.
15. Watts, *The Legacy of Asia and Western Man: A Study of the Middle Way* (London: John Murray, 1937), p. 61.
16. Ibid., p. 43.
17. Watts, *In My Own Way*, p. 132.

4. The Towers of Manhattan, 1938–1941

1. Alan Watts, *In My Own Way: An Autobiography* (New York: Random House, Pantheon Books, 1972), p. 160.
2. Ibid., p. 161.
3. Quoted in Rick Fields, *How the Swans Came to the Lake: A Narrative History of Buddhism in America* (Boulder, Colo.: Shambhala, 1981), pp. 180–81.
4. Watts, *In My Own Way*, p. 142.
5. Quoted in Fields, *How the Swans Came to the Lake*, p. 189.
6. Fields, ibid., p. 190.
7. Watts, *In My Own Way*, p. 145.
8. Ibid., p. 145.
9. Watts, *The Meaning of Happiness* (New York: Harper & Row, 1940), xxii.
10. Ibid., p. 65.
11. Watts, *In My Own Way*, p. 149.
12. Watts, "The Problem of Faith and Works in Buddhism," *Columbia Review of Religion* (May 1941).
13. Watts, *In My Own Way*, p. 157.
14. Ibid.
15. Ibid., p. 159.
16. Ibid., p. 158.
17. Ibid.

18. Ibid., p. 161.
19. Ibid., p. 156.
20. Ibid., p. 163.

5. Colored Christian, 1941–1947

1. Alan Watts, *In My Own Way: An Autobiography* (New York: Random House, Pantheon Books, 1972), p. 178.
2. Ibid., p. 176.
3. Ibid., p. 180.
4. Ibid., p. 183.
5. Ibid., p. 141.
6. Ibid., p. 186.
7. Watts, pamphlets describing the work at Canterbury House.
8. Ibid.
9. Watts, *Behold the Spirit: A Study in the Necessity of Mystical Religion* (New York; Random House, Pantheon Books, 1947), pp. 4–5.
10. Ibid., p. 13.
11. Ibid., p. 15.
12. Ibid.
13. Ibid., p. 16.
14. Ibid., p. 29.
15. Ibid., p. 70.
16. Ibid., p. 110.
17. Ibid., p. 155.
18. Ibid., p. 180.
19. F. S. C. Northrop, *Church Times*, November 2, 1947.
20. Watts, *In My Own Way*, p. 189.
21. Ibid.

6. Correspondence, 1947–1950

1. Eleanor Watts to Bishop Wallace Conkling, June 29, 1950.
2. Ibid.
3. Ibid.

4. Alan Watts, *In My Own Way: An Autobiography* (New York: Random House, Pantheon Books, 1972), p. 203.
5. Eleanor Watts to Bishop Conkling, June 29, 1950.
6. Ibid.
7. Ibid.
8. Carl Wesley Gamer to Bishop Conkling, July 20, 1950.
9. Alan Watts to Bishop Conkling, June 29, 1950.
10. Ibid.
11. Bishop Conkling to Alan Watts, July 5, 1950.

7. A Priest Inhibited, 1950–1951

1. Alan Watts, *In My Own Way: An Autobiography* (New York: Random House, Pantheon Books, 1972), p. 226.
2. Ibid., p. 213.
3. Ibid.
4. Ibid., p. 215.
5. Ibid., p. 217.
6. Ibid., p. 223.
7. Ibid.
8. Watts, *The Wisdom of Insecurity: A Message for an Age of Anxiety* (New York: Random House, Pantheon Books, 1951), p. 9.
9. Ibid., p. 52.

8. The Wisdom of Insecurity, 1951–1960

1. Alan Watts, *In My Own Way: An Autobiography* (New York: Random House, Pantheon Books, 1972), p. 244.
2. Ibid., p. 247.
3. Ibid., p. 246.
4. Ibid., p. 378.
5. Ibid., p. 251.
6. Ibid.
7. Ibid., p. 270.

8. Watts, *The Way of Zen* (New York: Random House, Pantheon Books, 1957), p. 14.
9. Ibid., p. 141.
10. Watts, *In My Own Way*, p. 276.
11. Watts, *Nature, Man and Woman* (New York: Random House, Pantheon Books, 1958), p. 70.
12. Ibid., p. 112.
13. Ibid., p. 199.
14. Watts, *In My Own Way*, p. 336.
15. Ibid., p. 339.
16. Ibid., p. 245.
17. Ibid., p. 304.
18. Watts, *The Wisdom of Insecurity: A Message for an Age of Anxiety* (New York: Random House, Pantheon Books, 1951), pp. 79–80.
19. Watts, *In My Own Way*, p. 306.
20. Ibid., p. 305.
21. Ibid.
22. Ibid.
23. Ibid.
24. Ibid., p. 307.

9. Counterculture, 1960–1968

1. Alan Watts, *In My Own Way: An Autobiography* (New York: Random House, Pantheon Books, 1972), p. 311.
2. Watts, speech at Varda's memorial service, January 1971.
3. Ibid.
4. *Pacific Sun*, January 1–7, 1982.
5. Watts, *In My Own Way*, p. 319 .
6. Ibid.
7. Watts, *Nature, Man and Woman* (New York: Random House, Pantheon Books, 1958), p. 70.
8. Rick Fields, *How the Swans Came to the Lake: A Narrative History of Buddhism in America* (Boulder, Colo.: Shambhala, 1981), p. 212.

9. Jack Kerouac, *The Dharma Bums* (New York: Viking Press, 1958), p. 104.
10. Timothy Leary, *Flashbacks: An Autobiography* (Los Angeles: J. P. Tarcher, 1983), p. 149.
11. Ibid., p. 195.
12. Aldous Huxley, *The Doors of Perception* (New York: Harper & Row, 1954), pp. 12–17.
13. Watts, "The New Alchemy," *"This Is It" and Other Essays on Zen and Spiritual Existence* (New York: Random House, Pantheon Books, 1960), p. 140.
14. Ibid., p. 143.
15. Ibid., p. 152.
16. Ibid., pp. 152–53.
17. Watts, *The Joyous Cosmology* (New York: Random House, Pantheon Books, 1972), p. 73.
18. Ibid., p. 43.
19. Leary, *Flashbacks*, p. 132.
20. Ibid., pp. 158–59.
21. Watts, *In My Own Way*, p. 367.
22. Theodore Roszak, *The Making of a Counter Culture* (Garden City, N.Y.: Doubleday, Anchor Books, 1969), p. 132.
23. Watts, *The Essence of Alan Watts* (Berkeley: Celestial Arts, 1974), p. 4.
24. Ibid., p. 23.
25. Watts, *The Two Hands of God* (New York: George Braziller, 1963), p. 168.
26. Watts, *Beyond Theology: The Art of Godmanship* (New York: Random House, Pantheon Books, 1964), preface.
27. Ibid.
28. Watts, *In My Own Way*, pp. 310–11.
29. Roszak, *The Making of a Counter Culture*, p. 30.
30. Charles Perry, *The Haight-Ashbury: A History* (New York: Random House, 1984), p. 55.
31. Ibid., p. 122.
32. *The Berkeley Barb*, January 13, 1967

33. Perry, *The Haight-Ashbury*, p. 125.
34. "Dateline," BBC TV, March 27, 1968.
35. Aelred Graham, "LSD and All That," *Conversations: Christian and Buddhist* (London: Collins, 1969), pp. 53–87. Conversation between Gary Snyder and Dom Aelred Graham, September 6, 1967.
36. Ibid.
37. Fields, *How the Swans Came to the Lake*, p. 256.
38. Watts, *Zen in America: An Unconditioned Response to a Conditioned World* (Zen Center brochure).
39. Watts, ibid.

10. The Home Behind Home, 1969–1973

1. Alan Watts, *Cloud-hidden, Whereabouts Unknown: A Mountain Journal* (New York: Random House, Pantheon Books, 1973), p. 13.
2. Watts, *In My Own Way: An Autobiography* (New York: Random House, Pantheon Books, 1972), p. 31.
3. Dom Aelred Graham, "Zazen and Related Topics," *Conversations: Christian and Buddhist* (London: Collins, 1969), p. 9.
4. Ibid., p. 8.
5. "LSD and All That," ibid., p. 82.
6. Watts, *Cloud-hidden*, p. 29.
7. Ibid., p. 184.
8. Ibid., p. 153.
9. Watts, *Cloud-hidden*, p. 17.
10. Ibid., p. 19.
11. Ibid., p. 20.
12. Al Chung-liang Huang, foreword to Watts, *Tao: The Watercourse Way* (New York: Random House, Pantheon Books, 1975), p. ix.
13. Ibid.
14. Watts to Bishop John Robinson, January 29, 1973.

15. "The Timeless Moment," BBC TV, August 10, 1973.
16. Mary Jane Watts to Laurence Watts, February 16, 1974.
17. Rick Fields, *How the Swans Came to the Lake: A Narrative History of Buddhism in America* (Boulder, Colo.: Shambhala, 1981), p. 360.

Books by Alan Watts

The Spirit of Zen; A Way of Life, Work, and Art in the Far East. London: John Murray, 1935.

The Legacy of Asia and Western Man: A Study of the Middle Way. London: John Murray, 1937.

The Meaning of Happiness: A Quest for Freedom of the Spirit in Modern Psychology and the Wisdom of the East. New York: Harper & Row, 1940.

The Theologia Mystica of Saint Dionysius. Worcester, Mass.: Holy Cross Press, 1944.

Behold the Spirit: A Study in the Necessity of Mystical Religion. New York: Random House, Pantheon Books, 1947.

Easter—Its Story and Meaning. New York: Henry Schuman, Inc., 1950.

The Supreme Identity. New York: Random House, Pantheon Books, 1950.

The Wisdom of Insecurity: A Message for an Age of Anxiety. New York: Random House, Pantheon Books, 1951.

The Way of Zen. New York: Random House, Pantheon Books, 1957.

Nature, Man and Woman. New York: Random House, Pantheon Books, 1958.

"This Is It" and Other Essays on Zen and Spiritual Experience. New York: Random House, Pantheon Books, 1960.

Psychotherapy East and West. New York: Random House, Pantheon Books, 1961.

The Joyous Cosmology. New York: Random House, Pantheon Books, 1962.

Beyond Theology: The Art of Godmanship. New York: Random House, Pantheon Books, 1964.

The Book: On the Taboo Against Knowing Who You Are. New York: Random House, Pantheon Books, 1966.

Myth and Ritual in Christianity. Boston, Mass.: Beacon Press, 1968.

The Two Hands of God: The Myths of Polarity. New York: Macmillan, Collier Books, 1963.

Does It Matter? Essays on Man's Relation to Materiality. New York: Random House, Pantheon Books, 1970.

In My Own Way: An Autobiography. New York: Random House, Pantheon Books, 1972.

Cloud-hidden, Whereabouts Unknown: A Mountain Journal. New York: Random House, Pantheon Books, 1973.

The Essence of Alan Watts. Berkeley: Celestial Arts, 1974.

Tao: The Watercourse Way. With the collaboration of Al Chung-liang Huang. New York: Random House, Pantheon Books, 1975.

Index

AVAILABLE FROM BETTER BOOKSTORES. TRY YOUR BOOKSTORE FIRST.

Inspiration

Finding Time for the Timeless: Spirituality in the Workweek
By John McQuiston II
Offers refreshing stories of everyday spiritual practices people use to free themselves from the work and worry mindset of our culture.
5⅛ x 6½, 208 pp, Quality PB, 978-1-59473-383-3 **$9.99**

God the *What*?: What Our Metaphors for God Reveal about Our Beliefs in God *by Carolyn Jane Bohler*
Inspires you to consider a wide range of images of God in order to refine how you imagine God. 6 x 9, 192 pp, Quality PB, 978-1-59473-251-5 **$16.99**

How Did I Get to Be 70 When I'm 35 Inside?: Spiritual Surprises of Later Life *by Linda Douty*
Encourages you to focus on the inner changes of aging to help you greet your later years as the grand adventure they can be. 6 x 9, 208 pp, Quality PB, 978-1-59473-297-3 **$16.99**

Restoring Life's Missing Pieces: The Spiritual Power of Remembering & Reuniting with People, Places, Things & Self *by Caren Goldman*
A powerful and thought-provoking look at reunions of all kinds as roads to remembering and re-membering ourselves.
6 x 9, 208 pp, Quality PB, 978-1-59473-295-9 **$16.99**

Saving Civility: 52 Ways to Tame Rude, Crude & Attitude for a Polite Planet
By Sara Hacala
Provides fifty-two practical ways you can reverse the course of incivility and make the world a more enriching, pleasant place to live.
6 x 9, 240 pp, Quality PB 978-1-59473-314-7 **$16.99**

Spiritually Healthy Divorce: Navigating Disruption with Insight & Hope
by Carolyne Call
A spiritual map to help you move through the twists and turns of divorce.
6 x 9, 224 pp, Quality PB, 978-1-59473-288-1 **$16.99**

Who Is My God? 2nd Edition
An Innovative Guide to Finding Your Spiritual Identity
by the Editors at SkyLight Paths
Provides the Spiritual Identity Self-Test™ to uncover the components of your unique spirituality. 6 x 9, 160 pp, Quality PB, 978-1-59473-014-6 **$15.99**

Journeys of Simplicity
Traveling Light with Thomas Merton, Bashō, Edward Abbey, Annie Dillard & Others
by Philip Harnden
Invites you to consider a more graceful way of traveling through life. PB includes journal pages to help you get started on your own spiritual journey.
5 x 7¼, 144 pp, Quality PB, 978-1-59473-181-5 **$12.99**
5 x 7¼, 128 pp, HC, 978-1-893361-76-8 **$16.95**

Or phone, fax, mail or e-mail to: SKYLIGHT PATHS **Publishing**
Sunset Farm Offices, Route 4 • P.O. Box 237 • Woodstock, Vermont 05091
Tel: (802) 457-4000 • Fax: (802) 457-4004 • www.skylightpaths.com
Credit card orders: (800) 962-4544 (8:30AM–5:30PM EST Monday–Friday)
Generous discounts on quantity orders. SATISFACTION GUARANTEED. Prices subject to change.

Children's Spiritual Biography

MULTICULTURAL, NONDENOMINATIONAL, NONSECTARIAN

Ten Amazing People

And How They Changed the World

by Maura D. Shaw; Foreword by Dr. Robert Coles

Full-color illus. by Stephen Marchesi

For ages 7 & up

Shows kids that spiritual people can have an exciting impact on the world around them. Kids will delight in reading about these amazing people and what they accomplished through their words and actions.

Black Elk • Dorothy Day • Malcolm X • Mahatma Gandhi • Martin Luther King, Jr. • Mother Teresa • Janusz Korczak • Desmond Tutu • Thich Nhat Hanh • Albert Schweitzer

"Best Juvenile/Young Adult Non-Fiction Book of the Year."
—*Independent Publisher*

"Will inspire adults and children alike."
—*Globe and Mail* (Toronto)

8½ x 11, 48 pp, Full-color illus., HC, 978-1-893361-47-8 **$17.95** *For ages 7 & up*

Spiritual Biographies for Young People

For Ages 7 & Up

By Maura D. Shaw; Illus. by Stephen Marchesi

6¾ x 8¾, 32 pp, Full-color and b/w illus., HC

Black Elk: Native American Man of Spirit

Through historically accurate illustrations and photos, inspiring age-appropriate activities and Black Elk's own words, this colorful biography introduces children to a remarkable person who ensured that the traditions and beliefs of his people would not be forgotten.

978-1-59473-043-6 **$12.99**

Dorothy Day: A Catholic Life of Action

Introduces children to one of the most inspiring women of the twentieth century, a down-to-earth spiritual leader who saw the presence of God in every person she met. Includes practical activities, a timeline and a list of important words to know.

978-1-59473-011-5 **$12.99**

Gandhi: India's Great Soul

The only biography of Gandhi that balances a simple text with illustrations, photos and activities that encourage children and adults to talk about how to make changes happen without violence. Introduces children to important concepts of freedom, equality and justice among people of all backgrounds and religions.

978-1-893361-91-1 **$12.95**

Thich Nhat Hanh: Buddhism in Action

Warm illustrations, photos, age-appropriate activities and Thich Nhat Hanh's own poems introduce a great man to children in a way they can understand and enjoy. Includes a list of important Buddhist words to know.

978-1-893361-87-4 **$12.95**

Spirituality of the Seasons

Autumn: A Spiritual Biography of the Season
Edited by Gary Schmidt and Susan M. Felch; Illus. by Mary Azarian
Rejoice in autumn as a time of preparation and reflection. Includes Wendell Berry, David James Duncan, Robert Frost, A. Bartlett Giamatti, E. B. White, P. D. James, Julian of Norwich, Garret Keizer, Tracy Kidder, Anne Lamott, May Sarton.
6 x 9, 320 pp, b/w illus., Quality PB, 978-1-59473-118-1 **$18.99**

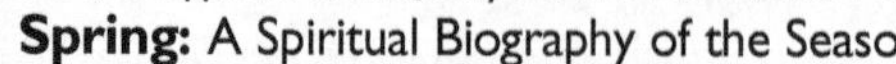

Spring: A Spiritual Biography of the Season
Edited by Gary Schmidt and Susan M. Felch; Illus. by Mary Azarian
Explore the gentle unfurling of spring and reflect on how nature celebrates rebirth and renewal. Includes Jane Kenyon, Lucy Larcom, Harry Thurston, Nathaniel Hawthorne, Noel Perrin, Annie Dillard, Martha Ballard, Barbara Kingsolver, Dorothy Wordsworth, Donald Hall, David Brill, Lionel Basney, Isak Dinesen, Paul Laurence Dunbar. 6 x 9, 352 pp, b/w illus., Quality PB, 978-1-59473-246-1 **$18.99**

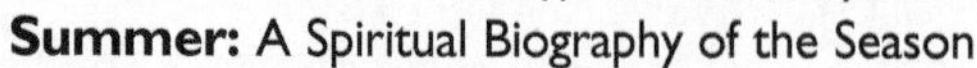

Summer: A Spiritual Biography of the Season
Edited by Gary Schmidt and Susan M. Felch; Illus. by Barry Moser
"A sumptuous banquet.... These selections lift up an exquisite wholeness found within an everyday sophistication." — ★ *Publishers Weekly* starred review
Includes Anne Lamott, Luci Shaw, Ray Bradbury, Richard Selzer, Thomas Lynch, Walt Whitman, Carl Sandburg, Sherman Alexie, Madeleine L'Engle, Jamaica Kincaid.
6 x 9, 304 pp, b/w illus., Quality PB, 978-1-59473-183-9 **$18.99**
HC, 978-1-59473-083-2 **$21.99**

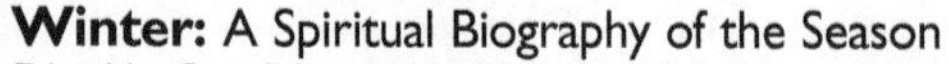

Winter: A Spiritual Biography of the Season
Edited by Gary Schmidt and Susan M. Felch; Illus. by Barry Moser
"This outstanding anthology features top-flight nature and spirituality writers on the fierce, inexorable season of winter.... Remarkably lively and warm, despite the icy subject." — ★ *Publishers Weekly* starred review
Includes Will Campbell, Rachel Carson, Annie Dillard, Donald Hall, Ron Hansen, Jane Kenyon, Jamaica Kincaid, Barry Lopez, Kathleen Norris, John Updike, E. B. White.
6 x 9, 288 pp, b/w illus., Deluxe PB w/ flaps, 978-1-893361-92-8 **$18.95**
HC, 978-1-893361-53-9 **$21.95**

Spirituality / Animal Companions

Blessing the Animals: Prayers and Ceremonies to Celebrate God's Creatures, Wild and Tame *Edited and with Introductions by Lynn L. Caruso*
5¼ x 7¼, 256 pp, Quality PB, 978-1-59473-253-9 **$15.99**; HC, 978-1-59473-145-7 **$19.99**

Remembering My Pet: A Kid's Own Spiritual Workbook for When a Pet Dies
by Nechama Liss-Levinson, PhD, and Rev. Molly Phinney Baskette, MDiv; Foreword by Lynn L. Caruso
8 x 10, 48 pp, 2-color text, HC, 978-1-59473-221-8 **$16.99**

What Animals Can Teach Us about Spirituality: Inspiring Lessons from Wild and Tame Creatures *by Diana L. Guerrero* 6 x 9, 176 pp, Quality PB, 978-1-893361-84-3 **$16.95**

Spirituality—A Week Inside

Lighting the Lamp of Wisdom: A Week Inside a Yoga Ashram
by John Ittner; Foreword by Dr. David Frawley
6 x 9, 192 pp, b/w photos, Quality PB, 978-1-893361-52-2 **$15.95**

Making a Heart for God: A Week Inside a Catholic Monastery
by Dianne Aprile; Foreword by Brother Patrick Hart, OCSO
6 x 9, 224 pp, b/w photos, Quality PB, 978-1-893361-49-2 **$16.95**

Waking Up: A Week Inside a Zen Monastery
by Jack Maguire; Foreword by John Daido Loori, Roshi
6 x 9, 224 pp, b/w photos, Quality PB, 978-1-893361-55-3 **$16.95**; HC, 978-1-893361-13-3 **$21.95**

Spirituality & Crafts

Beading—The Creative Spirit: Finding Your Sacred Center through the Art of Beadwork *by Rev. Wendy Ellsworth*
Invites you on a spiritual pilgrimage into the kaleidoscope world of glass and color. 7 x 9, 240 pp, 8-page color insert, 40+ b/w photos and 40 diagrams, Quality PB, 978-1-59473-267-6 **$18.99**

Contemplative Crochet: A Hands-On Guide for Interlocking Faith and Craft *by Cindy Crandall-Frazier; Foreword by Linda Skolnik*
Illuminates the spiritual lessons you can learn through crocheting.
7 x 9, 208 pp, b/w photos, Quality PB, 978-1-59473-238-6 **$16.99**

The Knitting Way: A Guide to Spiritual Self-Discovery
by Linda Skolnik and Janice MacDaniels Examines how you can explore and strengthen your spiritual life through knitting.
7 x 9, 240 pp, b/w photos, Quality PB, 978-1-59473-079-5 **$16.99**

The Painting Path: Embodying Spiritual Discovery through Yoga, Brush and Color *by Linda Novick; Foreword by Richard Segalman*
Explores the divine connection you can experience through art.
7 x 9, 208 pp, 8-page color insert, plus b/w photos, Quality PB, 978-1-59473-226-3 **$18.99**

The Quilting Path: A Guide to Spiritual Discovery through Fabric, Thread and Kabbalah *by Louise Silk*
Explores how to cultivate personal growth through quilt making.
7 x 9, 192 pp, b/w photos and illus., Quality PB, 978-1-59473-206-5 **$16.99**

The Scrapbooking Journey: A Hands-On Guide to Spiritual Discovery
by Cory Richardson-Lauve; Foreword by Stacy Julian Reveals how this craft can become a practice used to deepen and shape your life.
7 x 9, 176 pp, 8-page color insert, plus b/w photos, Quality PB, 978-1-59473-216-4 **$18.99**

The Soulwork of Clay: A Hands-On Approach to Spirituality
by Marjory Zoet Bankson; Photos by Peter Bankson
Takes you through the seven-step process of making clay into a pot, drawing parallels at each stage to the process of spiritual growth.
7 x 9, 192 pp, b/w photos, Quality PB, 978-1-59473-249-2 **$16.99**

Kabbalah / Enneagram

(Books from Jewish Lights Publishing, SkyLight Paths' sister imprint)

Cast in God's Image: Discover Your Personality Type Using the Enneagram and Kabbalah
by Rabbi Howard A. Addison, PhD 7 x 9, 176 pp, Quality PB, 978-1-58023-124-4 **$16.95**

Ehyeh: A Kabbalah for Tomorrow *by Rabbi Arthur Green, PhD*
6 x 9, 224 pp, Quality PB, 978-1-58023-213-5 **$18.99**

The Enneagram and Kabbalah, 2nd Edition: Reading Your Soul
by Rabbi Howard A. Addison, PhD 6 x 9, 192 pp, Quality PB, 978-1-58023-229-6 **$16.99**

The Gift of Kabbalah: Discovering the Secrets of Heaven, Renewing Your Life on Earth
by Tamar Frankiel, PhD 6 x 9, 256 pp, Quality PB, 978-1-58023-141-1 **$16.95**

God in Your Body: Kabbalah, Mindfulness and Embodied Spiritual Practice
by Jay Michaelson 6 x 9, 272 pp, Quality PB, 978-1-58023-304-0 **$18.99**

Jewish Mysticism and the Spiritual Life: Classical Texts, Contemporary Reflections
Edited by Dr. Lawrence Fine, Dr. Eitan Fishbane and Rabbi Or N. Rose
6 x 9, 256 pp, HC, 978-1-58023-434-4 **$24.99**

Kabbalah: A Brief Introduction for Christians
by Tamar Frankiel, PhD 5½ x 8½, 208 pp, Quality PB, 978-1-58023-303-3 **$16.99**

Zohar: Annotated & Explained *Translation & Annotation by Daniel C. Matt; Foreword by Andrew Harvey* 5½ x 8½, 176 pp, Quality PB, 978-1-893361-51-5 **$15.99**

Prayer / Meditation

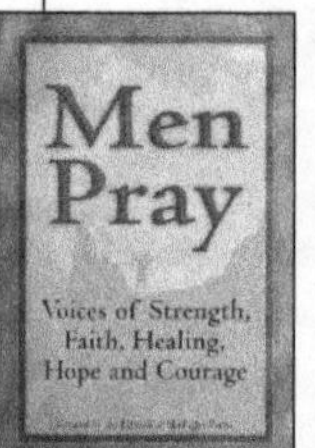

Men Pray: Voices of Strength, Faith, Healing, Hope and Courage
Created by the Editors at SkyLight Paths
Celebrates the rich variety of ways men around the world have called out to the Divine—with words of joy, praise, gratitude, wonder, petition and even anger—from the ancient world up to our own day.
5 x 7, 200 pp (est), HC, 978-1-59473-395-6 **$16.99**

Sacred Attention: A Spiritual Practice for Finding God in the Moment
by Margaret D. McGee
Framed on the Christian liturgical year, this inspiring guide explores ways to develop a practice of attention as a means of talking—and listening—to God.
6 x 9, 144 pp, Quality PB, 978-1-59473-291-1 **$16.99**

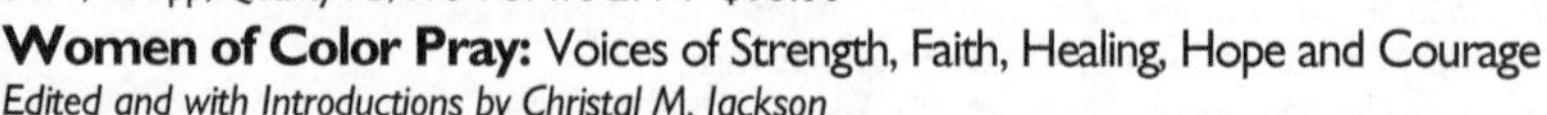

Women of Color Pray: Voices of Strength, Faith, Healing, Hope and Courage
Edited and with Introductions by Christal M. Jackson
Through these prayers, poetry, lyrics, meditations and affirmations, you will share in the strong and undeniable connection women of color share with God.
5 x 7¼, 208 pp, Quality PB, 978-1-59473-077-1 **$15.99**

The Art of Public Prayer, 2nd Edition: Not for Clergy Only
by Lawrence A. Hoffman, PhD 6 x 9, 288 pp, Quality PB, 978-1-893361-06-5 **$19.99**

A Heart of Stillness: A Complete Guide to Learning the Art of Meditation
by David A. Cooper 5½ x 8½, 272 pp, Quality PB, 978-1-893361-03-4 **$18.99**

Living into Hope: A Call to Spiritual Action for Such a Time as This
by Rev. Dr. Joan Brown Campbell; Foreword by Karen Armstrong
6 x 9, 208 pp, HC, 978-1-59473-283-6 **$21.99**

Meditation without Gurus: A Guide to the Heart of Practice
by Clark Strand 5½ x 8½, 192 pp, Quality PB, 978-1-893361-93-5 **$16.95**

Prayers to an Evolutionary God
by William Cleary; Afterword by Diarmuid O'Murchu
6 x 9, 208 pp, HC, 978-1-59473-006-1 **$21.99**

Praying with Our Hands: 21 Practices of Embodied Prayer from the World's Spiritual Traditions *by Jon M. Sweeney; Photos by Jennifer J. Wilson; Foreword by Mother Tessa Bielecki; Afterword by Taitetsu Unno, PhD*
8 x 8, 96 pp, 22 duotone photos, Quality PB, 978-1-893361-16-4 **$16.95**

Secrets of Prayer: A Multifaith Guide to Creating Personal Prayer in Your Life
by Nancy Corcoran, CSJ
6 x 9, 160 pp, Quality PB, 978-1-59473-215-7 **$16.99**

Three Gates to Meditation Practice: A Personal Journey into Sufism, Buddhism, and Judaism *by David A. Cooper* 5½ x 8½, 240 pp, Quality PB, 978-1-893361-22-5 **$16.95**

Prayer / M. Basil Pennington, OCSO

Finding Grace at the Center, 3rd Edition: The Beginning of Centering Prayer *with Thomas Keating, OCSO, and Thomas E. Clarke, SJ; Foreword by Rev. Cynthia Bourgeault, PhD* A practical guide to a simple and beautiful form of meditative prayer. 5 x 7¼, 128 pp, Quality PB, 978-1-59473-182-2 **$12.99**

The Monks of Mount Athos: A Western Monk's Extraordinary Spiritual Journey on Eastern Holy Ground *Foreword by Archimandrite Dionysios*
Explores the landscape, monastic communities and food of Athos.
6 x 9, 352 pp, Quality PB, 978-1-893361-78-2 **$18.95**

Psalms: A Spiritual Commentary *Illus. by Phillip Ratner*
Reflections on some of the most beloved passages from the Bible's most widely read book. 6 x 9, 176 pp, 24 full-page b/w illus., Quality PB, 978-1-59473-234-8 **$16.99**

The Song of Songs: A Spiritual Commentary *Illus. by Phillip Ratner*
Explore the Bible's most challenging mystical text.
6 x 9, 160 pp, 14 full-page b/w illus., Quality PB, 978-1-59473-235-5 **$16.99**
HC, 978-1-59473-004-7 **$19.99**

Bible Stories / Folktales

Abraham's Bind & Other Bible Tales of Trickery, Folly, Mercy and Love *by Michael J. Caduto*
New retellings of episodes in the lives of familiar biblical characters explore relevant life lessons. 6 x 9, 224 pp, HC, 978-1-59473-186-0 **$19.99**

Daughters of the Desert: Stories of Remarkable Women from Christian, Jewish and Muslim Traditions *by Claire Rudolf Murphy, Meghan Nuttall Sayres, Mary Cronk Farrell, Sarah Conover and Betsy Wharton*
Breathes new life into the old tales of our female ancestors in faith. Uses traditional scriptural passages as starting points, then with vivid detail fills in historical context and place. Chapters reveal the voices of Sarah, Hagar, Huldah, Esther, Salome, Mary Magdalene, Lydia, Khadija, Fatima and many more. Historical fiction ideal for readers of all ages.
5½ x 8½, 192 pp, Quality PB, 978-1-59473-106-8 **$14.99** Inc. reader's discussion guide
HC, 978-1-893361-72-0 **$19.95**

The Triumph of Eve & Other Subversive Bible Tales
by Matt Biers-Ariel
These engaging retellings of familiar Bible stories are witty, often hilarious and always profound. They invite you to grapple with questions and issues that are often hidden in the original texts.
5½ x 8½, 192 pp, Quality PB, 978-1-59473-176-1 **$14.99**

Also available: **The Triumph of Eve Teacher's Guide**
8½ x 11, 44 pp, PB, 978-1-59473-152-5 **$8.99**

Wisdom in the Telling
Finding Inspiration and Grace in Traditional Folktales and Myths Retold
by Lorraine Hartin-Gelardi
6 x 9, 192 pp, HC, 978-1-59473-185-3 **$19.99**

Religious Etiquette / Reference

How to Be a Perfect Stranger, 5th Edition: The Essential Religious Etiquette Handbook *Edited by Stuart M. Matlins and Arthur J. Magida*
The indispensable guidebook to help the well-meaning guest when visiting other people's religious ceremonies. A straightforward guide to the rituals and celebrations of the major religions and denominations in the United States and Canada from the perspective of an interested guest of any other faith, based on information obtained from authorities of each religion. Belongs in every living room, library and office. Covers:
African American Methodist Churches • Assemblies of God • Bahá'í Faith • Baptist • Buddhist • Christian Church (Disciples of Christ) • Christian Science (Church of Christ, Scientist) • Churches of Christ • Episcopalian and Anglican • Hindu • Islam • Jehovah's Witnesses • Jewish • Lutheran • Mennonite/Amish • Methodist • Mormon (Church of Jesus Christ of Latter-day Saints) • Native American/First Nations • Orthodox Churches • Pentecostal Church of God • Presbyterian • Quaker (Religious Society of Friends) • Reformed Church in America/Canada • Roman Catholic • Seventh-day Adventist • Sikh • Unitarian Universalist • United Church of Canada • United Church of Christ

"The things Miss Manners forgot to tell us about religion."
—*Los Angeles Times*

"Finally, for those inclined to undertake their own spiritual journeys ... tells visitors what to expect." —*New York Times*

6 x 9, 432 pp, Quality PB, 978-1-59473-294-2 **$19.99**

The Perfect Stranger's Guide to Funerals and Grieving Practices: A Guide to Etiquette in Other People's Religious Ceremonies *Edited by Stuart M. Matlins*
6 x 9, 240 pp, Quality PB, 978-1-893361-20-1 **$16.95**

The Perfect Stranger's Guide to Wedding Ceremonies: A Guide to Etiquette in Other People's Religious Ceremonies *Edited by Stuart M. Matlins*
6 x 9, 208 pp, Quality PB, 978-1-893361-19-5 **$16.95**

Spiritual Poetry—The Mystic Poets

Experience these mystic poets as you never have before. Each beautiful, compact book includes a brief introduction to the poet's time and place, a summary of the major themes of the poet's mysticism and religious tradition, essential selections from the poet's most important works, and an appreciative preface by a contemporary spiritual writer.

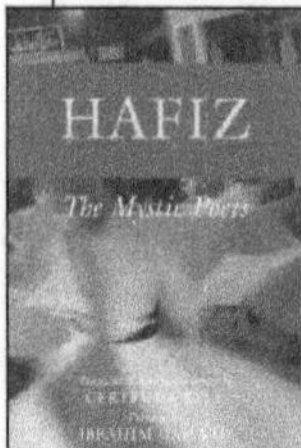

Hafiz

The Mystic Poets

Translated and with Notes by Gertrude Bell

Preface by Ibrahim Gamard

Hafiz is known throughout the world as Persia's greatest poet, with sales of his poems in Iran today only surpassed by those of the Qur'an itself. His probing and joyful verse speaks to people from all backgrounds who long to taste and feel divine love and experience harmony with all living things.

5 x 7¼, 144 pp, HC, 978-1-59473-009-2 **$16.99**

Hopkins

The Mystic Poets

Preface by Rev. Thomas Ryan, CSP

Gerard Manley Hopkins, Christian mystical poet, is beloved for his use of fresh language and startling metaphors to describe the world around him. Although his verse is lovely, beneath the surface lies a searching soul, wrestling with and yearning for God.

5 x 7¼, 112 pp, HC, 978-1-59473-010-8 **$16.99**

Tagore

The Mystic Poets

Preface by Swami Adiswarananda

Rabindranath Tagore is often considered the Shakespeare of modern India. A great mystic, Tagore was the teacher of W. B. Yeats and Robert Frost, the close friend of Albert Einstein and Mahatma Gandhi, and the winner of the Nobel Prize for Literature. This beautiful sampling of Tagore's two most important works, *The Gardener* and *Gitanjali,* offers a glimpse into his spiritual vision that has inspired people around the world.

5 x 7¼, 144 pp, HC, 978-1-59473-008-5 **$16.99**

Whitman

The Mystic Poets

Preface by Gary David Comstock

Walt Whitman was the most innovative and influential poet of the nineteenth century. This beautiful sampling of Whitman's most important poetry from *Leaves of Grass,* and selections from his prose writings, offers a glimpse into the spiritual side of his most radical themes—love for country, love for others and love of self.

5 x 7¼, 192 pp, HC, 978-1-59473-041-2 **$16.99**

Women's Interest

Women, Spirituality and Transformative Leadership
Where Grace Meets Power
Edited by Kathe Schaaf, Kay Lindahl, Kathleen S. Hurty, PhD, and Reverend Guo Cheen
A dynamic conversation on the power of women's spiritual leadership and its emerging patterns of transformation. 6 x 9, 288 pp, Hardcover, 978-1-59473-313-0 **$24.99**

Spiritually Healthy Divorce: Navigating Disruption with Insight & Hope
by Carolyne Call A spiritual map to help you move through the twists and turns of divorce. 6 x 9, 224 pp, Quality PB, 978-1-59473-288-1 **$16.99**

New Feminist Christianity: Many Voices, Many Views
Edited by Mary E. Hunt and Diann L. Neu
Insights from ministers and theologians, activists and leaders, artists and liturgists who are shaping the future. Taken together, their voices offer a starting point for building new models of religious life and worship.
6 x 9, 384 pp, HC, 978-1-59473-285-0 **$24.99**

New Jewish Feminism: Probing the Past, Forging the Future
Edited by Rabbi Elyse Goldstein; Foreword by Anita Diamant
Looks at the growth and accomplishments of Jewish feminism and what they mean for Jewish women today and tomorrow. Features the voices of women from every area of Jewish life, addressing the important issues that concern Jewish women.
6 x 9, 480 pp, Quality PB, 978-1-58023-448-1 **$19.99**; HC, 978-1-58023-359-0 **$24.99***

Bread, Body, Spirit: Finding the Sacred in Food
Edited and with Introductions by Alice Peck 6 x 9, 224 pp, Quality PB, 978-1-59473-242-3 **$19.99**

Dance—The Sacred Art: The Joy of Movement as a Spiritual Practice
by Cynthia Winton-Henry 5½ x 8½, 224 pp, Quality PB, 978-1-59473-268-3 **$16.99**

Daughters of the Desert: Stories of Remarkable Women from Christian, Jewish and Muslim Traditions
by Claire Rudolf Murphy, Meghan Nuttall Sayres, Mary Cronk Farrell, Sarah Conover and Betsy Wharton
5½ x 8½, 192 pp, Illus., Quality PB, 978-1-59473-106-8 **$14.99** Inc. reader's discussion guide

The Divine Feminine in Biblical Wisdom Literature
Selections Annotated & Explained
Translation & Annotation by Rabbi Rami Shapiro; Foreword by Rev. Cynthia Bourgeault, PhD
5½ x 8½, 240 pp, Quality PB, 978-1-59473-109-9 **$16.99**

Divining the Body: Reclaim the Holiness of Your Physical Self
by Jan Phillips 8 x 8, 256 pp, Quality PB, 978-1-59473-080-1 **$18.99**

Honoring Motherhood: Prayers, Ceremonies & Blessings
Edited and with Introductions by Lynn L. Caruso
5 x 7¼, 272 pp, Quality PB, 978-1-58473-384-0 **$9.99**; HC, 978-1-59473-239-3 **$19.99**

Next to Godliness: Finding the Sacred in Housekeeping
Edited by Alice Peck 6 x 9, 224 pp, Quality PB, 978-1-59473-214-0 **$19.99**

ReVisions: Seeing Torah through a Feminist Lens
by Rabbi Elyse Goldstein 5½ x 8½, 224 pp, Quality PB, 978-1-58023-117-6 **$16.95***

The Triumph of Eve & Other Subversive Bible Tales
by Matt Biers-Ariel 5½ x 8½, 192 pp, Quality PB, 978-1-59473-176-1 **$14.99**

White Fire: A Portrait of Women Spiritual Leaders in America
by Malka Drucker; Photos by Gay Block 7 x 10, 320 pp, b/w photos, HC, 978-1-893361-64-5 **$24.95**

Woman Spirit Awakening in Nature: Growing Into the Fullness of Who You Are
by Nancy Barrett Chickerneo, PhD; Foreword by Eileen Fisher
8 x 8, 224 pp, b/w illus., Quality PB, 978-1-59473-250-8 **$16.99**

Women of Color Pray: Voices of Strength, Faith, Healing, Hope and Courage
Edited and with Introductions by Christal M. Jackson
5 x 7¼, 208 pp, Quality PB, 978-1-59473-077-1 **$15.99**

The Women's Torah Commentary: New Insights from Women Rabbis on the 54 Weekly Torah Portions *Edited by Rabbi Elyse Goldstein*
6 x 9, 496 pp, Quality PB, 978-1-58023-370-5 **$19.99**; HC, 978-1-58023-076-6 **$34.95***

* A book from Jewish Lights, SkyLight Paths' sister imprint

Cut along dotted lines and remove, fold as shown at center, tape closed and mail to SkyLight Paths Publishing.

Place Stamp Here

SKYLIGHT PATHS PUBLISHING
SUNSET FARM OFFICES RTE 4
PO BOX 237
WOODSTOCK VT 05091-0237

(fold here)

Fill in this card and return it to us to be eligible for our quarterly drawing for a $100 gift certificate for SkyLight Paths books.

We hope that you will enjoy this book and find it useful in enriching your life.

Book title: __________

Your comments: __________

How you learned of this book: __________

If purchased: Bookseller __________ City __________ State _____

Please send me a free SkyLight Paths Publishing catalog. I am interested in: (check all that apply)

1. ❑ Spirituality
2. ❑ Mysticism/Kabbalah
3. ❑ Philosophy/Theology
4. ❑ Spiritual Texts
5. ❑ Religious Traditions (Which ones?) __________
6. ❑ Children's Books
7. ❑ Prayer/Worship
8. ❑ Meditation
9. ❑ Interfaith Resources

Name (PRINT) __________

Street __________

City __________ State _____ Zip _____

E-MAIL (FOR SPECIAL OFFERS ONLY) __________

Please send a SkyLight Paths Publishing catalog to my friend:

Name (PRINT) __________

Street __________

City __________ State _____ Zip _____

Printed in the USA
CPSIA information can be obtained
at www.ICGtesting.com
JSHW082157140824
68134JS00014B/281

9 781893 361324